# THE GAME OF OUR LIVES

## Peter Gzowski

Heritage
House

Copyright © 2004 by the Estate of Peter Gzowski
Introduction © 2004 by Michael P.J. Kennedy
Copyright © 1981 by McClelland and Stewart. Published by arrangement with
McClelland and Stewart Ltd., Toronto, Canada

National Library of Canada Cataloguing in Publication
Gzowski, Peter
The game of our lives / Peter Gzowski.
ISBN 1-894384-59-8
1. Edmonton Oilers (Hockey team)  2. Hockey--Canada. 3. National Hockey
League. I. Title.
GV848.E35G96 2004     796.962'64'0971     C2004-900908-7

"Hometown Hero" lyrics by Pete White, music by Paul Hann, reprinted with per-
mission. Excerpt from "The Hockey Sweater" by Roch Carrier, copyright © 1979
House of Anansi Press. Reprinted by arrangement with House of Anansi Press.

Heritage House acknowledges the financial support for our publishing pro-
gram from the Government of Canada through the Book Publishing Industry
Development Program (BPIDP), Canada Council for the Arts, and the British
Columbia Arts Council.

Heritage House Publishing Ltd.
#108-17665-66A Avenue
Surrey, BC, Canada
V3S 2A7
greatbooks@heritagehouse.ca
www.heritagehouse.ca

Printed in Canada

BRITISH
COLUMBIA
ARTS COUNCIL

Canada Council    Conseil des Arts
for the Arts      du Canada

# THE GAME OF OUR LIVES

For both my daughters and all my boys

# Acknowledgements

The scribes of hockey are a jolly lot, and I was pleased to be admitted to their number for the season described in these pages. I thank particularly Ken Brown, Dick Chubey, Jim Matheson, and Rod Phillips for their knowledge and their company. I spent time, too—or felt I did—with writers who have gone before, among them Ralph Allen, Jim Coleman, Stan Fischler, Trent Frayne, Foster Hewitt, Andy O'Brien, Gary Ronberg, Herbert Warren Wind, and Scott Young, nearly all of whom I cite at one point or another, and all of whom deepened my appreciation of the game we share.

The Edmonton Oilers themselves were kinder to me than I had dared hope—not only the players, coaches, and owner, who figure prominently in my story, and among whom, as the reader will no doubt discern, I now count many friends, but the backstage personnel: John Blackwell, Elaine Ell, Bob Freeman, Sue Hall, Bruce McGregor, Tina Scott, and, especially, Bill Tuele, the director of public relations.

Some of the material on Wayne Gretzky and Billy Heindl appeared in quite different form in *Saturday Night* magazine during the season, and I am grateful to Robert Fulford and Gary Ross for that. I am further grateful, as only an old editor can be, to Gary Ross for suggestions about the book, as I am to Michael de Pencier and Jan Walter and, perhaps most of all, Jack McClelland. Without any of them, although for separate reasons, there would have been no *Game of Our Lives*.

Joan Dixon, a Wayne Gretzky among researchers, was with me from beginning to end.

# Contents

# Introduction

## by Michael P.J. Kennedy

For millions of Canadians living in the latter third of the twentieth century, Peter Gzowski was synonymous with all that was good in Canadian radio. Indeed, his unassuming manner yet intelligent and insightful questions and comments made his Canadawide weekday broadcasts on CBC extremely popular. "This Country in the Morning," broadcast from 1971 to 1974, and later "Morningside," which appeared from 1982 to 1997, provided Canadians with an opportunity to view themselves in all their diversity from coast to coast to coast. He showed people in Toronto what life was like for their fellow citizens in Yellowknife. He had fishers in Nova Scotia or in British Columbia share their ideas and aspirations with farmers in Manitoba and Saskatchewan. Stay-at-home parents were exposed to the worlds of national politics, international finance, and professional sport as Gzowski provided his listeners with an eclectic yet distinctly Canadian view of the world.

Peter Gzowski on the radio seemed like a wise uncle or older brother, yet he was not patronizing; above all, he was a professional journalist. He posed serious questions for those he interviewed but always showed respect and warmth and at times humour in his approach. After graduating from Ridley College, he attended the University of Toronto, where he began his journalistic career editing *The Varsity*. Subsequent stints with newspapers in Timmons, Ontario; Moose Jaw, Saskatchewan; and Chatham, Ontario, led to a position with *Maclean's* magazine in 1958, where he became managing editor in 1962. He also worked for a time at the Toronto *Star* and the national *Star Weekly*. Despite this extensive range of experience, he never lost the small-town curiosity and sensitivity he developed as a boy in Galt, Ontario, in the years following his birth in Toronto in 1934. Peter Gzowski, journalist, broadcaster, author of a dozen books, champion of literacy, holder of twelve honourary doctorates, and a member of the Order of Canada, retired to freelance journalism in 1997 and passed away in 2002.

With the publication of *The Game of Our Lives* in 1981, Peter Gzowski showed Canadians hockey in all its diversity. This is a book about youth discovering the joys of the game and about a middle-aged man rediscovering that joyful game in his past. It is also a volume about a seasoned journalist experiencing a multi-talented, rising professional hockey team's daily activities in the National Hockey League. Never confused for a professional athlete, the middle-aged Gzowski becomes part of the Edmonton Oilers in 1980 and shares with his readers what it is like to play professional hockey with a team on the threshold of success, a team which, led by the peerless Wayne Gretzky in the 1980s, would become one of the most dominant in NHL history.

In subsequent years, the Oilers fell victim to the Canadian small-market syndrome, having finite revenue produced in Canadian dollars but ever-increasing players' salaries paid in American dollars. The result was the loss of Gretzky in 1988 and then other stars to larger market-based teams. The Oilers teams of the past decade and a half have been exciting to watch and have had potential, but invariably they seem destined to be disassembled as the players improve and make salary demands that cannot be met. Thus, the Edmonton Oilers teams of the early and mid-1980s were unique in that they were teams of players and coaches who matured together and used their talents to capture five Stanley Cups within seven years.

Gzowski's view of hockey is by no means a romanticized view. Indeed, in *The Game of Our Lives* when he reminisces about his boyhood and the anticipation of that first skate of the year on new ice, he touches something which many Canadians have felt for generations. Whether on a pond in rural New Brunswick or the interior of British Columbia; a slough on a farm in Manitoba, Saskatchewan, or Alberta; or an urban outdoor rink in Saskatoon, Toronto, Montreal, or Halifax, the outdoor experience related in Gzowski's descriptive prose is a part of being Canadian. Similarly, when he puts on the equipment and is on the ice with Gretzky, Lowe, and Messier, he at once fulfills the dreams of many hockey fans, yet he suffers the very real middle-aged aches and pains of practices and competition.

For many readers, *The Game of Our Lives* captures the essence of hockey for Canadians. Roy MacGregor in the *Encyclopedia of Literature in Canada* (University of Toronto Press, 2002) refers to the work as: "one of the best hockey books." Indeed, it was republished as a popular paperback in 1983. The fact that it was out of print denied countless potential readers the opportunity to share their roots with one of Canada's most respected journalists. With this new Heritage Group edition, readers in the twenty-first century now will be able to experience first-hand Gzowski's description of a part of the Canadian cultural fabric in prose that is at once intelligent and passionate.

Does hockey mean the same to Canadians in 2004 as it did over two decades ago? Canadians' overwhelming positive reaction to the women's and men's gold medals for hockey at the 2002 Olympic Games seems to indicate no dissipation in Canadians' visceral feeling for the game. It is interesting to note that the men's team was assembled under the guidance of Wayne Gretzky, who after playing for Los Angeles, St. Louis, and the New York Rangers retired from the game in 1999. Yet there he was in 2002, back in his own country creating what would be one of the two most important teams of the decade for Canadians.

In the fall of 2003, it was Gretzky again, along with fellow members of the Edmonton Oilers from the era described in *The Game of Our Lives*, who played an outdoor "Mega-Stars" contest against former members of the Montreal Canadiens at Commonwealth Stadium in Edmonton. The game, played before a record NHL crowd of more than 57,000 people, featured Oilers players from the 1979–1990 era. This "Mega-Stars" contest against former Montreal Canadiens players from the 1970s, '80s, and '90s preceded the regular NHL contest between the current Edmonton and Montreal squads. The latter game marked the first time in history that NHL teams played an official contest outdoors. For six hours, 57,167 people from across the country, and some from other countries as well, cheered, clapped, and stomped their feet throughout this unique afternoon and evening of hockey. The initial contest began in mid-afternoon with the temperature at -19 Celsius. Yet by evening when the second game was in full swing, hardly any of the people had left, despite a cold wind and dropping temperature.

This "Heritage Classic" was an event the late Peter Gzowski would have loved. Hockey Hall of Fame players donning toques, players shovelling snow off the ice surface between periods, and more than 2.747 million Canadian television viewers shared this country's game in a unique yet so typical way. To play pond hockey or to skate on a city neighbourhood outdoor rink is what the sport is all about. Indeed, in *The Game of Our Lives*, Gzowski lauds the outdoor rink experience as preparing Canadian youth to appreciate their hockey heroes in the NHL: "We understood; we knew what it felt like. All that separated us from our true heroes was that they were better at something we all had done. They belonged to us, as no other kind of hero ever could, at once more celebrated and more approachable because of what we shared. They were *of* us, playing the game of our lives."

Here it was, 2003, and heroes like Wayne Gretzky, Guy Lapointe, and Steve Shutt played "our game" in concert with the dreams and fantasies of the millions who watched live and on television. Canadians could share with Wayne Gretzky when he said the night before the big game that hockey is "the greatest game in the world and we never grow tired of it." They could share with Guy Lapointe when he stated unequivocally that the big game was "for the people … it brings back memories of when we were kids." And Canadians could share with Hall of Fame player Steve Shutt when he said the game illustrated "people going back to their roots. Everybody grew up on an outdoor rink and I think this stripped-down hockey takes the business away from it, all the marketing away. You just go back to when everyone was a kid playing pond hockey. I think that's what's caught everybody's imagination."

Fans by the thousands flocked to Edmonton on that cold day in November 2003. A newly married couple from Windsor, Ontario, on their honeymoon, a pair of unemployed workers in their twenties recently laid off in Labrador, retired men from central Canada, a family from Winnipeg, a couple from Montreal … all came, sometimes at great expense, to experience first-hand "our game" as it was meant to be played.

With the publication of this new edition of *The Game of Our Lives*, the spirit of Canada's sport reflected in the Heritage Classic of 2003, the Olympic victories of 2002, the wide-open Oilers hockey of the 1980s is captured in words. This book will once again enable Canadians of all ages, from all walks of life to join together and savour "the game of our lives," hockey, through the imagination, wit, and intelligent prose of one of this country's greatest journalists. Enjoy!

# Hometown Hero

*Lyrics by Pete White, music by Paul Hann*

We had a helluva team that year
We won us almost every game
We got ourselves a playoff spot
And a touch of small town fame
I had a helluva year that year
Everybody knew my name
And if I didn't make the Maple Leafs
I only had myself to blame

There was a pat on the back and a free beer
From every old boy in this old town
A teasin' smile—a rosy-cheeked cheer
From every young girl for miles around
Maybe it was just the breaks
Or not havin' what it takes
But this hometown hero
Didn't make it out of town

I guess we married kind of young
Maybe we had the kids too soon
Waitin' for the second one to come
I knew I had to make the money soon
Started workin' at the plant
Been there now since fifty-four
My father worked there too
His father long before …

Sometimes the oldest boy and I
We head down to the rink
But the old man's gettin' old
'Least that's what the young one thinks
He's havin' a helluva year this year
Everybody knows his name
And if he doesn't make the Maple Leafs
He's only got himself to blame

**1**

*… Their hands were a better sign of their profession than their faces*

Of all the young mercenaries who began the 1980–81 National Hockey League season with the Edmonton Oilers, only one, Mark Messier, had grown up in Edmonton. Messier was still a teenager that fall, although he had a body sculptors would kill for. On the ice, he played with what he liked to call "reckless abandon," probably unaware that the phrase echoed back to players as ancient as Sprague Cleghorn, a face-breaking defenceman of the 1920s. Messier sometimes played with reckless abandon off the ice, too. He had a wide-eyed look when he was excited, and his nostrils seemed to flare. In the dressing room he would occasionally break into song. With his head thrown back, his eyes closed, his Praxitelean body naked, one hand cupped over his genitals, he would bellow, "been down so long it looks like up to me." Messier's father was a schoolteacher who also coached hockey; sometimes Mark would stay at his parents' house in Edmonton and sometimes he would not.

Messier and Don Murdoch, a right-winger from Cranbrook, British Columbia, with a troubled past, were related on their mothers' side and had known each other casually when they were growing up. But the rest of the Oilers had met only when they came to Edmonton to play hockey. They had come from as nearby as Ponoka, Alberta, and as far away as Mantta, Finland. More of them, nine, came from Ontario than anywhere else. Although two of them had been born in Toronto, one in Winnipeg, and one in Chicago, the names of many of their birthplaces sounded like the timetable of an old-fashioned Canadian train, running from Charlottetown in the east to Nelson in the west, and passing on the way through such communities as Hawkesbury, Petrolia, Birtle, and Cold Lake.

They lived in various accommodations around Edmonton. A few of them were married and owned their own houses. Blair MacDonald, their handsome captain, spent much of the summer of 1980 working on a spacious old house he and his wife had bought across from the Provincial Museum, sanding the floors and tearing down a wall between the kitchen and what was to be a dining area. Lee Fogolin, a defenceman with wrists the size of some men's thighs, liked to stay at his suburban home and work with wood. The cabinet in which the team stored videotapes of its games was a product of Fogolin's home workshop. One or two of the bachelor crowd shared their quarters with permanent lady friends. Paul Coffey, a rookie, maintained a room at the Edmonton Plaza Hotel, partly out of shyness and partly because he was still not sure he would not be assigned to the minor leagues. But by far the most common arrangement was to live with other members of the team, in apartments or condominiums or houses. Housing was not cheap in Edmonton, a city enjoying the profits of the Alberta oil boom, but the Oilers lived high in the middle class. Bryan Watson, their coach, once drew up a map to see who lived close to which shopping centre, to facilitate personal appearances through the season. The map looked like a guide to the more affluent neighbourhoods of Edmonton, with clusters near the University of Alberta, in the prosperous west end, and around the Whitemud Freeway on the way to the airport.

Gathering for a road trip, the Oilers would often descend on the airport in groups. In concession to Edmonton's northern climate and rude setting, some of them drove Jeeps or panel trucks. Others settled for standard American cars. Cars were an important part of their lives, but those who owned exotic breeds—Wayne Gretzky, their young superstar, had a $57,000 black Ferrari—would leave them elsewhere; getting to the airport called for practical transportation. At the airport, the discrepancies in their lifestyles would disappear; they became an entity. They dressed similarly, in slacks and well-tailored sports jackets, or well-cut suits. Their clothes showed their slim hips. Their shoes or

cowboy boots were always shined. Even those who wore their hair long
never needed it cut. Three of their veterans wore neatly trimmed beards;
and as the season began, some of the younger players were trying to
grow beards, too, but even unshaven they looked kempt, like studiously
casual fashion models. All of them could have been described as handsome, though in different ways. Their colouring varied from the pale
blond of the Finnish defenceman Risto Siltanen to the swarthiness of
the shy rookie Coffey, and their height from Siltanen's five-eight to the
looming six-four of their square-jawed enforcer, Dave Semenko. Their
faces were sometimes emblazoned with cuts or scrapes or bruises, but
in the age of helmets—only four of them played without—they were
usually unmarked. One or two had complexion problems. Their hands
were a better sign of their profession than their faces; nearly all of them
had large hands.

Even their baggage was alike. They packed what they needed for a
week's road trip into a carry-on valise, with an extra jacket pressed into
a hanging bag, which they would stow in the aircraft locker, or hand
to a stewardess to store at the back. They called stewardesses "miss" or
"ma'am." Their seats were assigned by Rod Phillips, the bespectacled
play-by-play radio announcer who also acted as the team's travelling
secretary. Few of them would read, and those who did concentrated
on thrillers or science fiction. If there was a new edition of the weekly
*Hockey News*, they passed that around, and they shared the sports
section of the paper from whatever city they had just left. The front
section of the newspaper meant little to them, and the magazines that
attracted their attention almost all contained pictures of naked women,
which they chortled over. Their favourite movies were comedies; their
favourite music channels, rock and roll. A few of them would play cards
or backgammon for small stakes, but with extraordinary quickness;
they were all good at games. Often, they would doze. They could fall
asleep easily, their heads lolling against the seats, their ties now loos-
ened. But they would not be still for long. They were healthy young
men, in prime fettle, and even in the sedentary confines of an aircraft
they needed to move around. They expressed themselves physically,
wrestling, tugging, patting, slugging each other on the arm. For no apparent reason, one of them would suddenly wrap another's neck in the

crook of his arm and knuckle his hair. If anyone slept too long or too soundly, he ran the risk of waking up with his tie cut, or his cowboy boots filled with shaving cream.

The sense of pack that characterized them in airplanes was not confined to the road. The team was the nucleus of their lives. The rest of the world that spun around it—trainers, coaches, agents, writers, and, at the very outside, fans—was extrinsic. Even their families sometimes seemed less important to them than their playmates. After a trip of several days, during which they had travelled, eaten, dressed, drunk, played hockey, and roomed with one another, they were liable on their return to forsake their women and children and congregate in one of the Edmonton watering holes they favoured. Friendships were between the player and the team as a whole, rather than between individuals. For all their unity, no one wanted to become too close to anyone else, since a friend could be traded away without notice. As a result, the Oilers were virtually without cliques. On the road, roommates were rotated by management; recreationally oriented players were usually paired with the more dependable. After training camp, where veterans stayed aloof from rookies until it was clear who might belong on the team and who would go to the minors, social combinations would form and reform, so that the appearance of one Oiler at a particular bar or restaurant was no guarantee of the possible appearance of any other. The exception to this rule was the trio of Finns, Matti Hagman, Jari Kurri, and the squat defenceman Siltanen. The Finns formed a sort of club within the club, set apart by their inaccessible language. At training camp one morning, the coaches asked Hagman to count off the day's warm-up exercises in Finnish: *yksi, kaksi, kolmë, nelja, viisi* ... The fact that everyone followed his count was as close as the English-speaking majority came to a gesture of international friendship. At least one of the Anglos—Pat Price, a moustachioed defenceman given to cowboy hats and country music—grumbled about the divisiveness of the Finns' presence; but this rift was carefully hidden from outsiders, and was less important than the team's solid front.

The Oilers' most notable characteristic, as they set out on Edmonton's second season in the NHL, was their youth. Hockey players used to serve an apprenticeship before graduating to the NHL, arriving usually in their early twenties and staying, with luck, until their mid-thirties. As late as 1967, the last year of the old six-team league, the Toronto Maple Leafs won a Stanley Cup with a team built around such players as George Armstrong, Marcel Pronovost, and Tim Horton, all of whom were thirty-seven, Terry Sawchuk, thirty-eight, Red Kelly, forty, Allan Stanley, forty-one, and the remarkable Johnny Bower, who, if his birth certificate was to be believed, was forty-three.

The year after the Leafs' victory, the NHL doubled its enrolment, and in 1971 a group of outsiders started another professional league, the World Hockey Association. With the demand for competent players now far in excess of the supply, some veterans were able to stick around even longer. The owners also began raiding the junior ranks and, led by the barons of the WHA, lowering the age limitations on whom they could sign. On many teams, men played with teammates young enough to be their sons. (In the case of the Howe family, this generational bridge was actually made.) Then the supply of the young talent began to meet the demand, and good old players began to give way to good younger ones. By the late 1970s, the NHL was a booming market for Clearasil, a nonexistent one for Geritol.

Even in this juvenile environment, the Oilers were noteworthy. They were almost certainly (there were no statistics from the early days) the youngest team in NHL history. Only the goalie Ron Low had reached thirty, and with his heavy black beard, Low looked wizened among his colleagues. In a pinch, the Oilers could have iced a lineup of eligible juniors. One defenceman, Kevin Lowe, was twenty-one, and in his second year. Two rookies, Glenn Anderson and Jari Kurri, were twenty. And Coffey, Messier, and Gretzky were nineteen. Even excluding these six, the team's average age would have been just over twenty-five. In spite of their elegantly tailored clothes, the Oilers on the road resembled not so much a team of young professionals as a seminar of sturdy graduate students, fresh-faced and eager to meet their term assignments.

During the season, the Oilers travelled across scores of thousands of miles by airplane and bus. They visited each of the NHL's twenty other cities twice, and made three extra trips across the continent during the playoffs. In spite of their youth, there were few of these cities in which at least one of them had not spent some time playing for the home team, so that in almost every town they would quickly find a bar or café in which they could relax, often surrounded by fans; and the roster of fans usually included eager females. Occasionally, a few of the players would show up at practice with red eyes and tender heads. On one trip to Montreal, with no game for the next two days, a crew of them went to a bar whose chief feature was strip-tease dancers who came within body checking range of the customers. The next day some of the more boisterous Oilers were chuckling over the way these women had reacted to live matches lit near their pubic hair. But these occasions of late-night revelry were, considering the Oilers' youth and the amount of time they spent away from home, noticeable by their infrequency. Most of their time on the road was spent in hotel rooms or hockey arenas. Sometimes they would kill time shopping, and in places like Montreal or Los Angeles they would arrive at the rink before game time exchanging notes on their new apparel.

At least as much time was spent staring at television in their rooms, or trying to nap. Many of them were experts on the plot of *General Hospital*, and even on the rare evenings when they would gather with their mates in Edmonton, they would often play *Family Feud*, a TV game show they could follow in almost every city they visited. They were indifferent tourists. Museums and art galleries interested them not at all. Even Glenn Anderson, a rookie who had come to them from the Canadian Olympic team, who had spent time travelling in Europe and Japan, and who, in Edmonton, could be found from time to time sipping a soft drink in a University of Alberta pub and reading a book, tended to behave as if all cities were interchangeable. In Quebec City, the Oilers rode taxis from the Quebec Hilton, overlooking historic battlements, down through Lower Town to the arena, without lifting their eyes from the *Hockey News*. In New York, some of them walked briefly past the flesh-pots of Forty-second Street and one or two invested silver coins in peep shows featuring "live" girls, but after the game most of them congregated in a saloon on the street level of Madison Square Garden. They sampled steamed clams and lobster in Boston, wiener schnitzel in St. Louis, and filet of sole in Montreal, but more often they sought out the nearest hearty Italian meal, or steaks and baked potatoes with sour cream and chives.

On the ice, the Oilers had an exceptionally eventful season. At first they played so badly that management felt compelled to make a dramatic coaching change. They would beat teams they apparently had no business beating—sometimes by lopsided scores—and then lose to a team they ought to have defeated. In spite of a playoff structure so generous as to offend many hockey traditionalists—only five of the twenty-one teams weren't eligible to contest the Stanley Cup—they entered the last stretch of the season in danger of not making the playoffs. In that final stretch, however, they turned into a nearly invincible force, roaring through their final dozen games with as good a record as any team in the league. In the playoffs they surprised even themselves, managing one of the most remarkable upsets in the history of the Stanley Cup and coming breathtakingly close to another one.

Through this month-long surge of excellence, they caught the imagination of hockey fans everywhere. They played most of the year with a lineup that included only one player who drew attention, Gretzky, but they finished amid widespread affirmation of their strength as a team, and several of their youngest players became celebrities, the talk not only of the hockey world but of many spring dinner parties as well. There was something special about them, something about the magic of their youth. When they played on national television, ratings soared; people who had grown cynical of hockey learned their names and became their fans. When their season finally ended, some of the game's wisest and most experienced observers were hailing them as the team of the future and even going so far as to suggest that what had begun in Edmonton was a dynasty of Montreal Canadiens dimensions, even though they had yet to win their first Stanley Cup. With hindsight, a few of their supporters claimed to have foreseen this happy outcome all along. In truth, their year was as marked by false starts, wrong turns, and stretches of exasperation as it was by the steadiness of their triumphant march. The clues to what was to happen eventually, if they were there at all, were almost always obscured by the churning of their own personalities and those of the people who helped to guide their destiny.

**2**

*"If they weren't going to play me … I could have used one more day at home"*

Buffalo, New York, October 15, 1980: High in the press box, amid the rafters of the Buffalo Memorial Auditorium, Glen Sather, the Oilers' general manager, plays with the aerial of a walkie-talkie. On the creamy ice below him, the Oilers swirl in lazy arcs, loosening their muscles for the evening's fray. The sounds of their ritual fill the arena like the tuneless warm-up of a symphony, the *rask, rask* of their skates, the *thwock* and *clack* of the puck. A lunatic has been killing cab-drivers in Buffalo this fall, cutting out his victims' hearts. Even the Oilers, tough young athletes, with hardened bodies and a cocky air, have not walked the streets carelessly. The arena feels safe, comfortable, resonant with memory.

In the broadcast booth not far from Sather, Rod Phillips goes over his notes. Phillips may be the Oilers' ultimate fan. As he yells the games back to Edmonton, his glasses steam with enthusiasm. The Oilers have dubbed him Road Trip, in honour of his supervision of airplane tickets, and they treat him as one of their own. At practice this morning, Mark Messier, the irrepressible teenager, emptied the scotch from the mickey Roddy sometimes packs to relieve the tension of his broadcasts and filled it with water.

The Oilers are off to a depressing start. They lost their first two games of the season, both at home. The teams that beat them, Quebec and Colorado, both of whom finished behind them last year, are the sort they will have to handle if they are going to have a successful season. Already some tension is setting in. On the ice below, they look solemn and businesslike, even grim. Sather's walkie-talkie will keep him in touch with the Edmonton bench. As well as being their general manager, Sather is the Oilers' president. At thirty-seven, he is almost as young for his position as so many of his players are for theirs. Until this year he has also been the team's coach. But this season he has handed that job over to Bryan Watson, a friend from his playing days who stands below him, arms folded in tense concentration. Throughout the exhibition schedule and the first two games of league play in Edmonton, Sather has worked conscientiously at letting Watson direct the immediate fortunes of the team. The transition has not been easy for Sather, and at least in Watson's view, he has not been entirely successful at it.

Sather likes to run things. Competition throbs through everything he does. On airplanes he plays liars' poker for the price of a headset; in restaurants he turns the negotiations over who will pay the bill into a complex game of guessing numbers, for which he holds the pencil and explains the rules. Minor matters of office administration he sometimes settles on the racquetball court. Even in casual conversation, he seeks the edge, keeping his partner off balance with a barrage of lighthearted insults and cackling with delight when he scores a point. Like most competitive men, he enjoys the contest almost as much as the victory. He prides himself on being as scrupulous as he is tough.

At the Oilers' training camp in September, Sather had to bring both these characteristics into play almost daily. One incident involved Dave Archambault, a big, strong, handsome young man from Ontario, who wanted to give the pros a whirl after a successful career in United States college hockey. Like almost all the rookies who won invitations to the Oilers' camp, Archambault looked impressive on the ice, but to Sather's expert eye, and to the eyes of the coaches and scouts who worked with him, he lacked the aggressive nature that would have marked him as big-league material. Archambault sensed this. In his final practice he deliberately started a fight; as a result, he broke two bones in his hand on the helmet of a player whose name he did not

know. When Archambault returned from the hospital, Sather called
him in for a chat and, while Archambault sat with his broken hand
pulsing with pain, offered him a contract well down in the Oilers' minor
system, in Milwaukee, for a signing bonus of $4,000 and an annual sal-
ary of $10,000. For Archambault, whose college marks had fallen off as
his hockey career blossomed, the news meant the end of an ambition he
had nourished most of his life; players who go down as far as Milwaukee
almost never make it to the NHL. Yet when he went to the rookies' hotel
that evening, he was full of praise for Sather's generosity and fairness.
"He didn't have to give me any bonus at all," he said.

For the past couple of weeks, Sather has been concerned that
Watson, an extraordinarily decent man and a close and cherished friend,
has shown neither the ruthlessness that he feels the coach of a young
team needs nor the finesse to deal with situations similar to Sather's
meeting with Archambault.

Now, in anticipation of the game against Buffalo, Sather grins. He
has light hair and a pale complexion that rouges when he is emotional.
When he was a player, his nickname, Slats, which is still used by those
who are or would be his friends, occasionally gave way to Tomato. There
are blushes on his cheeks tonight.

"I played my first game as a pro in this rink," he says. "No, wait, I
played my first game as a defenceman here."

Sather sometimes has difficulty remembering the details of his career. He was a prototypical journeyman, a scrapper. In nine seasons, he
played for six teams: Boston, Pittsburgh, New York Rangers, St. Louis,
Montreal, and Minnesota. He racked up an impressive number of penalty minutes, 724, but a paltry number of goals, 80. Wherever he went,
he impressed both his coaches and his teammates with his competitive
zeal. "You can tell it's getting close to the playoffs," Vic Hadfield, then
the captain of the New York Rangers, wrote in a diary he kept for the
season of 1972–73. "Slats is getting bitchy." Hadfield, the thirty-second
highest goal-scorer in NHL history, sits down the pressbox from Sather
tonight, smoking a cheroot. In the off season, he is a successful golf professional, and the owner of substantial golfing real estate. But in hockey
he is a part-time scout for the Oilers and Sather is his boss.

"I thought you were a defensive forward," someone says to Sather. "Yeah, sure," he replies. "But sometimes they put me back on defence." His mind seems to be somewhere else for a moment. "Jeez, I liked playing," he says. "I always liked playing."

The emotionless voice of the Buffalo public address announcer begins calling out the names of the players who are listed in the program but not dressed for tonight's game.

"For Edmonton," he drones, "number six, Colin Campbell ..."

Soupy Campbell, twenty-seven years old, a solid defenceman widely liked by the rest of the team and respected for his tenacity, had been sent to the Vancouver Canucks just before the Oilers left for the first road trip of the year. Some of his friends are not happy with the way he was let go: called over to the boards in mid-practice and told the Oilers had released him and Vancouver had claimed him. Thanks, Soupy, and good-bye.

"... number twenty-three, Tom Bladon ..."

Bladon is back in Edmonton. He is twenty-seven, too, one of the older players in the Oilers' organization. Like Campbell, he is a defenceman and an established pro. He has never quite lived up to his early promise. The Philadelphia Flyers made him their second-round draft choice in the 1972 amateur draft, and he stayed with them for six undistinguished years before being traded to Pittsburgh and then, in 1979, to Edmonton. On paper, Bladon looked like just what the Oilers needed: a reliable veteran to settle their young team and perhaps lead their defensive corps. But at training camp the coaches seemed to notice only his mistakes. There are those who wonder if the coaches would have been as assiduous if Bladon had been a rookie. The Oilers have asked him to report to their minor-league affiliate in Wichita, Kansas. Pride is keeping him at home.

"... ten, Hagman, and seventeen, Kurri."

Two of the Finns. Matti Hagman is one of what some people call Sather's reclamation projects. He came to North America in 1976, when he was twenty, to play for the Boston Bruins, one of the first of his countrymen to try to crack the big payrolls of the NHL. He had what the

Oilers' media guide refers to as "difficulty adjusting to North American ways," which is to say he started drinking too much. Boston unloaded him and the Quebec Nordiques, then a member of the WHA, picked him up. On one road trip with the Nordiques, he missed the team's plane, an unforgivable breach of conduct in professional hockey. He went back to Finland. At home, he apparently turned himself around. He applied himself to life away from the hockey rink, studying for and acquiring a licence to be a fireman. He married and had a son. His hockey skills, meanwhile, remained intact. Last season he scored fifty goals in thirty-four games with his team in Helsinki, a national record, and the Oilers, who follow European hockey with an eager eye, persuaded him to give the big league another try. He is a serious young man, still only twenty-five, whose blond eyebrows turn up at the edges to give him a satanic look. So far, except for the unfortunate development of a skin eruption between his eyebrows ("do you need a contact lens for your third eye?" someone asked him at practice this morning), things have gone well for him. He and Kurri, a nineteen-year-old with a hair-trigger release to his shot, have been among the most impressive forwards in training camp. In the two losses that opened the season, however, the Oilers have given up nine goals. Finns, the wisdom goes, don't play a strong defensive game. The coaches have decided to rest Hagman and Kurri.

These are not easy decisions to make, and the coaches struggle with them all the time. At this stage of the season, teams often carry more players than they can dress. The rules allow only nineteen men in uniform for a game, and on this trip, which will take them from Buffalo to Long Island and New York, the Oilers have twenty-two. The twenty-second joined them last night. He is John Hughes, a stocky defenceman with bright eyes, a flourishing moustache, and a quick and winning smile. Tonight he is feeling vexed. He had been playing in Vancouver and, so far as he knew, playing well. After several years of knocking around teams in Phoenix, Cincinnati, Houston, Indianapolis, and even Edmonton for awhile when the Oilers were in the WHA, he had counted on Vancouver as a place to settle down. He and his wife spent most of the summer finishing a house they built for themselves in Coquitlam. Training camp had seemed to go satisfactorily. And then, suddenly, the chop. Vancouver made him available to any team that wanted him. When Hughes got home to tell his wife that they and their year-and-a-half-old son would be moving to Edmonton, his wife had been in the process of opening the last box of possessions for their new home. He caught the next plane to Buffalo. Since he has been able to practise only once with the team, the coaches have decided not to put him on tonight's list. His transfer is part of the life he has chosen. Talking of its suddenness, he smiles wryly. It is hard for him not to wonder at the turn of events in his own life and Soupy Campbell's that has, at whatever disruption to them and their families, meant in effect that two teams could exchange defencemen of similar size, style, ability, and—he realizes as he catches up on the veterans' speculation about the unsuitability of Campbell and Bladon—age. He wonders if the Campbells, whose daughter is just six months younger than his own son, would like to rent the house in Coquitlam this year. His smile grows tighter.

"If they weren't going to play me," he said just before tonight's game, glancing around as if to make sure no member of the coaching staff would hear even a mild complaint, "I could have used one more day at home. My wife's pretty upset."

There are cheers as the Buffalo Sabres come out on the ice. The Sabres are off to almost as bad a start as the Oilers, having lost one and tied one of their first two games. But those games were on the road, and they have an awesome record at home: No one has beaten them in a regular season game at the Aud since last January. They are a puzzling team, stocked with competent players and a few who are much more than competent, yet they are somehow incapable of, as they say, winning it all. Already, Scotty Bowman, the former Montreal coach who has been hired as general manager to breathe some life into the Sabres, is rumoured to be looking for trades to shake them up. He has his eyes on some of the young Oilers, but the lineup he has sent out tonight looks menacingly mature.

Gilbert Perreault draws the loudest cheers. Perreault is one of the most exciting players in the league, able to launch himself on long, dervish-like rushes, but far too often his adventures end pointlessly.

This week, *Sports Illustrated* has run a piece about the new season that calls Perreault the most overrated player in the game. Today, the Buffalo papers, or those parts of them not given to the fate of slain cab-drivers, have been full of counterattacks, at least one of them pointing out that the author of the *Sports Illustrated* piece is, God forbid, a woman. Even the Oilers have been buzzing about the insult, and they fear Perreault will answer his critics with the kind of explosive game of which he is still capable.

The Oilers quicken their pace, trying to break sweat before they must pose for the opening ceremonies. Their away uniforms, predominantly royal blue, look crisp and fresh. Their names, stitched in white across their shoulders, are less dominant than the orange numbers on their backs.

Number 2 is Lee Fogolin, the brawny, wood-working defenceman. One of his eyes looks vaguely askance, but no one teases him about it. Fogolin is as strong as he appears, and every day after practice he works with weights. He was born in Chicago, where his father, also Lee, was a hockey player, but he spent most of his youth in northern Ontario. Lee the son—universally Fogie—is a devout Catholic and family man, and the most dedicated hockey player on the team. One night last season, he awoke in Hartford, Connecticut, with a screaming toothache. He called long-distance to his sister-in-law, a dental hygienist. "Wait till morning," she said. "I can't," said Fogie, "I have to play tomorrow." Then he went to his hotel-room closet, dismantled a coat hanger, made a small hook, and ripped the cap off his offending molar. In the game the next night, he beat up Hartford's Warren Miller, whose errant stick had cut him for six stitches—outside the mouth.

Number 4 is Kevin Lowe, called Vicious, or Vish, by his teammates, because he isn't. Kevin's mother lives in Quebec, reads the *Hockey News* every week, and is a devoted fan. The first time she heard the nickname she thought it was Fish, and wondered why. Tall and angular, Kevin was the Oilers' first draft pick in 1979, and scored their first NHL goal, one of only two he got last year. There is a gentlemanly air about him, and the look of a future star, although he still has much to learn. He is a young man of innate class and is fluently bilingual. Sometimes he fights to upgrade the television tastes of his Edmonton apartment mate, Wayne Gretzky, for whom he cooks. His easy, aristocratic smile serves to cover a bashfulness that he is struggling to conquer.

Number 5 is Doug Hicks, a workmanlike, bearded defenceman, now entering his eighth season in the NHL. He is one of the few native Albertans on the team, having been raised in Cold Lake. He is also a connoisseur of tailoring establishments around the league, and a splendid, if conservative, dresser who helps to set the Oilers' collegiate style. Along with his Edmonton roommate, Dave Lumley, he leads an active bachelor life. Although he suffered bruised ribs at training camp, it is already evident that his steady play on the blueline, though not much noticed by the press, is an important ingredient in the Oilers' scheme of things.

Number 7: the shy, young Coffey. *The* rookie. Coffey was Edmonton's first draft pick in the spring, and they expect wonders from him. So far, however, he seems bottled up, as tense on the ice as he is reticent off it. He first came to Edmonton over the summer, along with his agent Gus Badali, whom he shares with Gretzky. In the limousine that picked them up at the airport and drove them downtown, he said not a word, staring at the Edmonton skyline as if it were Babylon. At training camp he looked unsure of himself, although he is such a fluid skater that he is obviously capable at any moment of living up to his promise. He is nineteen, but seems much younger than Gretzky. A handsome young man with deep brown eyes, he still keeps much to himself. Badali says he could be the next Bobby Orr, but, of course, all agents say that of all their defensive stock.

Number 8: Risto Siltanen, in terms of service the Oilers' senior Finn, although he will turn twenty-two only at the end of this month. This is Risto's third year with Edmonton. His diminutive height and gleeful grin give him the look of a Viking pixie. He is an impressive skater, maintaining extraordinary balance with the quick, choppy strides that characterize European-trained skaters; contrary to the conventional wisdom about his national proclivities, he is a defensive rock. His English is the best of the three Finns' and sometimes he serves as the team's Finnish-English translator. Matti Hagman, with his earlier experience, is quite comfortable in English too, but the teenage Kurri, who is apparently quite unschooled even in his first language, has yet to be heard from at all.

Number 9 is Glenn Anderson, still another vaunted rookie—perhaps too vaunted. At Lake Placid last year, Anderson was the most exciting player on the Canadian Olympic team, and when the Oilers signed him to a professional contract this summer, the scout who'd followed him made a flattering comparison between his speed and that of Guy Lafleur. Sather reacted vehemently, but the comparison had already been published. Still, if anyone can handle the pressure that kind of comparison entails, it is Anderson. He is fey. He comes either from Vancouver, as his birth records show, or from another planet; he seems incapable of giving a straight interview—he doesn't take the process seriously enough. He told the Oilers' publicity department that his childhood idol was Wayne Gretzky, who is younger than he is. He has told other reporters that he dropped out of boyhood hockey because his feet got cold. Anderson bears an uncanny resemblance to the television comedian Robin Williams, and since he does not appreciate being called Mork, he is in the process of growing a beard.

Number 11: Mark Messier. He is so young in many ways—only eight days older than Gretzky—and so old in others. He can be the best player on the ice, or the worst, and sometimes he is both on the same shift. In conversation he can be solemn, reflective, articulate, or as surly as a punk rocker, just as in a game he can be as thrilling as any player on the team or, without apparent reason, can decide to go for a leisurely skate.

Number 12: Dave Hunter is as unassuming as Messier can be cocky. Hunter walks splayfooted, and when he skates he hunches his shoulders and turns the inside of his elbows to the front. He is a stalwart defensive forward and just the kind of indestructible journeyman the team needs to anchor its freewheeling offence. The son of a farmer from Petrolia, Ontario, he has a brother who has been drafted high by the Quebec Nordiques and who some people think might have the goal-scoring ability Dave seems to lack, but Dave is too pleasant a young man to be jealous.

Number 14: Blair MacDonald, called B.J. The captain. In street clothes, and wearing, as he sometimes does, steel-rimmed spectacles, B.J. looks more like an airline pilot than an athlete. Married to a model, he occasionally models professionally himself. Although he is only twenty-six, B.J. is feeling middle-aged this fall. Last year, playing on Gretzky's wing, he scored forty-six goals and was named to the league's all-star team. But at training camp, when the team was divided into lines and squads of different coloured jerseys, he was often assigned black. Black means you're on the outer edges of the team. His place on Gretzky's line, who wore red jerseys, was often taken by Anderson or Kurri. He has had trouble negotiating his contract over the summer and the press has played it up. At least one important person in management has called him a whiner; his wife hopes he'll be traded, although she would hate to leave the house they're fixing up near the museum.

Number 15: Curt Brackenbury, called Brack. A right-winger known as good hit, no score, he has been acquired from Quebec only a few days ago, and has joined the team just before this trip. He remains a stranger, but Sather is counting on him to play an important role. Brackenbury has been around professional hockey for seven years, and he has run up more than twenty hours in penalties, but he has a cheery, enthusiastic disposition that contrasts with his gun-slinger's reputation. As the players get to know him, Sather hopes, he will provide them with the emotional spark they often need.

Number 18: Brett Callighen, proud of his post as the players' representative—a sort of shop steward, as opposed to the captain, who is appointed by management. His nickname, Key, refers not to this position but is an abbreviation of Monkey, and was given him in tribute to a jaw so simian as to be almost beautiful; Key does commercials on Edmonton TV. Unlike Glenn Anderson, he really did drop out of the game in boyhood—to ski, in his case—and came back to it only in college. (The fact that he'd been at college would have made him a rarity only a few years ago.) He's been a pro since 1974. Tonight, he has a secret: An eye that was injured last season and that kept him out of the final twenty-one games has not fully recovered its sight. He wears a clear plastic face-guard when he plays but, unknown to the coaches, he is having trouble seeing the puck and is labouring on the ice.

Number 20 is Dave Lumley, Doug Hick's bachelor partner, and a solid two-way performer. Like Hunter, Lumley is the kind of worthy tradesman who plies his way up and down his own wing, not sparkling but not noticeably weak either. Like Callighen, he is a college man, having graduated from the University of New Hampshire, from where he was swept up in the Montreal organization. Montreal kept him in the minors for two seasons, but with Edmonton, which acquired him upon their own entry into the NHL, he had an impressive rookie season, scoring twenty goals. Like MacDonald, though, he felt a little pressure at training camp from younger players (he is only twenty-five). His worst problem is a tendency to get down on himself and sulk.

Number 21: Stan Weir, at twenty-eight the wily veteran of the forward platoons. (All veterans are wily.) Weir even looks like a throwback to an earlier age; he is the only Oiler to play without his front teeth, and that, coupled with his red Edwardian beard, gives him a menacing appearance. He is a capable golfer, an effective penalty killer on the ice, and a bit of a loner. Although he is playing out the option year of his contract with the Oilers, hoping perhaps to go elsewhere next season, he works as hard as anyone when he plays, and his major concern this season is that he tends to lose weight over the long months of travel.

Number 26: Pat Price. One of the most highly regarded juniors ever to come out of the west—he was a star at fourteen—Price signed a contract for more than a million dollars when he turned pro in 1974. For awhile, he lived high, driving a Ferrari and picking up a lot of tabs. He was a disappointment, even to himself. He wrecked the Ferrari and was sent to the minor leagues. When the Oilers joined the NHL, Sather, in another of his reclamation projects, plucked him away from the New York Islanders, with whom he was seeing limited ice time. For all the cowboy boots and western music, he is a serious young man (he, too, is still only twenty-five), who studies the game painstakingly and is already talking about someday going into coaching.

Number 27 is Dave Semenko. It is easy to regard Semenko as a goon. He is six-four, weighs 215 pounds, and has fierce, dark eyes and a powerful jaw. He keeps his hair long, and at training camp wore a headband that added to his Ukrainian gypsy air. On the ice, he is the team's enforcer; and there are those who claim he is, or could be, the heavyweight champion of the NHL. Off the ice, though, he has a quiet, off-hand wit that is difficult to capture in print. Rod Phillips likes to tell the story of getting into an elevator with Semenko in Philadelphia last season and encountering Wilt Chamberlain, the basketball star, who at seven feet is eight inches taller than Semenko. Dave looked Chamberlain up and down and then, in his deep, bass voice, said to Phillips: "If he played in our league I'd have to score goals." One morning at training camp, he sat looking out over the ice, talking of what he'd done that summer, which turned out to be nothing much (he is married and has a young son), and then he said: "Do you know what I used to think about? Making a perfect pass. I'd think about coming out from our own end"—he gestured toward one blueline—"and just as I came out sending it right across to the other side"—another gesture—"and hitting my other winger in full stride just as he hit the other line. I'd dream about that play."

Number 47, Don Murdoch, is the ultimate Sather reclaimee. In 1977, when he was a rising young star with the New York Rangers, Murdoch was apprehended at the Canada-U.S. border, searched, and charged with the possession of 4.8 grams of cocaine. (A charge of trafficking was later reduced.) He has been more than sufficiently punished. The NHL suspended him for a year, then lifted the suspension because of good behaviour after half a season. But wherever he went he was taunted with jeers and signs—"Junkie Go Home." His play, once brilliant, deteriorated. Sather picked him up for a middle-of-the-road forward and a draft choice. The drug affair obviously still bothers him. In 1978, Earl McRae published a detailed and sympathetic account of Murdoch's tribulations in *The Canadian* magazine. One of the most moving scenes described Murdoch in tears of remorse. Murdoch hated it. All he would like to do now is play hockey. He has pudgy cheeks and long dark hair, which flows behind him when he skates. At training camp he was skating wonderfully. After one particularly clever goal he scored in the voluntary scrimmages, he hurled his stick thirty feet in the air in glee and remarked, loudly but to no one in particular, "It's been a long summer."

Two of the remaining three players dressed for tonight's game are goaltenders, and no one needs to look at their sweater numbers. Ron Low, who will start, would be recognizable anywhere, even behind his mask, by his beard. This will be his first start of the regular season. A minor injury during the exhibition schedule kept him out of the two games at home. Remarkable among goalies, most of whom stand aloof from their teams, Low is the leader of the Oilers, a tough old pro who's been rattling around various leagues for a decade, doing time in places like Tulsa, Oklahoma, and Richmond, Virginia, before establishing himself in the NHL. He never played better than he did for Edmonton last year. As the trading deadline approached in March, Sather was so desperate for an experienced goaltender that in order to get Low from Quebec he gave up Ron Chipperfield, one of the most popular of the Oilers, who was a fixture in Edmonton, and whose mother was dying on the day Sather had to tell him he was going to Quebec. Chipperfield, who still lives in Edmonton, seems not to have forgiven Sather or the Oilers for dealing him off, but Low anchored the team all spring, holding them together through a drive to the finish, and then playing well enough in the first round of the playoffs that they scared mighty Philadelphia, taking two of three games into overtime. Last summer, when some people in Winnipeg organized a benefit game for a former player and one of the goalies showed up under the weather, Low got off his tractor near Foxwarren, drove 220 miles across the prairie to don his goaling tools, played the game, and drove back the next night to finish his chores. He shows the same kind of dedication on the ice and in the dressing room, and the younger players look up to him with affection and respect.

Low's substitute tonight is Eddie Mio, a twenty-six-year-old from Windsor, Ontario, with a pock-marked face and the voice of a young Don Corleone. Mio grew up in a working-class family. His father was a labourer who had emigrated from Italy to Windsor. When Eddie started playing hockey, he found that he could get equipped free if he played goal, so he played goal. Later, he discovered he liked it, and he was good enough to make a couple of city all-star teams, and to attract the attention of u.s. college scouts. Having exceptionally high marks, he was approached by Harvard, where he qualified for a full scholarship of $4,200. But since tuition alone at Harvard was more than $5,000, that was out; he settled instead for Colorado College, where he got all his expenses paid. Now, he is one of the few Oilers to read more than the sports pages of the newspapers. In spite of a pre-game temperament like a nervous diva's, he is popular with the other Oilers.

Number 99 is Wayne Gretzky, and no one in the arena has to look at a program to check it. Gretzky has worn 99 since he was a junior in Sault Ste. Marie, Ontario, and he has made his number so famous that even many people who don't follow hockey are as familiar with it as they are with Pierre Trudeau's boutonniere. Only a few years ago, when he was a child in Brantford, Ontario, Gretzky held Gilbert Perreault among his idols, and kept Perreault clippings in his scrapbook. Now the clippings in the family's home in Brantford, which are stored in a room his father built especially to hold his trophies, are mostly about Wayne. Gretzky was the most celebrated prodigy in the history of hockey, attracting local attention from the time he was six and national publicity at ten, when he scored 378 goals in one season. Unlike many other phenomena, he has continued to live up to his astounding promise. In his first season in the NHL, he tied for the scoring championship with Marcel Dionne of Los Angeles. Only an unpopular ruling by the league's mandarins, who claimed that the season Gretzky had spent as a seventeen-year-old in the WHA had rendered him ineligible, prevented him from winning the Calder Trophy as the rookie of the year. But he won the Hart, as its most valuable player, and the Lady Byng, as its most gentlemanly. The sweep of the laurels by so young a player was unprecedented, and there are those who think that Gretzky has already established himself as the heir to a tradition of superheroes that dates back to Howie Morenz, whose magic helped the league move from its Canadian beginnings to the bright lights of Broadway, or, before Morenz, to Joe Malone, who scored forty-four goals in the first season the NHL ever played. Gretzky's importance to the Oilers is impossible to exaggerate. The 137 scoring points he accumulated last year meant he was involved in 44 per cent of their goals. On each of the fourteen occasions in which he was kept off the score sheet the Oilers lost.

Gretzky is sprinting now, in the last minute of the warmup. Technically, he leans too far forward as he skates. Audrey Bakewell, a figure skater and hockey technician who worked with the Oilers at training camp, sometimes shook her head as she watched him. But, as Ms Bakewell was among the first to acknowledge, he has a physique that allows him to perform easily manoeuvres that would be awkward for ordinary mortals. For one thing, he is still teenage slender in the upper body, and almost hollow of chest, but his legs are solid and muscular, giving him a low centre of gravity. For another, he is unusually supple, and the forward lean is comfortable for him.

At whatever clip he skates, his elbows fly up behind him. Since he almost always has his head up and is constantly peering around his environs, he looks a bit like a chicken-hawk on the prowl. But, also like a hawk, he is deceptively fast; in wind-sprints up and down or across the ice at training camp he was seldom if ever beaten. Around the league, and even on the Oilers' own roster, there are players who might out-race him over a distance or who, once they had gained their momentum, might pass him on an open stretch, but no one ever beats him to an open puck. He is as quick as a whisper. His suppleness seems to extend to his ankles. As a young boy, he was kept by his father in soft-booted skates. As a result, he is able to swerve suddenly without appearing to move his upper body. Often, though, he leans into these turns, dropping one shoulder so low that it seems inevitable he will fall, but catching himself at the last moment, and scooting off in a different direction. There are opponents who swear he can move sideways.

Gretzky has been in the limelight since prepubescence. So far at least, he has handled it with aplomb, as if bred to it. He is polite to the point of diffidence, calling his seniors "mister," and remembering more names than he should be expected to. In private conversation, he is relaxed and occasionally funny. He enjoys his own skills as much as other people do, and takes pleasure not only in their results but in their performance. At training camp, he was often the last to leave the practice ice, staying out late to run some extra drills by himself, or with a chosen teammate. People watch him all the time, not only at the hockey arena but in airplanes, in restaurants, or just on the street. He is on display. He knows it, and sometimes he shows off. But there is so much joy in what he does that it is impossible to resent him. His teammates like him. The Kid, they call him—even those who are scarcely older than he is—or the Franchise, or simply, Gretz. For all the attention that is paid to him, he remains one of them, a member of the team.

As the national anthems end, Sather leans forward over the ledge of the pressbox. He looks down the way to check Phillip's microphone. Then he cups his hands to his mouth and yells to his players below.

"Come on," he shouts. "Come on, you mothers, let's go!"

**3**

*… Watson had seemed the perfect man to put some toughness and fire into the Oilers*

When Glen Sather approached Bryan Watson to act as coach of the Oilers, Watson was working with handicapped children. By the time the Oilers' caravan had moved from Buffalo to Uniondale, New York, where they would face the New York Islanders, defending champions of the Stanley Cup, Watson's doubts about the decision to return to hockey had risen to the surface. He was on edge.

"I think," he said as he stood in the lobby of the Uniondale Holiday Inn on the day before the game, "that I'll go see some kids in a hospital. That might put my troubles into perspective."

The Oilers had lost to Buffalo, 2–0. The game had been dull and frustrating. After jumping off to an early lead, the Sabres had gone into a defensive shell. Even Perreault, apparently spurred on at the beginning by the support of the fans, had begun to concentrate so hard on checking Gretzky that he had neglected his offensive duties, and by the end of the game, which the Sabres locked up with a third-period goal, the fans had been restless. Sather had chattered into his walkie-talkie through much of the first two periods. "Fogie looks flat-footed," he said at one point. "Get Risto out there." At another moment: "Have Mark take that face-off," and when Messier lost the puck to Perreault: "Damn." But by the middle of the third period his comments had stopped; the flush had faded from his cheeks. He left before the final buzzer.

Watson, in an attempt to cheer his players, had ordered them to go for a beer together after the game, and had offered to buy the first round. Even that apparently generous gesture had gone sour. A number of the players' relations and friends had driven down from various parts of southern Ontario for the game. The biggest contingent had been Gretzky's, and included not only his parents and an aunt and uncle, but his agent, his agent's wife, and his accountant and his wife. As a result, and with the usual delegation of fans waiting around the dressing room for autographs, Gretzky had been late getting to the team bus, and some of the players, waiting for the trip to their compulsory beer, had begun chanting rhythmically, "Let's go, let's go," and suggesting no team bus would have waited for them. B.J. MacDonald, filling his captain's role, had managed to cool things down, but the tension had risen to the extent that Gretzky, in an uncharacteristic outburst as he clambered aboard, told some of his teammates to screw off.

No one felt the pressure of the Oilers' third consecutive loss more than Watson. At the morning practice in Buffalo after their defeat by the Sabres, he had felt out of control of the team. At least one player, who had apparently not settled for just a beer after the game, smelled of booze in the morning. Watson was angry with them, and disappointed. After the Islanders, the team would face the New York Rangers in Manhattan before returning to Edmonton. The prospect was daunting.

"O and five," Watson said. "We would go home O and five."

Just a few months earlier, Watson had seemed the perfect man to put some toughness and fire into the Oilers. He must have been one of the most voracious competitors ever to have played the game. Small (five-ten) and stocky—he played at 170 pounds—he set league records for penalties; until Dave "The Hammer" Schultz came along to lead Philadelphia's Broad Street Bullies in the 1970s, he was the most penalized player in NHL history, with 2,212 minutes—more than thirty-six full games—in the box. Yet no one regarded him as a bully, or an intimidator. He shared many of Sather's characteristics as a player; in a book called *The Violent Game*, published in 1975, the American sportswriter Gary Ronberg singled out the two of them. Ronberg described them as "relatively small rogues," and went on to write that, "They intimidate few players, but have a knack of unnerving them with an impertinent word or gesture, an annoying slash or cross-check. When they fight, it is usually against a bigger or stronger man, but the mismatch is in one sense an advantage—little men are usually beaten, and when they manage to avoid a thrashing it seems like a victory."

Although Watson played with nine different teams in his seventeen years in the league, the most vivid memory most fans have of him was as the Detroit Red Wing who stuck so closely to Bobby Hull in a 1966 playoff series that, in one crucial game, Hull was kept to two shots and no goals. The tactic, sending one defensive specialist out to hobble a superstar, was not new at the time but no one had seen it used to this degree before, and it drove Hull to distraction. As a result of the punishment he received in the course of that and other assignments, Watson's face looks like that of a battered pug. The bridge of his nose is concave; scar tissue crinkles over both eyes. He looks, as his nickname Bugsy suggests, like some small-time hood in a Hollywood gangster movie. For all that, though, there is a boyish vitality about his rearranged features, despite their brutish history. Women find him inordinately attractive.

Watson was a medley of contradictions. When his NHL career ended, he settled in Washington where he helped the Kennedy Foundation set up its program for mentally challenged children, and he was full of praise for the Kennedy family. But he was a devout Reagan Republican. He read little, but he liked to tell an amusing story on himself, of sitting next to historian Barbara Tuchman on an airplane, and asking her, in innocence, if the galley proofs she was working on were for a friend. He was capable of making the most outrageous racial remark—presumably in jest, but always worrisome—and then following it with a story about meeting Rosa Parks, the woman who had refused to sit at the back of the Birmingham bus, for whom he had undying admiration. Jest for jest, he could match Sather. At dinner in Buffalo, a waiter accidentally bumped his elbow. When the waiter left, Watson changed seats with someone else at the table, and deliberately moved his shoulder so that the waiter could not avoid bumping him again. When the inevitable collision occurred, Watson rose in mock wrath and, with his eyes glaring from under their scar tissue, threatened to throw the

waiter through the nearest window. Yet he could become blatantly sen-
timental over a song or a memory. He would flirt tantalizingly with any
passing female; but he was obviously true to his wife, whom he referred
to only as Lindy, as if the whole world knew her by name. And for all
his reputation as a scrapper, he seemed to care deeply about the game,
and about playing it well.

"That Semenko," he said in the hotel lobby before the Islanders
game. "I wish I knew how to get him going. I almost wish Gillies [the
Islanders' Clark Gillies was almost Semenko's size] would take a run at
him and wake him up."

On his first road trip as a coach, Watson was having difficulty
adjusting to the social distance he felt he ought to maintain from the
players. For seventeen years he had been one of the boys; now, he missed
the fraternity. Executive robes did not rest easily on his shoulders. In
Uniondale, he wanted to go shopping for some blue shoes to match the
grey slacks and dark blazer he liked to wear behind the bench, and he
was having difficulty finding anyone to accompany him.

"There's a great mall just across the highway," he said.

But the problems of his new career kept inserting themselves into
his entreaties, and he was finding it hard to keep his conversation in a
straight line.

"The Finns," he said. "I should have played the Finns in Buffalo.
Pocklington wants them in the lineup." Peter Pocklington is the Oilers'
owner, a millionaire who made his fortune in used cars and real estate.
He had seen only one professional hockey game before he bought the
Oilers. His advice to his coaches about running his team was not always
technically sound.

"He's going to be here for the game," Watson said. "Doesn't anyone
want to go shopping?"

"Are you going to dress Semenko?" asked one of the Edmonton
newspapermen. Semenko was not favoured by Pocklington, who sometimes said he skated "like a Zamboni."

"Sure, I'm going to dress him," said Watson. "He can play his way
right off the team if he wants."

NASSAU VETERANS MEMORIAL COLISEUM, UNIONDALE, NEW YORK, SATURDAY, OCTOBER 18: Semenko is not only dressed for the game, he goes out for the first shift, playing on a line with Gretzky and B.J. MacDonald. This is Brett Callighen's usual place, but Watson, in consultation with Sather and assistant coach Billy Harris, is searching for a combination that will break their string of losses. Callighen is dressed, but will serve only on spot duty. Matti Hagman and Jari Kurri are dressed, too; they will form a line with Glenn Anderson. John Hughes is also in the line-up. Taking their places on the sidelines are Paul Coffey, who looked tense in Buffalo, Dave Lumley, who is struggling, and Curt Brackenbury, who, when he learned this morning that he would not be dressing with the team, responded by staying out on the practice ice by himself for close to half an hour, blasting up and down the rink until the sweat rolled down his nose and drenched his jersey.

The Islanders strike early, as Butch Goring beats Low. BOING! BOING! BUTCH GORING! the electronic scoreboard flashes, and the crowd clamours its appreciation. The Islanders fans are among the noisiest in the league, as partisan as if their suburban houses were bet on the final score. Many of them wear Islanders' sweaters, with the names of the Islanders' stars—Bryan Trottier, Mike Bossy, Denis Potvin—or, in some cases, their own names emblazoned on the backs. They are here not so much to appreciate the game as to ensure the desired outcome, and to assist in their rooting they ring cowbells and toot horns and wave glasses of beer in the air.

At 7:29, Duane Sutter, one of the three lusty brothers from Viking, Alberta, now in the NHL—there are more on the way—draws a boarding penalty, and Watson sends out his power play: Gretzky at centre, Pat Price and Risto Siltanen on defence, MacDonald and Semenko on the wings. As the power play proceeds, Semenko hovers near the front of the Islander net, trying simply to get in the way. MacDonald gets the puck and slips it back to Price on the defence. Price fires—wide. It goes behind the goal and there, suddenly, is Gretzky on his own. For a moment, the play seems to freeze. Billy Smith, in goal, looks mesmerized. Gretzky darts to his right, then draws the puck back and around, moving as if to the front of the goal, then twists his stick and tucks the puck into the corner of the net. 1–1. Price and MacDonald draw assists, but Semenko's cumbersome presence in front of the net has helped to create the goal.

Penalties continue to influence the game. At 10:11, Glenn Anderson, who is playing, as are nearly all the Oilers, with an assertiveness that was missing in Buffalo, gets into a heaving incident with the Islanders' John Tonelli. Both go off for roughing. Almost immediately after they return, Pat Price is called for hooking. Edmonton sends out its steady penalty killers, Stan Weir and Dave Hunter, but the Islanders' power play buzzes around them, and almost inevitably, Bossy scores. 2–1 Islanders.

Before the period ends, Edmonton ties it on a goal that would please the hearts of benchwarmers everywhere. Hagman goes into the corner and digs out the puck for Kurri, who drills it without pause just under the crossbar for his first NHL goal. To Hagman's assist is added one by the defenceman who put it in the corner in the first place: John Hughes. All three of the men involved on the scoring play were on the sidelines in Buffalo.

Between periods, Sather is interviewed on the radio by Rod Phillip's colour-man, Ken Brown. The talk turns to the unruly Long Island fans, and Sather is asked if the din is upsetting the Oilers.

"Huh," he snorts, "Canadian fans should be like this." His cheeks are glowing.

Just twenty-six seconds into the second period, Gretzky takes the puck behind the Islanders' goal again. This time, the defencemen start to come back on him, to close in. Somehow, he pushes the puck out from between his legs and in front of the goal where Semenko pushes it home. It is not a graceful goal, but it gives the Oilers the lead.

Not for long. At 2:04, Messier takes a hooking penalty—*Messy-er*, the PA announcer calls him—and the Islander power play strikes again. 3–3.

For the rest of the period, play roars back and forth. At 8:27, Anderson and the Finns put on a passing display, flipping the puck around like Globetrotters on ice, but getting no real chances. At 11:19, Kevin Lowe goes off for holding, but the penalty killers this time do their job. At 15:36, Gretzky cuts in across the blueline, and Gordie Lane—

Lois, as the fans have been calling him in a rare show of non-affection—clutches at him. Gretzky takes a dive, and Lane is called for interfering "with Gretzky," as the PA announcer duly notes. These dives—overreacting to attempted checks—are part of Gretzky's repertoire. Since the referees are aware of how closely he is followed, they tend to believe him when he plays the victim. This time, the trick backfires. After Anderson and the Finns move the puck again with rare but inconclusive excitement, the Islanders score short-handed. Then, with the Oilers still on a power play, Gretzky loses a face-off to Bossy, whips around to steal the puck right back, and goes in alone to tie the score again, 4–4.

Just before the period ends, Anderson leaps across the front of the Islanders' net like Superman and barely fails to set up Kurri. During the intermission, a New York newspaperman says to Dick Chubey of the Edmonton *Sun*, "Anderson is the most exciting player on the ice." Chubey, a gruff veteran of hockey journalism, scarcely looks up from his typewriter.

"The second," he says.

The third period is something of an anti-climax. Semenko, although he now has his name on the score sheet, plays listlessly, and fights neither Gillies nor anyone else. Pat Price and Gord Lane do mix it up briefly, but dispiritedly, as if they do not want to be away from the action too long. The NHL has put in a curious new rule this year: When a fight breaks out, all non-combatants must retreat instantly to neutral zones near their benches. Since few of the players are accustomed to this rule, they tend to linger on as they always have, watching the fisticuffs and trying to stay out of trouble. To avoid giving these innocent bystanders ten-minute misconducts, referees often fail to call fights fights, and this time they sentence Price and Lane to two minutes each for "delay of game." Now, with extra space to manoeuvre, Risto Siltanen dances up the ice and fires a slapshot past Smith. 5–4. Not long after, however, the Islanders' Steve Tambellini works his way unmolested to the front of the Edmonton net, fakes once, and rips a clever backhand past Low to tie it up.

And a tie it remains, although not without incident. Just eighteen seconds after Tambellini's goal, the Islanders have a goal disallowed for a high stick, and with just a minute and a half left in the game, Gillies breaks into the clear. With the fans roaring, he moves to his left, seems to have Low beaten cleanly and hits the goalpost.

To the Islanders, the tie is routine; they remain undefeated and on top of the league. To the Oilers, it is a godsend; their losing streak has ended, and they have played evenly with one of the best teams in the NHL. In his post-game press conference, Watson is beaming.

"I had to tear up part of my game plan," he says. "I didn't have to pull the goalie."

"What about Gillies' shot on that last breakaway?" someone asks him.

"I could have kissed him," says Watson, and breaks into a boyish giggle.

**4**

*… Murdoch had a long story to explain what happened before his arrest*

The Oilers stayed at the Uniondale Holiday Inn that night, and left the next morning by bus for New York. Once there, they would play the Rangers in the evening, sleep briefly at their midtown hotel, then head for home. As far as Sather was concerned, even this lightning visit to the evil city was too long; he was reluctant to expose his young charges to New York's temptations. His judgement was not a moral one. He had enjoyed his own days as a Ranger—as he had, indeed, enjoyed most of his playing days—but, like a father who turns strict with his children when his own oats have been sown, he was not confident of the Oilers' ability to live well and play well at the same time. "One of the things they can't do," he said once, "is play with guilt. On some of the older teams, we'd have guys who practically had to be carried to the rink in the morning, but sometimes it seemed they played better in that condition than if they'd been sleeping all night. It was as if they wanted to prove they hadn't hurt themselves. But these kids are liable to suffer for a week."

It was not only the danger of late drinking sessions that bothered him. Last year, on their first-ever visit to Manhattan, the Oilers had been overwhelmed by the blatant display of sexual commerce they saw on the streets. "They couldn't get over it," Sather said. "They just about went crazy on the bus. I knew on the bus we were going to get blown out." He had been right. The Rangers had won that first game 10–2.

Many of the Rangers revelled in a lifestyle whose excesses worried Sather. Although they were not the street-corner heroes they might have been if they had played in Canada several of them achieved a different kind of celebrity, appearing on talk shows, winning tables at the best restaurants, staying late at the trendiest discos. In 1980, the Ranger in the centre of the most fashionable spotlights was Ron Duguay, a tall, handsome, twenty-two-year-old centre from Sudbury, Ontario. In January, Duguay had sat down at the Quo Vadis restaurant to talk about his lifestyle with a group of people from—appropriately—Andy Warhol's *Interview* magazine.

"Doogie," said *Interview* in introducing a transcript of their conversation, is "number 10 on the NEW YORK RANGERS ... the sexy one with the curly locks in the Oo-la-la SASSOON commercials. He's also an ELITE model. Waiting for him at the table at Quo Vadis among the flowers is a note from BIANCA JAGGER saying she would like to meet him at HALSTON's after dinner."

"Oren & Aretsky' s is our favourite restaurant," said Warhol when the tape was rolling. "It's really butch."

RON: "I have to go at least three times a week because I never have anything at home."
CATHERINE GUINESS [from the magazine]: "What do you have in your fridge at this moment?"
RON: "Probably a bottle of ketchup, a jar of mustard, and maybe a little cheese."
SCOTT [COHEN]: "Where would you go on a dream date?"
RON: "Probably to Oren & Aretsky's."
SCOTT: "And then?"
RON: "Herlihy's."
SCOTT: "In your heart of hearts, when you go into these bars do you feel you can pick up any girl you want?"
RON: "Well, I know they know we come in here and the reason they come in here is to meet hockey players, so if they're there to meet the hockey players then they're probably willing to go home with them. So when I go to a bar I just flash my Ranger ring."

SCOTT: "Do you get the most girls on the Ranger team?"
RON: "I'd have to say Donny Murdock does."

Not long after the *Interview* article with Duguay appeared, Donny
Murdoch (*Interview* spelled it wrong) was traded to Edmonton. He left
New York in ignominy. He had arrived for his rookie season, 1976–77,
with huge promise, a welder's son who had burned up his junior league
and become the toast of Medicine Hat, Alberta. New York took him
as their first pick in the draft and lavished money on him. With his
signing bonus he gave his father and sister new cars, put $15,000 in his
father's bank account to start a new business, and another $8,000 in
his mother's. He got an $11,000 Corvette for himself and a comfortable
apartment in Long Island to drive it to. He started his playing career
with rocketing excitement: sixteen goals in his first sixteen games, thirty
in his first forty—more than any rookie had ever scored. The New
York media loved him. He was cute, with long, Lochinvar locks and
full, chubby cheeks that always seemed about to burst into dimples. His
high voice would break readily into laughter. He said colourful things:
that he started off his evenings "with a dozen beer or so," or that some
bars where groupies hung out were good to go to "in case you're not too
excited about the ones waiting around after the game." He danced with
Margaret Trudeau. The players called him Dock. The fans called him
Murder and brought him gifts.

Then in February, he broke his ankle, and stayed in New York to
recuperate. There are those who believe that was his downfall. "He had
a lot of idle time and he ran into a celebrity crowd," Dave Farrish, who
played with Murdoch on the Rangers, told William Houston of the
Toronto *Globe and Mail* much later. "New York is a fast-moving city
and it isn't hard to get involved in a few illegal things. He [Murdoch]
wanted people to like him. He came from a small town and … he was
an instant celebrity … You can get caught up in it so fast. It moves like
a tornado." In the August after his rookie season, Murdoch was arrested
at the Canadian border, on his way to teach at a hockey school in British
Columbia, and his life fell apart.

Murdoch had a long story to explain what had happened before his arrest. There had been a boozy party at his place on Long Island, he said. After going to bed at 4:30 in the morning, he had risen again at 6:30 to find people still hanging around. He had asked them to clear out, and started pushing some of them out the door. Someone had slipped a cellophane packet into his shirt pocket. Later, still hung over, he had tucked the packet into a pair of socks in his dresser drawer. When his girlfriend had come to pack for him she had inadvertently slipped the socks into his suitcase. But when he was caught, he did not deny that he knew the packet held cocaine. Nor did he deny ownership of the five joints of marijuana that were also on his person. In court, he pleaded guilty. What there was doubt about, to those who knew him well, was the picture of the drug-crazed freak that had emerged in the press and in the minds of the jeering fans. He was not so much guilty as stupid, they said. Dumb. And, indeed, there was about him a curious sense of innocence, an eagerness to please. He was a follower; while he never led any of the Oilers' social excursions, he was always a part of them. He couldn't say no to anything, his friends said. Earl McRae, in his research for *The Canadian* magazine, discovered with amazement that Murdoch, under heavy pressure because of his arrest, had gone drinking at a New York bar about which even the NHL's security men had warned all the players. He was like a puppy that had been spanked, but remained friendly to everyone who approached it.

On the Oilers' bus, rolling into Manhattan from Uniondale, he was as happy as he had been all season, and all the way down from Long Island he discoursed on the wonders of the city that had once done him in. The trip was his first time back since he had been traded to Edmonton the previous spring. He had risen early in Long Island, waking at eight o'clock for an eleven o'clock call.

For once, the press had been reasonably good to him. A New York *Post* reporter had done a preview of the Ranger game and had suggested that the Rangers could have used Murdoch this year. The story had made no mention of drugs, only certain "off-ice indiscretions" that forced the Rangers to let him go. Furthermore, the *Post* went on, "he had an outstanding pre-season with Edmonton and, according to team sources, has become more responsible, more of a model citizen."

"Hey, guys, know what that is?" he cried as the bus emerged from the Queens Midtown Tunnel.

"What?" said his cousin Mark Messier, who had been distracted for a moment, soliciting extra quarters for the flesh machines of Forty-second Street.

"It's the Empire State Building," said Murdoch.

"Big deal," said Messier.

"Hey, bussy," Murdoch shouted, using the athletes' universal name for men who drive buses. "Go down from Thirty-fourth to Thirty-first. That's the quickest way to the Garden. Look, guys, there's where they have the Steuben parade every year."

"What in God's name is that?" someone asked.

"It's German, dildo."

"Hey, Dock, look at that. Did you ever score with her?"

"I wasn't that hard up. What a hog!"

The spirit started catching all of them. "Okay, guys," said Doug Hicks. "A dollar for the freakiest things you see."

"This isn't even the right neighbourhood," said Murdoch. "We ought to go downtown and see the Village."

"I got that guy with the blanket and bare feet," said Dave Lumley.

The bus pulled up at a stop-light. There was a Chock Full O' Nuts on the corner. In the doorway a ragged man sprawled. There was a tear in his pants. He had dirtied himself.

"I win," said someone from a front seat. "The guy with the chocolate bar."

"You haven't seen *nothing*," said Murdoch, and began to tell the bussy how to park at Madison Square Garden.

MADISON SQUARE GARDEN, NEW YORK CITY, SUNDAY, OCTOBER 19: Lars-Erik Sjoberg, a Ranger scout, was in Long Island last night, watching the tie game. In the press room at the Garden tonight, he was asked if he learned anything.

"Sure," he says. "They told me when I went up there that to stop Edmonton you have to stop Gretzky behind the net."

" And?"

"And," he says, "now I know you have to stop Gretzky behind the net. It's just that I don't know how you do that."

For all the good spirits on the bus this morning, the team was tense at practice. Mark Messier appeared to get things off on the right note by striding purposefully out onto the glistening ice and shouting, "And now, live, from Madison Square Garden, it's the pesky Edmonton Oilers," but no one responded. Practice was desultory. People worked alone. Kevin Lowe took out a bucket of pucks and, like a golfer at the practice range, worked on his slapshot. Billy Harris set up a drill for Semenko, trying to get him to move the puck out of his own end more effectively. A pretty young woman showed up to wait for Murdoch. She turned out to be a reporter from one of the papers, but Murdoch gave her an autographed stick anyway. Curt Brackenbury, who has still not dressed as an Oiler but who works harder at practice than anyone, had an asthma attack and went to the dressing room to get a canister of spray. Sather called down from the stands for a look at the label. It was Hydro-Bromide. "Just curious," Sather said. Watson had said the work-out was optional, but when Glenn Anderson sat it out there was grumbling. "I'd like to see him do that if he played for Montreal," said Dave Lumley, who was benched in Long Island. Rod Phillips did an imitation of Watson behind the bench, mumbling confused requests for direction into an imaginary headset. A couple of players took up the theme.

"Uh ... get ready ... uh, Risto and Fogie," someone said.

"*Lee* and Fogie," said Lee Fogolin.

Now, as the game begins, it is evident that the fans—or just the heady atmosphere of the Big Apple—have set Murdoch off. On his first shift he sends Anderson in for a clear chance, then, when Anderson misses, digs to back-check. Sixteen minutes into the first period, he nearly gets a breakaway himself. He looks as exuberant as he did at training camp, but nothing quite clicks. The Oilers have to kill off three penalties in a row before the Rangers draw one, but the period ends scoreless.

At 8:17 of the second period, the crowd, which has been almost as flat as the hockey, comes to life as Steve Vickers pots one for the Rangers. On a power play that follows, Hagman and Kurri, playing

again with Anderson—while Pat Price, Brackenbury, and once again
Lumley sit out—create several good chances. Then, with time running
out before the intermission, Gretzky, behind the net, fakes once, twice,
and flips the puck out to Semenko in a traffic jam in the front. Semenko
pushes it home.

With the score tied at one, Sather paces in the pressbox. His face
is pink. He has been busy on the walkie-talkie to Watson.

"We're going to win," he says. "I can feel it coming."

The third period presents a new set of forward lines. Brett
Callighen, who has needed a spot since Semenko went to Gretzky's
wing, moves in with the two Finns. Semenko stays with Gretzky, but
on their right wing they now have Anderson. The third line is made
up of Stan Weir at centre, Dave Hunter at left wing, and Murdoch at
right—two checkers and a potential goal-scorer. B.J. MacDonald and
Messier, ordinarily two of the strongest offensive threats, are being
rested. If Murdoch is ever going to open fire it will be tonight, for he
has continued his early pace and is the most exciting player on the ice.
Well, the second.

Early in the third period, the most exciting one does it again, this
time taking the puck behind the net. Instead of passing to the front, he
fakes a pass, circles, and shoots into a narrow crack in the armour of
Wayne Thomas, the Ranger goalie. Semenko, who helped to push the
puck behind the net, gets an assist.

Now, with six minutes left, the pace of the game has picked up.
Sather is flushed.

At 15:57 Eddie Johnstone, a fine young winger, beats the valiant
Low, and it is 2–2. But at 17:36, Gretzky sets up Semenko. The second
assist goes to Ron Low, who cleared the puck to Gretzky after a Ranger
shot. With his assist, his second in only three games, Low is now the
leading scorer among the league's goalies. And outshot in last night's tie,
30–20, and tonight by an even wider margin, he is an important reason
the Oilers' losing streak has now ended and they are on the verge of
their first win.

More remarkable, though, are Semenko's statistics. In two games
with Gretzky he has racked up four points; his three goals are exactly

half the total he scored last year in the sixty-seven games he dressed for. But he is not finished. In the last minute, trailing by a goal, the Rangers pull Thomas and send out six attackers. The Oilers counter with the Gretzky line. The Rangers fire away. Low withstands the assault. Then, with less than half a minute on the clock, Gretzky intercepts a pass at his own blueline, and upper body bent, elbows working furiously, he sets out for the New York goal. A lone defender chases him. From centre, he has an almost certain shot on the empty net. He declines it. Barrelling down his wrong wing comes Semenko. Gretzky slides a pass across the ice. In full flight, Semenko picks it up and heads for the open goal. He shoots, he scores. The hat trick, and the highlight of a convincing 4–2 win.

After the game, the Oilers' dressing room is a strange scene. For one thing, there are more reporters around Dave Semenko than there are around Wayne Gretzky. The fact that Gretzky has assisted on all Semenko's goals as well as scoring one himself is less important than the fact that the Oilers have given the press something to write about, other than the Kid. Semenko is relishing his moment, handling the questions with ease and good humour. It is his first hat trick since he was a junior.

Even more strange is the presence of women in the locker room. In New York, this is a familiar situation; at least five women are writing hockey regularly now for the New York press, and while there are still some holdouts—St. Louis, Buffalo, Toronto—most of the visiting teams now open their dressing rooms to them. To the young, and now mostly nude, Oilers, the new liberalism is of little comfort. If there is a common reaction to standing ballocks bare in front of females, it is embarrassment. Some of their shyness they try to cover up with gross remarks, and there are muttered threats to stand on a table and introduce the New York *Daily News* to the pride of Edmonton, Alberta. But mostly, they just cover up.

In one corner stands a naked Murdoch, towelling himself and being interviewed. In spite of being kept off the score sheet, he has played a wonderful game, and there are some fans who want to see him afterward. In his interview, both he and the female reporter seem to be working very hard at maintaining eye contact.

The bus left the hotel at 5:30 the next morning, and all of the Oilers showed up for it. For the time of morning, they were remarkably bright, and it was impossible not to observe that among the brightest was Don Murdoch. He was clear-eyed and clean-shaven, bubbling with enthusiasm. The fans he had met after the game had presented him with a T-shirt bearing the letters MURDER bent sinister, and a handsome colour picture of himself in Ranger regalia.

Ron Low was still thirsty. In his cumbersome gear, Low loses as much as twelve pounds of moisture during a game, and he must spend time deliberately putting it back. In the dressing room he usually has a beer, and perhaps some salted water, but sometimes he must continue to take fluid for hours. In the dark Manhattan morning, he was carrying a can of Coca-Cola in one hand and a half-pint container of milk in the other. The Garden had been warm during the game, and Low had been, as he said while he waited for the bus, "as bloody well hot as I've bloody well ever been."

Mark Messier, along with one or two of the other young players, had taken advantage of some free time on the afternoon of the game to go shopping, and he had acquired a pair of stereophonic headphones. He was wearing them now, grinning in apparent enjoyment, and offering samples of their sound quality to anyone who cared to listen. Low, Messier's roommate for the trip, was regarding him with benign amusement. Messier got on the bus, humming contentedly to himself, and took a seat. Low moved paternally in beside him. The bus left for the airport, where there was time for coffee, or, in Low's case, a tomato juice and another container of milk.

As the team waited in the aircraft line-up, Messier was still helmeted by his earphones.

"Pretty good sound, eh, Mark?" another passenger said.

Messier smiled in silent reply, pointing to his covered ears, and snapping his fingers in rhythm. The line moved forward, then stopped. Someone ahead was asking Gretzky for an autograph. Messier took off his earphones and offered them to the passenger, who placed them carefully over his ears. There was no sound in them.

**5**

*"They're playing road hockey ... just like a bunch of kids on the sidewalk"*

In Toronto, a month after they'd left New York, the Oilers shaved Paul Coffey. In theory, this was an honour, a ritualistic welcome to the big league. Coffey had been playing well, gradually easing the tension that had seized him through the opening weeks of the season, skating more and more with the puck, firing confident, low slapshots from the point. In fact, the shave hurt; and although he had half-known and half-hoped it was coming, the experience frightened him. Two of his teammates— Callighen, the players' representative, and Brackenbury, who was emerging as a leader of locker-room enthusiasms—grabbed him when he returned from practice and lifted him onto a trainers' table, where they had prepared a bed of ice. He was blindfolded. Unseen hands held him in place; his legs were pried apart. He felt the warm stickiness of shaving lather. Someone ran a razor through his pubic hair. When the blindfold was removed there was a clear pink path running north through his dark shrubbery. Getting up from the training table, Coffey was not sure whether to strut naked around the dressing room showing off his mark or to ask the trainers for some calamine lotion.

All hockey players get shaved—some painfully and some more than once. Bryan Watson was welcomed to the Montreal roster three times. Some Boston Bruins once did Derek Sanderson in a hotel elevator, while two stewardesses watched with interest.

Almost every year there are stories about a shaving gone wrong.

In the 1980–81 season, a Winnipeg rookie was so badly razor-burned that his legs turned black and blue and he couldn't walk. Occasionally, someone has the hair on his head removed, or parts of it. But mostly the area of concentration is the loins, and mostly the attitude involved is one of brotherhood and sport—as it is, for example, for the University of Toronto fraternity that still jovially welcomes new members by imprinting its insignia into their arms with a branding iron.

One season, when Glen Sather was with Minnesota, he helped to shave a writer who was working out with the team. The writer was enormously proud of his mark of honour. "Listen," Sather told him, "if you write to Clarence Campbell [who was then the president of the NHL] and tell him that you've been done, he'll send you a membership card in this special club, and if you carry the card you'll never get done again." His victim complied. Campbell was outraged. No such thing took place in the NHL, he wrote back.

Last year, Paul Rimstead, one of the better-liked writers around the NHL—his column is carried in the Toronto, Calgary, and Edmonton *Suns*—got into a barroom discussion with Bill "Cowboy" Flett, then with the Oilers, about Flett's strength.

"I can lift five hundred pounds with one arm," Flett said.

"Want to bet?" Rimstead said.

"Put up your money."

Rimstead got some cash. So did some Oilers. Wagers were placed. Rimstead was led to the dressing room.

"How much do you weigh?" asked Flett.

"Oh, about one-seventy," said Rimstead.

"Lie down here. I'll pick you up and two other guys too. We'll get Semenko and Driscoll."

Semenko weighed well over two hundred. Peter Driscoll, who has since been sent down to Wichita, was almost as large. Rimstead lay down. They spread his arms. Semenko lay on top of one arm, Driscoll the other.

"Let's just tie you so I can lift you all together," said Flett. "Now, let's fasten your legs."

Then Flett went to get his razor.

"The only thing that really bothered me," said Rimstead later, "is that I wasn't as, well, you know, as well equipped as a hockey player."

For all his improved play, Coffey wasn't scoring goals; by the time the Oilers reached Toronto he had only one, plus one assist. It was symptomatic of the Oilers' plight that Ron Low, having by now picked up a third assist from his goalie's post, was tied in team scoring with Price, Lumley, Lowe, and Murdoch, and *ahead* of a handful of others.

The Semenko rocket had fallen quickly back to earth. After scoring two more against Calgary in the Oilers' first game after their return from New York, each assisted by Gretzky, Semenko had stalled. Worse, in the opinion of the coaches, he hadn't been beating anyone up, as if in his new-found role as a scoring ace, his old one of enforcer was beneath him, and he was skating around with a dismayingly Christian air. "Put this in the paper," Bryan Watson told Allen Abel of the Toronto *Globe and Mail.* "If I was playing on a line with Gretzky, and they put someone out there just to check him, I'd take the guy out. I can't go in there and tell my players to do it. But I'd like them to know that if I was playing and Gretzky was on my line, I'd go after the guy." Semenko was taken off Gretzky's wing.

The Calgary game, in which Semenko ended his streak, threatened to be the last high point of the season. The Calgary team was, in fact, the former Atlanta Flames, purchased and moved to Alberta over the summer by Nelson Skalbania, Peter Pocklington's former partner in Edmonton, still his good friend and forever his arch foe. The NHL, confident of a natural rivalry between teams in Calgary and Edmonton, could scarcely have picked two fiercer antagonists as owners. As if to demonstrate the depth of their feelings, they bet each other two thousand dollars on the outcome of their teams' first meeting. When Edmonton won, 5–3, Pocklington strode instantly to the Oilers' dressing room and told his young mercenaries he'd buy each of them a side of beef in celebration.

After that, trouble begat trouble. On October 24, eight months to the day after he had hurt his eye, Brett Callighen finally told the coaches the truth: His vision was desperately bad. "It's like there's a film over one eye," he said. "In the sunlight I can't see at all." In games, the puck would appear to him to be on the ice when it was in fact bouncing, and more than once, he had flailed at the air when Gretzky had set him up in front of the goal, only to have the puck slide under his stick. A cataract had developed; he would need a sophisticated operation. The Oilers, who had been suspicious of his clumsy play for some time, arranged for a Calgary specialist to leap Callighen over a six-month-long waiting list, but Callighen would still be away from the team for a minimum of six weeks. From Wichita, the Oilers summoned Don Ashby, a winger who had once been drafted high by Toronto, but who had not been able to stay long with an NHL club.

Two days after Callighen's diagnosis, Doug Hicks broke his wrist while going into a corner in Los Angeles. Even with Coffey now playing regularly, the team was down to a minimum of defencemen. They sent another call to Wichita for Charlie Huddy, a twenty-one-year-old of some promise.

And they couldn't win. They lost to Minnesota, went into a dreary and frustrating run of ties, lost to Vancouver, barely beat Winnipeg—*everybody* was beating Winnipeg—lost to St. Louis, and, the night before they came to Toronto, were trounced by Philadelphia 8–1. They were in sixteenth place and barely holding on.

MAPLE LEAF GARDENS, TORONTO, WEDNESDAY, NOVEMBER 15: All seventy-six seats in the pressbox are full, and so are most of the 16,307 seats of the paying customers. The Gardens has not had an *unsold* seat since February 27, 1946, but in recent years, with the Leafs playing lacklustre, losing hockey, some of the season's subscribers have had trouble giving their tickets away. Not tonight. Outside, scalpers are asking eighty dollars for a pair of golds, and when one of them is asked why, he looks disdainful, spits on the ground, and says simply, "The Kid."

The Kid. This week, General Publishing has brought out a book called *The Great Gretzky*, by Terry Jones of the Edmonton *Journal*. Although his agent, Gus Badali, is mildly annoyed that Wayne was not cut in for a piece of the price, the Kid has been autographing the copies brought to him at practice this morning. He is already on the cover of the *NHL 1980/81 Guide*, the *Hockey News Year Book*, the Oilers' media guide, *Goal Magazine*, an NHL publication distributed in various arenas, the Leaf program for tonight's game, and the current issue of *Saturday Night* magazine. Counting advertisements, his picture runs an average of three times a week in the *Hockey News* and is on at least the sports pages in every city the Oilers play in, so that the impression accumulated by the people who travel with him—and which he must get himself—is that he is in every paper, every day, like a reflection in an infinite mirror. His image stands life-size in department stores before displays of GWG jeans, with a crotch-wrinkle he had trouble with during the photo session smoothed out. A poster of him in his Oiler sweater urges you not to smoke. On television he supports the Heart Fund, the Red Cross, the United Appeal. He is a visible sponsor of the Ontario School for the Blind and the Canadian Association for Community Living, a cause to which he feels particularly attracted because he has an aunt who is mentally challenged and of whom he is particularly fond. He endorses 7-UP, Neilson's "Mr. Big" chocolate bars, Bic razors, Jofa helmets, Perfecta skate blades, Titan sticks. He looms from billboards and winks from the backs of trucks. The Toronto *Sun* has posed him for a colour front page of tomorrow's edition and *Hockey Night in Canada* has scheduled a feature on how he spent his summer for this evening's first intermission. He is everywhere.

But, by the standards that have come to be expected of him, he is not playing very well. In thirteen games he has only seven goals and sixteen assists; while this means he has been involved in just under half the team's forty-eight goals, and that he is far and away its leading scorer, in the league points race, which he almost must win to justify his reputation, he is tied for tenth. Marcel Dionne, his rival from last year, is eight points ahead of Gretzky's pace, and Charlie Simmer, one of Dionne's wingers, is three points ahead of that. The Islanders' Mike Bossy, well on his way toward a record, has nineteen goals.

As is usually the case, Wayne arrived at the Gardens this afternoon well after most of his teammates. On his way in, he passed through one of the corridors of history that lie under the Gardens stands. Many of the pictures on the corridor walls show men who were memories before Gretzky was born: Sweeney Schriner, Busher Jackson, Charlie Conacher. As he walked beneath them, he looked reverently upward; he has a better sense of these men and the glories of their times than he might be expected to, as if conscious of the heritage he carries.

When he turned the corner leading to the visitors' dressing room, though, his mood of ancestor worship disappeared, and he broke into a grin. Outside the room, some of the young Oilers were involved in a playful ritual that was becoming part of their pre-game preparation. Its instigator was Dave Lumley, who for all his troubles on the ice could still show flashes of buoyancy. Lumley would come early to the rink on game days. He would go into the dressing room and take a wad of the padding the Oilers used inside the knees of their shin pads. He would wrap the wad in adhesive tape, shaping it like a puck. Then he would borrow a catching glove and a blocking glove from the goalkeepers' equipment and repair to the hallway. There, Kevin Lowe and Doug Hicks would join him, carrying their sticks. No one knew when this protocol had first been designed; it had simply evolved. By the time the Oilers arrived in Toronto it was formally established. Lumley would designate a goal; in Toronto he used an overturned bench. First Lowe and then Hicks—it had to be in this order—would shoot the white, padded puck at him. Other members of the team, arriving later, would sometimes join them, and before Watson or Sather would call them in to get dressed, they would all become absorbed in their play, ignoring the tenseness of the professional game for which they would shortly have to dress.

They were doing this today, when Gretzky turned from the corridor. With his grin spreading, he went into the dressing room for his own endorsed red and white Titan stick and re-emerged to join them. For nearly fifteen minutes this afternoon they played, their sticks clacking on the concrete floor, their shouts and laughter breaking the afternoon gloom of the historic Gardens.

"They were playing *road* hockey, for Chrissake," said one of the older members of the Toronto press corps when he heard of their afternoon's adventure. "Road hockey. Just like a bunch of kids on the sidewalk."

Now, on the ice, it is instantly evident how the Leafs plan to stop Gretzky. They have assigned Darryl Sittler to check him. Almost everywhere he has gone, Gretzky has found himself shadowed—by Perreault in Buffalo, by Ryan Walter in Washington, by a full checking line in some places. But tonight seems different, as if Sittler, the second highest scorer in the Leafs' long history, has no offence in mind at all. Since the home team has the last change of personnel on the ice, there is no way Watson can get Gretzky away from Sittler. Once, Watson pulls Gretzky off in mid-shift, and Stan Weir jumps over the boards to replace him, but Sittler goes off, too, and is replaced; when Gretzky returns, so does Sittler.

At 12:07, Pat Hickey, a Leaf acquisition who, like a lot of recent arrivals, does not seem to play as well in Toronto as he did elsewhere, puts the Leafs ahead. Two minutes later, Don Ashby, playing in Callighen's spot, scores for Edmonton. The period ends in a draw.

During the intermission, Stan Obodiac, the Gardens' publicity director, spots a sign someone has hung from a Gardens' wall, celebrating Gretzky as "Mr. Big." The reference reminds Obodiac that Mr. Big, Neilson's chocolate bar, is one of Gretzky's sponsors. He rushes to order the sign removed. "We could get a thousand dollars for that space," he says.

Early in the second period, the Leafs go ahead again. At 14:20, Gretzky, on an Edmonton power play and briefly out of Sittler's shadow, ties it again. But not long afterward, Laurie Boschman, a young Leaf of promise, puts Toronto ahead. In the third period, Sittler tears himself away from his defensive duties to score an insurance goal, and the game ends 4–2 for Toronto. It has been an unsatisfying display, with the Oilers restricted to twenty-one shots on goal, two of them—including one that went in—by Gretzky.

While the Oilers do not necessarily win all the high-scoring games they play (or lose all the low-scoring ones), they do not respond well to the sort of close checking the Leafs have inflicted on them tonight. They can hit, if they have to, and play defensively themselves, and they are aware that this is the aspect of the game they must master if they are to succeed. But they are not as attractive when they are bottled up. More than most teams, they still need room to win, and to be exciting.

Outside the dressing room, where the Oilers were playing road hockey this afternoon, Watson holds court for the press. He decries Toronto's use of Sittler as a checking forward, and *Hockey Night in Canada's* selection of Sittler as one of the stars of the game, presumably as much for neutralizing Gretzky as for his own unimportant goal. If Gretzky is the most valuable commodity the NHL has right now," says Watson, "and if they're going to tolerate what went on tonight, we're all in trouble." No one seems to notice that the man making this pronouncement was also the player who, if he did not invent star-shadowing, brought it, against Bobby Hull fifteen years ago, to its highest state.

CHICAGO STADIUM, CHICAGO, ILLINOIS, NOVEMBER 16: Jari Kurri went to Edmonton last night. He has the flu. As he left the Hotel Toronto, clutching a sheet of notes to help him with cab-drivers at both ends of the trip, he looked red-eyed and miserable, a study in twenty-year-old loneliness. Jari has been doing almost nothing but playing hockey in the dark Finnish winters since he was in his early teens, and he has missed the classroom time that would have equipped him to live in North America. With his salary close to $50,000 a year, he now dresses with the same tailored look as his teammates, and the bowl-shaped haircut with which he reported to training camp has now been razor-cut to a more fashionable style. As the Oilers travel in a pack it is impossible to sort him out from, for instance, Kevin Lowe, until a ripple of laughter spreads through the team at some shared wisecrack, and Jari stands in the middle, his expression serious and blank. He and Paul Coffey, who, even shaved, is still reticent with more established members of the team, have moved together into the same apartment building as Gretzky and Lowe, but last night Jari went home to it alone, with a temperature of 101°.

Lee Fogolin has a bad back, Messier has a puffy knee (which he has been trying to conceal from the trainers), and Stan Weir's groin is tender. But the coaches have decided to dress all of them tonight and instead rest healthy players with whose play they are unhappy: Matti Hagman and Pat Price. Hagman has looked timorous; some of the press corps say he plays with a three-second buzzer, and is determined to get rid of the puck before it sounds. Price is fighting himself. He is an intense competitor, but sometimes his intensity brings him harmful penalties; he gets too many early in the game when the pattern of play is just being established. He and Watson are not getting along. Price seems to be trying to begin his coaching career while he is still a player. He speaks of "the rookies I've brought into the league." He talks on the ice too, peppering the play with advice to his younger teammates. Sometimes the youngsters are grateful; Kevin Lowe says he has learned much from watching Price and listening to him. At other times, however, the coaches are convinced Price is getting on his pupils' nerves, and they wonder if he is not contributing to Coffey's tension.

Sather has now moved down to join Watson behind the bench. Sather seems closer to taking full control each day. In Toronto, he went on the ice at practice, the first time since training camp. Watson said the move had been his idea, that he wanted Slats's advice, but not even the Toronto newspapermen believed him. On the bus to the stadium this afternoon there was no doubt who was in charge. The bussy had a Chicago Bears football game on the radio and as soon as Sather got on board he told him to change it. "I want their minds on *tonight's* game," he said. When the bussy found some semi-classical music, someone yelled from the back: "*That's* supposed to get us thinking about *hockey?*" And Sather snarled. "Get *into* it," he said, "get emotional."

Something has worked. The Oilers are playing their best hockey of the season tonight, skating like butterflies, hitting like trucks. Charlie Huddy, the replacement from Wichita, scores from the point, and in the pressbox, Price, whose place Huddy is taking, nods in appreciation. "I like to see hockey played well," he says, "even when I'm not playing it." The first period ends 2–0.

Before the first minute of the second period has elapsed, it's 3–0. Coffey fires from the blueline and the puck is deflected into the net. The scorers give the goal to Gretzky, but the consensus in the press box is that it went in off one of the Black Hawks and should go to Coffey. Chicago scores before the period is over, but the Oilers remain in command.

As they skate off for the intermission, Murdoch raises his stick and slaps it on the ice in frustration. He has been in and out of the line-up all season, playing only eleven games, and he has scored only one goal. He has never been able to regain the form he showed against the Rangers in New York. In eleven games as a rookie, he had eleven goals. When the rest of the team is skating as well as it is tonight, he seems left behind, as if he isn't thinking quickly enough.

The journey from the bench to the dressing room also allows Semenko and Curt Brackenbury to stretch their legs. Neither has been on the ice during the first two periods. Things have gone steadily down for Semenko since his outburst of scoring, and now he is relegated to what Brackenbury has christened the Swat team, held in reserve in case the game gets too tough. The role is not noticeably bothering Brackenbury, who sets an example of hard work during every practice and even yells encouragement from the bench. Semenko keeps within himself. He needs playing time to keep loose. His confidence is slipping.

As the teams come back for the third period, Gretzky skates to the scorers' bench to report that he did not touch Coffey's shot before it went into the goal. The scorers make the change, but Gretzky, who was involved in the play that set up Coffey's shot, gets an assist. Every point matters to him now. He is well behind Simmer and Dionne in the scoring race, but not out of reach. He is as happy with the assist as with a goal. The decision to give Dionne the scoring title last year was based on Dionne's greater number of goals in their equal points total, but he knows that this year his best chance of winning it all will come from the number of goals he sets up. With every team in the league now keying its defence on stopping him, he has more chances to find an open team-mate. Some day he would like to break Bobby Orr's all-time record for assists in a single season, 102. But this year the record looks a long way off; the change in attribution for Coffey's goal gives him his seventeenth, in seventeen games.

Eddie Mio is playing goal tonight, and in the second period has been felled by a high stick across the mask but he has stayed in the nets. Last season, Mio sat out a string of games with a broken cheekbone, and the night he came back to play, Semenko hit him in the throat during the warm-up. Some of the players think he is better when he has been hurt, and Sather is convinced that the best time to start him is when he is complaining about an injury or an upset stomach. Tonight he has shaken off the blow to his face and is playing strongly.

Dave Lumley scores to make it 4–1. And although Chicago storms back for two goals, the outcome is never in doubt. At 9:47, Anderson combines with Coffey and Gretzky to make it 5–3. The goal is Anderson's sixth of the year, not far from the pace the coaches have hoped he would set, but on many nights he plays as if nothing matters. The NHL has not yet become as important to him as the Olympics; on the road he still wears the red and white parka of Canada's national team, and the dreamy look seldom leaves his eyes. But his weaknesses are also his strengths; on the ice, his blithe spirit makes him creative and unpredictable, and he is capable of making rushes of electric excitement.

With just three minutes left, the nimble Chicago rookie Denis Savard dances around Huddy and goes in alone to bring Chicago within one, but the Oilers hold on to salvage a win out of what has otherwise been a disastrous road trip. As they head for the bus back to their hotel, they are chattering happily again. The only thing missing from the evening's show, says Ron Low, who has had time to look over the sparse crowd from his seat at the end of the bench, was the presence of Chicago Shirley in the stands.

Chicago Shirley is the most legendary of the NHL's groupies. She has broken in rookies in all sports since the early 1960s—some say even before that. Once, when asked who, of all the athletes she had known, had pleased her the most, she said "the 1968 college football all-stars." But hockey has been her specialty, and Low had intended to point her out to some of the new members of the lodge. Now he says: "You wouldn't have wanted to see her anyway. She's gone to fat. Sex must be fattening after all."

The cheerful mood of the dressing room continued on the long bus ride out to O'Hare Marriott Hotel, from where the Oilers would get an early start for the trip home in the morning. Perhaps sparked by Low's remarks about Chicago Shirley, the talk turned to women.

Times have changed in the hockey world, as they have everywhere else, but even the youngest Oilers continued to divide women into two groups: their wives or girlfriends (or other men's wives or girlfriends) on the one hand and, on the other, the women who made themselves available in bars. One of the younger players once held a locker-room session spellbound with a tale involving a groupie, his own roommate, and a dog, but when an older listener pointed out that the tale-spinner had just lost any chance of being introduced to *his* daughter (not to mention his dog), the tale-spinner reacted with astonishment: "No one's *daughter* would do *that*," he exclaimed. The groupies, and their excesses, continued to fascinate all of them, and when they were feeling pleased with themselves, as they were after their convincing win in Chicago, they would swap yarns incessantly.

"The best days were in the WHA," said one of the veterans at the front of the bus, "when we used to take road trips that would last two or three weeks, just to save airfare, and we'd hang around some cities for days. One time when we were in _____, we were sitting around the hotel bar at night, just killing time, when this real good-looking chick turned up and said she was looking for the goaltenders. 'How come you want the goalies?' I said, and she said, 'Because I'm a goalie myself.' 'Get *off* it,' I said, but it turned out she was, for this girls' team they had at the university there. So anyway, she found our two goalies sitting together in the bar and she joined them.

"Well, I'll tell you, they really started hitting on her. She'd say, 'Tell me what you do on a breakaway,' and they'd say, 'Listen, do you play the stand-up style or do you like to go down?' and it went on like that all night, but they couldn't get anywhere. She threw them a shut-out. So when the bar closed, the goalies went up to bed and left her in the lobby.

"Next day at practice, one of the defencemen had a real smile on his face, and he kept winking at the goalies. Finally one of them said, 'Don't tell me you ...' and the defenceman said, 'Sure, I asked her to come up to the room after you guys left, but she wanted to go back to her place. So I went back with her and ... well ...'

"'What?' said this goalie.

"'She wanted to put her pads on first.'

"'Her *goal* pads?'

"'Yeah, everything. Leg pads, belly protector, gloves. She said that was her fantasy.'

"'But no skates,' said the goalie.

"'No,' said the defenceman. 'No skates.'"

Each outrageous story would beget another, and the players would laugh over each recounting, and pass the punchlines up and down the bus. The veterans were the stars of these occasions, and the yarns would spread to the front seats where, by unspoken rule, the coaches and trainers and writers and broadcasters sat. Sometimes, the men who had played professional hockey but were now on the sidelines would tell the best stories of all; nostalgia, it sometimes seemed, improved history. And in the back, the rookies would absorb it all, like young hunters at the knees of their shaman.

"She did *what?*" someone would say, and when the end of an adventure was repeated: "No *kidding!*"

"It's too bad Chicago Shirley wasn't there," said Ron Low. "I hear she's breaking in her daughter."

## 6

*... an exemplar of the city's new breed of high-rolling, high-living millionaires*

On the day after the Oilers returned to Edmonton from Chicago, Peter Pocklington sat in his penthouse office on top of the Sun Life building, playing backgammon. The man he was playing against was Nelson Skalbania, and although the stakes were $1,000 a game, Pocklington's mind was not on the board. Skalbania had brought him into hockey in the first place, selling him a half interest in the WHA franchise for $700,000 and the assumption of half the Oilers' $1.6 million debt. Pocklington had paid for his share partly with a diamond ring he had pulled off his finger in the middle of their negotiations—"it's worth a hundred and fifty thou, easy," he had said—and partly by throwing in a Rolls Royce phaeton that had been used in *The Great Gatsby*, a film that had deep meaning for both the young millionaires.

Later, as Skalbania had moved on to other sporting interests, Pocklington had taken over full ownership of the Edmonton franchise. So far at least, he was pleased with his hockey investment; the Oilers filled Northlands Coliseum for every home game, and even as newcomers they led the NHL in attendance. Furthermore, he felt he had outsmarted Skalbania on the deal that had brought him Gretzky. But Skalbania was a tough man to stay ahead of; his investments had already spread to major league baseball—Pocklington had a surprise in store for him there—and his Calgary Flames were well ahead of the Oilers, tied for tenth place with the Montreal Canadiens, while the Oilers, even with last night's win in Chicago, were well back in the pack. He wished he could do something to shake them up. But first things first.

Pocklington won the first game of backgammon, and Skalbania wrote out a cheque.

"Double or nothing?" said Pocklington.

"Sure," said Skalbania, and shook the dice.

Pocklington had won at almost everything he tried since he was a boy. He grew up in London, Ontario, the son of a prosperous insurance agent—Basil Pocklington bridles at references to Peter's poverty-stricken youth—and he had begun making deals before his voice changed. He used to sell his Christmas presents. When he was fourteen, he traded his bicycle, plus $100 in cash, for his first car, a 1928 Model-A roadster. He sold the roadster for $500 and sensed his calling. When he was fifteen he went on holiday to his grandfather's place in Carberry, Manitoba, and discovered that cars on the prairies were in better shape than those of the same vintage that had been driven on the salted roads of Ontario. So: "I would buy at $25 a copy, ship them east for $150, and sell them for $500." He did not stop there. Once, his father returned from a business trip to discover that Peter had unloaded the family car for $2,800 in cash, plus a 1956 Plymouth. "His mother and I were annoyed," Basil said later, "but since $2,800 was all I'd been offered on a trade, and we eventually got $800 for the Plymouth, we made money." When Peter was sixteen, and finally had a licence to drive the cars he was now peddling the way other kids traded marbles, he was called into a meeting of his schoolteachers and, as he likes to say, "I was fired from school." He went into the car business full time and began dabbling in real estate, buying houses, then duplexes and apartments, in London. As he said later, however, he was "naive enough to sell cars on time and then sell the contracts to a finance company, guaranteeing the loans myself. I thought everyone naturally paid his bills. When some didn't, I went broke. I was twenty-one."

He tried working for other people for a while. Eaton's fired him as a sales clerk, he likes to boast, and so did one or two other concerns. But as a car salesman he was *sans pareil*. In three years he worked his way up to manager of new-car sales at the largest Ford dealership in London, asked for a better deal, and got, instead, fired again. Unperturbed, he went to a bank, said he had a dealership of his own locked up in Tilbury, a small town west of London, then told Ford he had the bank's approval. At twenty-three, he was in business for himself. While Ford was not pleased by his youthfulness, or, when they discovered it, the way he had swung the deal, they did like his sales, which were four times what the previous owner's had been. Within a year, he had eight people working for him. The following year, he took over the Ford dealership in Chatham, a larger city in the same part of Ontario, and repeated his success, building his empire to sixty employees. He pestered Ford for an even bigger dealership; they introduced him to a man with a franchise for sale in Edmonton, and Pocklington, with what now appears to be an instinct for the upcoming western tilt of Canadian money, jumped. Foreseeing the rapid expansion of Edmonton that would accompany its oil boom of the 1970s, he moved his new franchise, Westown Ford, to the suburbs, and the city followed. By 1972, he was in the real-estate market again, first in Edmonton and then throughout Alberta and the west. He bought everywhere, and sold just as quickly, getting a reputation as a man of fast decisions with an ability to work out details as he went.

By 1977, real estate accounted for 80 percent of his time. He assembled around him the brightest men he could hire, but took no partners. He and Skalbania, who had been his friend for years, decided to go separate ways in their sporting lives; Pocklington took over the Oilers for $500,000, with an agreement to pay another $500,000 if they should ever be admitted to the NHL.

By the summer of 1980, Pocklington was an established and renowned figure in Edmonton, an exemplar of the city's new breed of high-rolling, high-living millionaires. While he still owned Westown Ford and continued to grind out real-estate deals, his interest had spread to the oil patch. The year before, he had taken over a prairie financial institution called Fidelity Trust. Through the purchase of Gainer's Food Limited, he was also involved in meat packing. Altogether, his businesses were grossing $350,000,000 a year.

He had gone into the hockey business, he admitted, because he wanted to be recognized on the streets, and his sports investments—if that is the right word for something that was losing so much money—had spread to the National Soccer League, where he was proprietor of a team he had named the Edmonton Drillers. When the government had failed to finance a cancer detection unit called a thermograph at the W.W. Cross Institute in Edmonton, Pocklington had stepped into the breach and told the institute to bill him $1,000 a month until it was paid for. Not long after he was appointed to the board of the Citadel theatre, he donated Oilers seasons' tickets worth $40,000 to that cause.

He lived well. He was known as a collector of paintings and a connoisseur of wines. He had a strikingly beautiful wife, his second, named Eva, and a handsome son named Zachary. They lived in an airy house on Edmonton's south side, with a view down the North Saskatchewan River. At dusk, sunlight would reflect off their windows, and the house would be visible for miles. He also had a $240,000 condominium in Hawaii. He was friends, and shared a passion for racing boats, with the movie star Paul Newman. Around town, he drove a Rolls Royce convertible, often faster than the law would have encouraged; Eva drove a white Mercedes.

The office where he was playing backgammon with Skalbania was listed under his major holding company, Patrician Land Corporation Limited. Two walls of glass overlooked the winding river valley. Behind his glass-topped desk hung a portrait by Cornelius Krieghoff; on the other walls, five oils by Emily Carr. There were eighteen other Carrs in his office suite. Emily Carr oils at the time were going for as much as $30,000.

Pocklington wears his sandy-coloured hair fashionably long but razor cut, and he has a full, neat beard. He is not a tall man, but he holds himself, even while sitting, with military erectness. By far his most noticeable features are his pale, blue eyes, which that afternoon bore straight across the backgammon board at Skalbania. His unblinking gaze had the concentrated energy of a laser.

Skalbania rolled doubles, enough to clear four of his last men.

"Okay?" he said.

"Okay," said Pocklington, and tore up the cheque. "Stay for lunch?"

"I can't," said Skalbania. "Got to get back to Vancouver."

"Too bad," said Pocklington. Today was his thirty-ninth birthday, and Cal, his office chef, had prepared a special lunch of the light but healthy foods he favoured: fresh fruit salad, a won ton soup, and rice pudding.

"See you later," said Skalbania. "Hope your team does better."

"They will," said Pocklington. "They will."

A HOLIDAY INN ON THE OUTSKIRTS OF PHOENIX, ARIZONA, WEDNES-DAY, NOVEMBER 19: Pocklington is sitting at one point of a group of tables arranged in a υ. He is wearing a double-breasted blue blazer, white on white shirt, red and blue striped tie, grey slacks, and oxblood loafers with gold buckles. On the table in front of him, unopened, is a slim briefcase, inside which are a few files of baseball information and an even slimmer pocket calculator. The men seated around the υ, whose dress varies from sports jackets to crested windbreakers, are the owners of the teams in the Pacific Coast Baseball League. The Pacific Coast League is rated as Triple A, one notch below the major leagues. Pocklington is applying to take over a defunct franchise in Ogden, Utah, and move it to Edmonton. On his left sits Mel Kowalchuk, a young Edmonton advertising salesman and baseball fanatic who has brought Pocklington to the table.

Kowalchuk is already a devotee of his new boss. He approached Pocklington at an Oilers game in the Coliseum and asked him if he would be interested in baseball. Pocklington said yes. The first time he met with Kowalchuk in the penthouse office, Pocklington took only one telephone call. The call was from his banker. Kowalchuk could not help thinking that it was exactly like the discussions he had had with his own banker. Only the numbers were different. "I've just closed a deal for some land in Calgary," Pocklington said on the phone in the same tone of voice Kowalchuk might have said if he had just got a fifty-dollar raise at his advertising job. Then Pocklington mentioned sums in the several millions of dollars. When Kowalchuk pointed out to Pocklington the similarity with his own dealings, Pocklington agreed. "It *is* the same," he said. "I just add a few more zeroes."

On the way down to Phoenix this morning, Pocklington was in an expansive mood.

"These suckers climb like a homesick angel," he said as they roared off the runway at Edmonton in his Lear jet, and all the way down he wanted to talk not only about his plans for baseball in Edmonton but about his philosophy of business. For all the complexities of the deals he arranges, Pocklington is a man of extraordinarily simple ideas. He believes in positive thinking. In the Oilers' first year in the NHL he arranged for the players to take a course in self-motivation called Omega. He urges Omega on many of his business and social acquaintances. He believes also in the power and innate goodness of business, and there is no more pejorative word in his vocabulary than *socialist*. He thinks business, if left to its own devices, could solve many of the world's ills. Politics interests him, and he has been approached by more than one political party to apply his mind and his ambitions to public life. So far, he has found all the parties to be too "socialistic," and too conventional for some of his ideas, such as the flat 10-per-cent income tax he thinks everyone should pay. Politicians amuse him. Sometimes he invites Peter Lougheed, the premier of Alberta, to join him at the Oilers' home games, and once he invited Pierre Trudeau to ski at a lodge Pocklington had bought in British Columbia—one of the few business ventures that has not worked out for him. But Trudeau, he said, was not his kind of man. He had "too many socialist ideas." That was one of the things he liked about hockey owners; they were greedy and he knew how to deal with them. In the plane, he told Kowalchuk that he hoped the baseball men were the same. "If they are," he said, "I'll wrap this thing up in an hour. We'll just put on the dog and pony show."

He took the slim calculator out of his briefcase. "Look, we'll sell season's tickets and have a draw," he said. "Let's say—how many?—six thousand season's tickets at $350 each and then I'll give away fifty cars at seven thou each—I can get 'em from Westown Ford—is 350 thou, and six thousand tickets at ... let's see, we make ... that's over two mill. We could do it, right? Why not a hundred cars? Let's see ..."

The calculations had amused him for nearly half an hour, playing with percentages, chortling to himself.

"King Ringer would be proud of me," he said.

"King Ringer?" Kowalchuk asked.

"Ah, the King," he said. "Best car salesman there ever was. He used to come into the place I worked in London to give a course. I lapped it up. I used him as an instructor all the time."

"What did he do?"

"Well, everything started with writing. You had to write your customer—get him to sign an offer. Then you did what the King called the Sorry. What that meant was you went into the sales manager's office and stood around for a few minutes, and then you came back and said, 'Sorry. That would be okay for unit 8231, but it won't do for this one.' Then the guy would write another offer, and you'd go into the office again and say, 'Look, my limit is $15,975. Your offer is $9,500. Somewhere in the between we can make a deal. I'd take the nine-five, but it's just not up to my limit.'"

And on he went, reliving the joys of selling cars.

"It's *all* just selling cars," he said. "Only with more zeroes. Like the difference between your bank loans and mine. Same game, more zeroes. I learned very early on that you can sell when everyone else is buying. Always give people more than they're asking, and get it back on the terms. If you offer what sounds like enough, you can give them zero interest and they'll take it. Greed overcomes good judgement. Remember that. Greed overcomes good judgement."

On the way to the baseball meeting, he gave Kowalchuk a tour of downtown Phoenix, one of the first places outside Edmonton he had bought real estate. "See that block," he said. "I bought that whole thing for $2.7 mill in 1974, when they thought Phoenix was going to stagnate. Later, I sold it for $7 mill, and in that hotel there, there was a wonderful collection of art deco furniture. That was the real pleasure for me. Making the money was easy."

Now, in the Holiday Inn meeting room, the dog and pony show begins. Patiently, he waits till the preliminaries are over, the introductions made, and the chairman has called on him. Then, without rising, he fixes his blue eyes on the chairman and begins to talk of Edmonton's appeal. It is very simple stuff. There is no formal presentation, no charts, no maps. He quotes a few figures about average temperatures—the Pacific Coast League plays in places like Tucson and Hawaii and the owners are worried about being frozen in the prairie spring. He says he'll pay a travel subsidy for teams that have to travel farther than they've been accustomed to, and when that doesn't seem enough to the owners, he sweetens his offer. "And don't worry about the Alberta economy," he says. "It's on fire—in spite of some socialist tendencies of the government."

The spiel finished, he waits for questions. To Kowalchuk's amazement, the owners do not instantly rise to welcome him among their ranks. They ask him to leave the room for a moment, while they deliberate.

"Well, I'm trying to get back to a hockey game tonight," Pocklington says.

When he and Kowalchuk return, they see what the trouble is. The owners have never seen anything like him before. They are baseball men, interested in nurturing their game and running their minor-league franchises from summer to sweet summer, against the tide of the televised majors. And now, this bearded Canadian has descended from the sky and thrown figures at them like a spitball pitcher in the spring—except that, unlike a spitball pitcher, he seems to care nothing for their game, and to see it only as a place to play with money.

"I guess you're interested in running your purchasing of the Ogden franchise into a big-league team, Mr. Pocklington," one of them says.

Pocklington, his bearded jaw jutting toward his inquisitor, says yes.

There is a pause. Someone says there have been a lot of promises of money, and the league has only met Pocklington today. Could they, could he—?

"Look," says Pocklington. "I've lost fifteen mill in sports up to now, and a few hundred thou more won't hurt me."

After some more discussion, Pocklington writes a personal cheque for $5,000 as a token of good faith ("What's the name of this league again?" he whispers to Kowalchuk) and leaves for the airport.

"Let's fire up some Coors for the plane," he says, and not long after they are airborne, he gets a phonecall in the jet telling him his application has been accepted. "Good," he says. "I'm very pleased." Then, to Kowalchuk: "Want to play some crib?"

The Oilers lost to Vancouver that evening, 6–4. Of ten games at home they had won one; the loss dropped them to eighteenth place.

The next evening Pocklington had a birthday party at home with some close friends. Sather and his wife, Ann, arrived barely in time for the cake. Sather's cheeks were flushed. He had spent the afternoon with Watson, and after dinner he huddled with Pocklington.

On Saturday, the team gathered at the Coliseum for its official group picture, the players in uniform, the executives in mufti. In blazer and tie, Watson met with Sather and Pocklington in Sather's office. They were down to the last strokes of Watson's dismissal. Various offers flew back and forth. Pocklington told Watson he could stay on at his Oilers salary and run a junior achievement program Pocklington was interested in. Watson said he'd stay if they'd guarantee him an unfettered job behind the team's bench. In the end, Watson was given two years' salary and his freedom. In the elevator, as Sather and Pocklington prepared to attend the picture session, Pocklington stared absently at the ceiling. Watson, the man who had checked Bobby Hull to a standstill, said: "Don't be too down about it, Peter. You should think positively." Then, still wearing his shirt and tie, he went home to Lindy; the team picture was taken without him.

That afternoon, Sather told the press that firing Watson, his friend, had been among the most difficult things he had ever done. "But the most important thing is the team," he said. "If my own brother was coaching this club, or playing on it, and it wasn't working out, I'd let him go too."

*... all of us dreamed of hockey glory*

In the winters of my boyhood, my life centred on a hockey rink in Dickson Park, across the road and down the hill from my parents' duplex apartment. The rink lay on a low stretch of the park, between the baseball diamond and a low, grey building used to exhibit farmers' wares during the fall fair. Even before freeze-up, workmen would set up boards around the rink's space, and the boards would stand there through the last days of autumn, pale against the darkening grass, waiting for the season to begin. Metal light standards sprouted along their edges. With the first frost, the workmen would begin to flood, so that well before Christmas we could skate, and each day after school and all day on weekends, until spring softened the ice, we would give our lives to our game.

Weekends were the best. I would wake early Saturday morning, and pad down the hall to the sunny kitchen at the back of the apartment, careful not to wake my parents. I would slither down the back stairs for the milk, reaching one goose-pimply arm out to clutch the cold bottles, from which, as often as not, the frozen golden Guernsey cream had pushed the tops. Then upstairs again for cereal with brown sugar and, if I felt leisurely, a piece of toast. Into my clothes: warm corduroy trousers, a plaid shirt and heavy sweater, thick woollen socks. Down the stairs again, where my skates and outer clothing had steamed overnight on the radiator. I would lace on the skates, stretching out my leg with each eyehole to get the laces tight enough to stop the circulation. A good pair of laces could be pulled tight enough to be looped around the ankles twice and tied in a double bow in front. Stand on the linoleum to get the feel. Up on the toes. Good. Then into coat and toque, earmuffs if the day was cream-popping cold, then on with the mittens—wool, unfortunately, with a hope of hockey gloves for Christmas—and out across the squeaky snow.

If I was lucky, I would get to the rink before anyone else. Then, I could move around by myself, revelling in the clean air and the early light, and the untrammelled freedom I would feel as my body swayed with the rhythm of my strides. My hockey stick was an extension of my body, swinging back and forth in front of me as I moved. Counter-clockwise I went at first, moving on the right wing along the boards and down along the end, making ever longer strides as I built up speed, dig-ging in with the pushing foot, hearing the *rask, rask* as I glided into each step. Around the corners, crossing the right leg over the left, leaning into the turn, building up momentum for the straightaway, then harder even down the boards, bent at the waist, getting my shoulders into it. Head down, with the stick held horizontal in front. Dig, dig, then turn again, my body warming as I moved. Now some turns the other way. Kitty-corner across the diagonal of the rink, swerving around rough patches, skates biting into the good ice, bumping ratchet-quick across the choppy islands. Tighter turns now, smaller circles, raising the outer leg to swing with centrifugal force. Back onto the long stretch of open ice, glass smooth, its surface cleared by the overnight winds, exulting with jumps and hops, scissoring in the air, heading breakneck toward the boards to stop in a spray of snow and stand laughing and panting in the morning sun.

Dickson Park was in Galt, a small industrial city in southwestern Ontario, long since swallowed up (though not in spirit) by the munici-pality of Cambridge. But the rink where I spent so much of my boy-hood could have been at Eighty-sixth Street in Edmonton, or on the mill-pond of Richibucto, New Brunswick, or in the parish schoolyard of Sainte-Justine-de-Dorchester, Quebec, where Roch Carrier set a classic short story that translated my experience into French. Swapping memories in later years, I would sometimes imagine one great outdoor hockey game, stretching from just inside the Rockies to the shores of the Atlantic, detouring only around the too temperate climate of a few of the bigger cities. Or, perhaps, a hundred thousand simultaneous games, all overlapping as our own used to overlap at Dickson Park, kept separate only by the carved initials, inlaid in snow, on our pucks.

There were, to be sure, regional variations. In the west, a rule provided that if a frozen puck shattered against whatever was serving as a goalpost, the destiny of the biggest portion would determine if a goal had been scored. Western kids often wore what they called "garbage mitts"—padded for heavy duty by city workers—instead of hockey gloves; Maritimers used their father's work gauntlets, with heavy leather up the wrists. But the essential rules were the same everywhere: no goal-sucking, no raising, unless whoever's younger brother was stuck in goal was also foolish enough to wear shin-pads, no long shots, no throwing your stick to stop a breakaway. We began our games the same way, by choosing up sides, and we played the same infinite hours, and kept the same infinite scores. The initials on our pucks were in fact superfluous, for we knew how to stick-handle and keep track of our own game without looking down; we had learned it playing keepaway, where you held your head up or lost the puck forever. Wherever we played, we knew the same pleasures: the thrill of carrying the puck at top speed, cradling it with your stick pushed out like a probing lance; the satisfaction of a well-executed pass; the joy of slipping past a defenceman to go in on the open goal.

Our best sticks were made of rock elm, but since they cost as much as $1.25 each, we settled for grey ash or ordinary elm, and wrapped them thick in tar tape; when the tar tape wore through at the bottom and made moth's wings on the blades, we taped them with adhesive tape from our families' medicine chests, and the sticks lasted all winter. We would wear them down to what we all called toothpicks, then use them through the spring for road hockey. On the rinks, we secured our shin pads with rings from our mothers' sealers, or strips cut from inner tubes, and the agony of a puck that caught us just under the kneecap—worse even than the searing ache of frozen feet—was as common to all our experiences as was winter itself.

I sometimes wonder if the fervour with which we pursued our game moulded us more than we realized. In 1976, in *The International Review of Sports Sociology*, a Canadian named Howard L. Nixon wrote of "those who are consumed by this passion," and concluded that "the culture of hockey will profoundly affect their values, attitudes, and behaviour ... as they mature." I think, for example, of the way we looked on girls, with their white skates and their hours on the nearby—but separate—"pleasure rink," or of those few of our own sex who chose not to play hockey at all, and were branded forever as outsiders. And I wonder if those attitudes, formed on the rinks and rivers and sloughs, have not stayed with us into our marriages and our boardrooms.

I know that it was in hockey that we found our heroes. We collected their images on Beehive Golden Corn Syrup cards and tore their history from the pages of newspapers and magazines we delivered. Sometimes we touched them. In Galt, Syl Apps, the captain of the Maple Leafs, addressed our hockey banquet and gave out advice I can still recite—"shoot low and on the stick side." We watched an awkward Gordie Howe make his first shy (and illegal, since he was a transfer from Saskatchewan) forays into junior hockey, with the Galt Red Wings. And one memorable summer afternoon, Marty Pavelich and Harry Lumley, two Junior Red Wings who would later go to Detroit—and who played on the same team as Lee Fogolin's father—tossed a gang of us, squealing, into Willow Lake. We could, all of us, recite the lineups of our favourite teams, and on Saturday nights, we huddled by our radios to hear Foster Hewitt limn their skills. For their skills were our skills; in our dreams, and sometimes alone on the evening ice, we would score over and over again the winning goal in overtime of the Stanley Cup's deciding game, and in our own scratchy voices we would hail the astonishing debut of the lanky rookie from Edmonton or Richibucto or Galt.

The boys I played hockey with have gone on, the more successful of them, to run newspapers and department stores, to become chemists and lawyers. But there is not one who would not have been a hockey player if he could have been. As we matured, we chose other heroes, and even in the days of our boyhood there may have been those among us who dreamed of other futures. But all of us dreamed of hockey glory.

Later, when Elvis Presley sang or Pierre Trudeau made his way through adoring throngs, we envied and admired them. But when Bobby Hull wheeled down the wing, his sweater bulging in the wind, we were there with him. We understood; we knew what it felt like. All that separated us from our true heroes was that they were better at something we all had done. They belonged to us, as no other kind of hero ever could, at once more celebrated and more approachable because of what we shared. They were *of* us, playing the game of our lives.

In 1949, I left both Galt and my boyhood, or at least the part of it that I had spent on skates. But my fascination with the game continued. At high school and university, and later, as I travelled about the country working on newspapers and magazines and eventually on radio and television, I followed it with interest and enthusiasm. Occasionally, I managed to turn my passion into part of my work. I wrote about hockey for most of the journals I worked for, though never, alas, as a full-time sports writer, and in broadcasting I seized every chance to talk to its latest stars or dig into its newest trends. Hockey was the common Canadian coin. Though the men who played it for a living came from what the sociologists called the lower or lower-middle classes ("66.2 percent ranked 39 or less on the Blishen Socioeconomic Index for Canada," one study reported in the 1970s) the men—and sometimes the women—who followed it came from every class and every region. Wayne and Shuster made jokes about it on their own television shows and popped up as guests on *Hockey Night in Canada*. John Allen Cameron burst into his televised presentations of Cape Breton music to show himself proudly—and surprisingly gracefully—skating with the NHL Old Timers; on other shows and with other teams, other hosts repeated the same act, Allan Thicke in Vancouver with the Los Angeles Kings, Tommy Banks in Edmonton with the Oilers; in Montreal, Lise Payette, just before she left late-night television to become a Parti Québécois cabinet minister, strapped her ample body into goalie's pads and, with more bravado than good sense, let the Canadiens fire pucks at her. Television was only one mirror of hockey's appeal. Hugh Hood, the Montreal novelist whose stated ambition was to write a fictional series of Proustian dimensions, took time out to write a worshipful book about Jean Béliveau. Mordecai Richler followed the Canadiens with as much passion as he delved into St. Urbain Street. Peter Pearson made a film with a vignette of the real Max Bentley. Rick Salutin wrote a play about *Les Canadiens*, "with an assist from Ken Dryden." Nancy White sang about hockey on CBC radio's *Sunday Morning*. Robert Charlebois wore a hockey sweater on the cover of his most popular album. When John Robert Colombo set about compiling the best-known Canadian images, he chose, among the grain elevators and Niagara Falls, Ken Danby's magical print "At the Crease." At *Maclean's*, the editors used to say, if there was no excuse to use the Queen on the cover, they could always get Gordie Howe.

Hockey was us.

As my own Toronto-born sons reached wobbling age, I, along with a million other fathers, began to take them to the local arena on Saturday mornings, and even stayed to coach; and when I could cadge tickets to the Gardens, or when we watched on television, I would try to pass on to them my own enthusiasm for the game and its heroes.

In the early 1970s, with the sudden expansion of professional hockey, things began to sour. The novelty of teams from Oakland, California, and Cleveland, Ohio, quickly wore off. "I'm not a drinking man," said Conn Smythe, "but I know if you pour too much water in your whisky, the whisky gets weaker." At first, it had seemed, the beauty of the game would transcend the ineptitude of the new instant professionals. To be sure, there were still some instances of what Ralph Allen, the novelist and editor who set so many of our standards, had called "a tough but lovely form of art." But those instances became rarer and rarer: The loveliness gave way to the toughness. Unable to find players who could skate with the genuine stars, the owners reached out for people who could knock them down. Big, rugged, tough guys, or "goons" as even their most excited fans called them, set out to intimidate the better, quicker players. In response, other teams acquired more goons, agents of protection. The definitive offensive play became throwing the puck into the other team's zone and seeing who was big enough to go in and root it out. This was not new to the game, of course. The pages of hockey history were studded with bloodthirsty sagas, and some of its earliest heroes, from Eddie Shore to Sprague

Cleghorn, were known as much for their abilities to maim as for their offensive skills. (Cleghorn, said Conn Smythe, could have broken any of the modern tough guys in two.) Some of the teams we had admired most fervently as youngsters had played the game savagely, and many of our idols, from Red Horner and Black Jack Stewart to Bill Ezinicki and later, John Ferguson and Lou Fontinato, were renowned for violence. What seemed to differentiate the new wave of enforcers was the fact that they could do nothing else. Traditionally, the man who protected his teammates was also expected to score twenty goals, or play a solid defence. In the post-expansion era, he could only brawl.

The team that understood this system best was the Philadelphia Flyers, and the Flyers quickly rose to the top of the expansion pyramid. While there were some fine hockey players in their lineup, the team was characterized by such thugs as Bob "Houndog" Kelly, who spent more than six hours in the penalty box in two years, and Dave "The Hammer" Schultz, who spent more than ten. By the season of 1973–74, the Flyers had wrestled the Stanley Cup away from the original six teams. The fans in Philadelphia loved them and celebrated them as the Broad Street Bullies.

What the Philadelphia fans were, of course, was American, and the Americanization of the game was something we had had to live with for a long time. The NHL admitted its first u.s. franchise, Boston, in 1924, and two years after that a majority of the teams were playing out of u.s. cities. But somehow, with their virtually all-Canadian rosters, playing in cities that at least had snow in the winter, the Rangers, Bruins, Red Wings, and Black Hawks seemed part of the Canadian game, part of the tradition. Their fans, while perhaps less knowledgeable, were at least watching and enjoying the same aspects of the game we were. The fans in the new cities were not; they were there for the roller derby on ice. They didn't *know*.

Meanwhile, from another flank, the Russians were attacking. The highlight of hockey in the 1970s—one of the highlights of hockey in *any* period—was the victory of Team Canada '72 over the Soviet national team. Almost every Canadian I knew could tell you exactly where he was at the moment Paul Henderson jammed the puck past Vladislav Tretiak with thirty-four seconds left in the final game. But even as we relished the victory, some truths were sinking in. Team Canada had won the series, yes, with four victories to the Russians' three, and one tie. But the Russians had outscored us, 32–31, and, in at least some senses, outplayed us; they took fewer penalties and made prettier passes. Where even our all-stars were trying to shoot the puck into the corners and then to shove the Russians off it, the Russians were carrying it in and, as they did so, making plays with a rare combination of discipline and creativity. The game with which so many of us had grown up had been taken over from across the pole, or was about to be; and the hordes in Philadelphia and all the other American cities, clamouring for blood and punishment in place of grace and skill, were battering it from the south. In 1976, Paul Henderson, the hero of '72, left Canada and went to play for a WHA team called the Bulls in Birmingham, Alabama. Someone there started a boys' league. After a goal, the boys would drop their gloves and, holding out their naked hands, would slap each other's palms.

Neither the NHL nor the WHA, as far as one could tell, was bothered by the disintegration of the game. Players continued to dump the puck into the corners. With the single exception of the Montreal Canadiens, teams continued to respond to the Philadelphia syndrome by hiring enforcers of their own. The junior ranks continued to swell with brawny six-footers who looked, and behaved, like bouncers. In 1974, Canada sent into the international fray an all-star team that, although representing the WHA, included many of the finest NHL players of all time; the Soviets defeated them handily. Attendance at most professional games in North America, however, continued to flourish, and the press, some of whose members had crowed in dismay over the two series against the Russians, continued to write about the game as if it had never lost its sheen. But at the foundations of hockey, changes began to take place that, taken cumulatively, amounted to a counter-revolution.

    The first place I noticed these changes was at my own neighbourhood arena. I had become, by then, fairly deeply involved with minor hockey. The experience had been both rewarding and frustrating. It was rewarding because of the great fun of playing with the boys—with the littler ones we actually went out on the ice during games—and of setting, or trying to set, various strategies for the games. It was frustrating because, for all my involvement with the game, there was very little I could teach. Having learned my hockey by osmosis, I was ill-equipped to instruct. In half an hour of expensive ice time in Toronto, I could no more impart what I had absorbed at Dickson Park than a Tahitian, given a morning in a rented, chlorinated pool, could have taught a band of Inuit to swim. The boys I drove to the rink on Saturday mornings spent, literally, less time on the ice over a season of Toronto league play than I had spent on a single winter afternoon. Far too often, they would waste their energies imitating what they had seen on television, up to and including the little victory dances executed by players like Dave "Tiger" Williams of the Maple Leafs.

By the mid-1970s, however, it was impossible not to notice around the local hockey arenas a new breed of coach: younger, in better condition, and, most important, better trained than we were. Many of them had learned the game under similar conditions to our sons, playing on artificial ice and wearing full equipment. Many were university trained, and had played college hockey. To the arenas that had been run mostly on our feeling for the game, they brought not only knowledge but an ability to communicate what they knew. They read books by Anatoly Tarasov about the Russian system and by Tom Watt, a Canadian university coach who had won seven national championships. They studied. In 1973, 940 coaches in Ontario alone attended clinics set up by the hockey establishment, which itself was responding with an unprecedented barrage of studies, pamphlets, films, and video material.

Reforming hockey became a Canadian sub-industry. Much of what was produced was a frenzied restatement of the obvious. "Much status or prestige in society is attained by out-performing (on the basis of skill) others under similar conditions," one report stated portentously. But a great deal of the material took hockey apart and put it back together again, and the coaches who were now appearing at the rinks, with their *Level 2* badges proudly stitched to their windbreakers, were a different breed from those of us who had shown up on Saturday mornings, bleary-eyed and nostalgic, to tell our sons about how we used to play. They came to practice with notes and plans on clipboards. They drew diagrams. They spoke of zones and boxes and systems for moving

the puck out of your own end. They found extra time to teach something they called "power skating." They began to use all the available ice
time to improve the game.

The word was spreading elsewhere. I remember, toward the end
of my own coaching career, preparing a team of fourteen-year-olds
for an exhibition game against a team from Amherst, Massachusetts.
I gave them a fatherly lecture, emphasizing the importance of taking
it easy against the foreign visitors. I should have seen what was coming in the pre-game warm-up, when Amherst ran through a complete
set of formal exercises that bore a remarkable resemblance to what the
Russians had done before each of their games against the NHLers, while
our own kids skated in circles and rattled the glass with slapshots. The
Americans were ahead of us 5–0 before I could get any word to my
team. They came at us like wolves on the fold, sweeping in on our blueline in combinations of two and three and making devastatingly creative
plays as they crossed it. I think the final score was 8–2, kept down by
Amherst in the interests of international good will.

The pros, too, were finally admitting the existence of a pool
of well-trained hockey talent outside not only Canada but North
America. In 1973, the Toronto Maple Leafs signed Borje Salming from
the Swedish national team, and Salming rapidly proved himself one of
the league's finer defencemen, personally demolishing the theory that
he and his countrymen were "chicken." The next year, the Winnipeg
Jets brought two of Salming's former teammates, Anders Hedberg and
Ulf Nilsson, to the WHA to combine with Bobby Hull on one of the
best forward lines in all hockey. The Toronto Toros helped to smuggle
Vaclav Nedomansky out of Czechoslovakia. All over both leagues, well-
coached graduates of American colleges, many of them American-born,
were suiting up regularly. And, however begrudgingly, Canadian fans
recognized that these non-Canadians were, like the Soviets, playing the
game as well as anyone did, playing it, moreover, in a manner that was
closer to the game of our boyhood than were many of the Canadian-
born players.

The season of 1979–80 began a new era for professional hockey. The
men who had backed the upstart WHA had faced reality: their invasion

of the south had been repelled. The owners of the only healthy franchises they had left, in Winnipeg, Quebec City, Edmonton, and Hartford, Connecticut, agreed to join the NHL. Each of the top twenty-one teams in North America would now face each of the others four times during the regular season, and a complicated playoff schedule would declare one champion of them all. To those of us who still had difficulty dealing with the fact that there were more than six teams in the NHL, this seemed very diluted whisky indeed, and as the season played itself out we saw some pretty dreadful games. Defensive hockey suffered in particular; teams in the new lineup averaged more than three and a half goals per game each—nearly a full goal more than the six members of the traditional NHL had scored in 1966–67. The results that came over the radio each morning often sounded more like football scores than hockey: 9–7, 10–2, 8–6. Shutouts by goaltenders, which had once been a regular feature of the game (Terry Sawchuk registered 103 of them himself in the 1950s and 1960s), became almost as rare as no-hitters in baseball. Eight players scored at least fifty goals, an accomplishment that had, only a generation before, been reserved for such immortals as Maurice Richard and Bobby Hull.

On the whole, there was much to deplore. But there was also much to celebrate. As athletes, the players in the new league were much superior to their predecessors: bigger, better nourished, better trained. They skated faster. In Ottawa, an archivist named Bill Galloway worked out a way to compare movies of old skaters with videotapes of the new. By adjusting for film speed, Galloway discovered that there was as much difference between, say, Yvan Cournoyer and Howie Morenz as there would be between any of the modern track's easy four-minute milers and Glenn Cunningham, who stunned the world in 1934 by running a mile in 4:06:8. Conn Smythe notwithstanding, Mark Messier, bigger and better trained, might very well have been able to take Sprague Cleghorn on in a fight and thrash him.

In every aspect of the game, the young players were becoming dominant. Only five years earlier, the average age of the league's top twenty-five scorers had been twenty-nine; in 1979–80 it was just over twenty-five, and at the season's end, none of them had yet turned thirty.

The most pleasurable aspect of the changing NHL, however, was one the statistics couldn't reflect. Nearly everyone was playing, or trying to play, a hockey that was very close to the game of Dickson Park. Nearly every team had a *bouquet garni* of European-born players, and many of the more attractive aspects of what we now recognize as the European style were being incorporated in the NHL. As well, the American-trained college players were adding their own skills to the stock. By the 1979–80 season, fully 25 percent of the NHL players had been born outside of Canada. Instead of plodding up and down their wings, forwards were criss-crossing as they attacked, swerving and soaring, freelancing. Drop passes, where one player would whip across a teammate's path and leave him the puck, became more common. Stick-handling improved. Dumping the puck into the opponents' zone became not so much an end in itself as a part of the game's tactics.

For the lack of defence, there were at least two explanations. One was that Bobby Orr, the most thrilling player of his day, had changed the role of the defenceman by carrying the puck up the ice, directing traffic from his place on the point, feeding his forwards—and in the process blasting apart the old record for assists by *any* player—and in general turning his position into one from which launching goals was at least as important as preventing them. The younger players had copied him, to the extent that all the leading defencemen of the expanded league—Larry Robinson, Denis Potvin, Ray Bourque, Salming—were noted for their offensive skills first and their abilities and willingness to block shots second. Another explanation was that all players could shoot better—harder and more accurately—than their elders. While there were other sides to this interpretation (a theory, for instance, that goaltending skills had declined), there was no doubt that the show the new, young pros were putting on was an exciting one.

In the summer of 1980, I decided to go have a look at it. In a way, I would be returning to Dickson Park, trying to look from the perspective of middle age at the game of my boyhood. But at the same time I might be able to find out something about the heroes of the new game, and the world in which they operated. In that context, I could scarcely avoid following Wayne Gretzky; it was already evident that he was a candidate for the pantheon of all-time superstars. When I mentioned my plans to him—I had met him during his early teenage years—he suggested that if I wanted to follow a team for a season, the Oilers might be the perfect choice: young, improving, and very much representative of the themes I wanted to explore. I wrote to Peter Pocklington, their owner, and a man who, it seemed from what I read, embodied the new breed of high-rollers who were taking over the ownership of hockey as much as his players embodied the changes on the ice. He invited me to visit him and, after checking with Glen Sather, agreed to let me join his team for a year. In September, I reported to rookie camp at Edmonton Gardens, a ramshackle building in the shadow of the glistening new Northlands Coliseum.

By agreement with the powerful Players' Association, the sessions at Edmonton Gardens were for unseasoned players only: the rookies selected by the Oilers in the spring draft, the men who had played last year for one of their minor-league affiliates, and a collection of hopefuls from various levels of hockey who had talked Sather into looking them over in person. The "veterans"—a rubric that covered even the teenaged Messier and Gretzky—could not be ordered onto the ice until their own camp began in Jasper a week later. But nearly all of them showed up anyway. Wearing cut-off jeans and T-shirts, they would arrive in mid-morning, while the aspirants were slogging through the first of two daily sessions, and congregate in the Gardens lobby. They looked brown and fit and confident. While many of them had seen each other in the summer, at golf tournaments or charity baseball games or at the hockey schools where they taught, the gathering together in the fall was still a sort of class reunion for them, and they would move around the arena as a group, sitting together in the stands and looking aloofly at the new boys on the ice.

"Look at that bag of hammers," one of them would say. Or, "I guess *your* job's safe, Murder"—or Lummer or Vicious or Key—and the others would guffaw appreciatively.

Then, while the hopefuls broke for lunch, they would move to the dressing room and don their hockey gear for an hour-long skate. On the ice, they would play. Without bothering to choose up sides, they broke easily into teams. Except for the presence of their fully equipped goalies, the game these teams waged was essentially the game of Dickson Park and Eighty-sixth Street. There were no referees and no offsides. No one bodychecked. Forwards lurked near their opponents' line and called for the puck by banging their sticks on the ice until someone hollered goal-sucking. Defencemen soloed deep into the attacking zone. After each goal, which was celebrated by taunts of defiant jubilation, the team that had been scored against took the puck from behind its own net and started once more up the ice, and the play would range on until the coaches reclaimed the ice for the resumption of the rookies' practice.

During these games, the Oilers would smile and laugh, feeling their muscles begin to work themselves back into playing shape and sensing once again the simple pleasures of the game they played. But as the days rolled by, the play turned to work, and the training program settled down to the long grind that would last till spring.

Like most teams in the modern NHL, the Oilers had tried to turn the assessment of the players available to them into a scientific process. The process began with a bureaucratic-looking form, printed in triplicate, called a "Player Evaluation Report." There was a file of these reports on every player who showed up for camp, established pro or dream-filled rookie, rating each of them in seventy-four different aspects of hockey promise. Skating alone was broken down into stride, speed, balance, acceleration, change of pace, lateral movement (left and right), sharpness of turn (left and right), quickness of cutting (left and right), and the ability of the prospect to stay on his feet. Each of these components of the skating skill was rated on a scale of one (poor) to nine (exceptional). So were the components of shooting ability, puck-handling, checking, passing, positional play, aggressiveness, use of his body, sense of anticipation, and—by less visible criteria—attitude, desire, and potential as a team leader. At the conclusion of these forms, which the players never saw, was an ominous bottom line, which on the same scale of one to nine rated his "Prospects of Playing Professional Hockey." No one who was invited to training camp was a big enough bag of hammers to be given a one on this scale ("reject") although there were a few twos ("reject with one good quality"). Most of the players at camp had overall ratings ranging from three or four (which gave them a chance at playing in the minor professional leagues) up to seven ("NHL prospect with good potential") or eight (simply "NHL"). Gretzky was a nine.

At the 1980 training camp, the coaches were beginning to feed the notations on these forms into a computer. In the future, they hoped, they would add data on players from other teams, and the computerized information would serve them during the league's draft, and when trades were being negotiated. But the judgements that were recorded on the PERS remained human ones, and they spelled out the futures of the prospective hockey players as clearly as a road map. While a few days of superior play could turn a three into a four, or a few bad practice sessions could suddenly threaten a veteran's job, no one could move up or down more than one or two categories over the course of the camp; they were labelled.

A few of the men who filled out these forms—Vic Hadfield was one—had been sevens and eights themselves, and all of them had played some hockey. But Barry Fraser, the Oilers' chief scout, would scarcely have registered in the system he had masterminded. Fraser is a deceptively naive-looking man who, with his pompadour and generous belly, resembles a contented Elvis Presley. His own playing career stopped in B, where he broke a leg while trying to make a team in Cochrane, Ontario. After his injury, he retired to an office job with Ontario Hydro, but he maintained his interest in hockey by coaching young boys, and gradually the canny reports he sent in on prospects from his neck of the woods drew so much attention that he was swept into full-time scouting, ending up as a senior official of the Houston Aeros of the WHA. By the time the WHA folded, he had achieved such a reputation as a bloodhound that Sather snapped him up to head the Oilers' scouting staff. Kevin Lowe, who had been the first draft he recommended, had worked out well, but the 1980–81 season would be a full test of Fraser's powers of discrimination; it was on his word that the Oilers had spent their valuable first-round draft choice on Coffey, had courted Anderson, and had gambled yet another draft choice on being able to talk Jari Kurri into coming to North America. It was on his system, which Sather had urged him to perfect, that the future of the team and its young personnel would depend.

Before moving to Jasper, the Oilers trimmed all the lowest-rated players from their roster. This blood-letting ended the dreams of a number of young men. But it also ended, as it did each year he had to do it, a dream of Sather's. Like all hockey men, Sather still cherished hopes that ran counter to his own computerized bureaucracy, that somewhere there would be a player, unscouted and unranked, who would show up at training camp with the size of a Semenko, the abandon of a Messier, and the skills of a Gretzky. In 1980, as every other year, he faced the fact that the men he called walk-ons had served only as bodies to test the skills of the players his scouting system had already found and measured.

At Jasper, the serious work of selection began. Coffey, Anderson, and Kurri all began working out with the returning veterans. Such others as Don Ashby and Peter Driscoll, who had served with the Oilers the year before, found themselves lining up with the players who would go to Wichita. And nearly all in-between players felt the tension of fighting for a job or establishing a position.

From outside the sanctum of the team, not much of this tension or the manoeuvring that was producing it was evident. Each day, I would try to read the signs: Who was wearing what colour sweater? Who was playing on whose wing? Who, in a desperate attempt to attract attention, was trying to start a fight? But the coaches, caucussing each night in their private suite to pore over their notes and charts, remained close-mouthed. And the players, intent on their own struggles, were remote. The rest of us were excluded. I was having a hard time getting a sense of the team.

On the Wednesday morning of their week in Jasper, I put into effect a scheme I had concocted with Joe Black, an amiable photographer who had been taking pictures around the NHL for more than a generation, and who was in town as part of a tour of all the NHL's training camps. As instructed by Black, I showed up early for the Wednesday practice and sat in the bleachers while he set up his lights on the ice.

Sather saw me sitting there.

"What are you doing here so early?" he said.

"I came to get my picture taken," I said, "for my bubble-gum card."

"Okay," he said. "Go ahead."

I swallowed hard. I had not thought he would rise so easily to the bait. I suddenly remembered I had not been on skates since I stopped coaching my sons.

"Get some equipment on and get ready," Sather said. "You're never going to know these guys unless you get right in with them on their terms."

I wondered if his coaching instincts had led him to know exactly what I was up to.

"I'll make a fool of myself," I said.

"Of course," said Sather.

I went toward the dressing room. The trainers issued me clean long underwear, a fresh pair of white socks, a jockstrap. I padded down the corridor of the Jasper arena, seeking a place where no one else was changing. I settled for a spot next to Doug Hicks's gear. Hicks had injured a rib and wouldn't be suiting up for the day's practice. Next to Hicks's spot was space for Paul Coffey. A couple of other rookies were further down the bench.

"Are you the mayor?" asked one of them.

"No," I said, "why?"

"I thought you might be the mayor, getting dressed for a picture."

"A writer," I said.

"Why, it's Peter Plimpton," I heard someone else say from down the line.

"*George* Plimpton, you turkey," said B.J. MacDonald from across the way.

The garter belt was giving me trouble. The device that holds up stockings in today's NHL is a major advance from the inner tubes of my youth. It is intricate and flimsy enough to have come from Frederick's of Hollywood. I got mine on, laid the shin pad over the legs of my underwear, and pulled on the footless blue, orange, and white stockings. Hicks's pants, light as parachute silk, came up over the shin pads. Laced at the waist, modern pants rise to your rib cage, protecting the kidneys and liver. Braces. Shoulder pads over the head.

"Uh, excuse me," said Coffey. "Those are my ... uh, I think you've got the wrong shoulder p—"

"Sorry, Paul," I said.

"Doesn't matter."

My—well, Hicks's—elbow pads presented an unexpected problem. In my day, even the best-quipped players just had elbow pads. Today, there is a right elbow pad and a left one. Coffey helped me out. He finished dressing and clumped off toward the ice.

And now came the real crisis, the skates. After some negotiation—skates come in different sizes from shoes, and hockey players wear them as tight as skin—I had arranged to borrow Vic Hadfield's. Now I bent to put them on.

I couldn't get down. Partly because of the tightly laced pants, but also because of my middle-aged girth, I couldn't bend over to slip on my skates—or, rather, Hadfield's. I thought of Plimpton—George—trying to play football with the Detroit Lions, and having trouble pulling his helmet open to get his head in.

Helpless, I suspended the left boot from my left thumb and forefinger, trying to slip it over my foot. It wouldn't slip. The skate fell to the floor.

"Having trouble?" It was Jim Crosson, twenty years old.

"Uh … well … "

"Let me help you."

And there I sat, leg outstretched on the bench, while a man younger than two of my children bent over my skates, lacing them up, tying them neatly and tightly at the top, in a reversal of a time-honoured, Saturday-morning Canadian scene. Finally, I stood up.

"Are you the new wily veteran?" asked B.J. MacDonald.

"I'm younger than Gordie Howe," I said.

"Who isn't?" said B.J.

I had borrowed Dave Semenko's sweater. I needed his size to accommodate my midriff.

"Twist the arms so the numbers show," said Semenko.

"You really want people to see me in this?"

"Any publicity helps," he said.

"One more thing," said Jim Crosson. "You have to know the look."

"What?"

"The look. For pictures, you pull the tongue of your skates out and up. It looks flashy. We all do it. Here, let me give you a hand."

Skate-tongues pulled, sweater-numbers twisted, my greying hair brushed neatly into place, I waddled down the hall. A trainer handed me a Sherwood PMP 5030, right-handed, slick-black with tar tape on the blade. I bent to test its springiness against the floor.

"For Chrissake, don't do that," a trainer snarled.

"Why not?"

"You just don't *do* that to a professional hockey player's stick."

I remember the hours the players spent working on their sticks, sanding them, shaping them, blasting off the rough edges with a blow torch, like hunters with weapons on which their lives would depend.

"Sorry," I said.

Hand over hand, I made my way out the gate, and joined the line waiting along the boards. A Zamboni was adding a finishing gloss to the ice.

I took a tentative step outward. As well as being tighter, pro skates are sharper than any I had ever worn. You have to *dig* to stop. I turned instead, moving in what I took to be a graceful curve, leaning my Sherwood across the tops of my shin pads. From the boards came hoots of what might have been appreciation. Players I had not yet spoken to called my name. "Sign him," someone cried. "*Help* him," cried someone else. The cheers, if they were cheers, mounted. Sather and I had both been right. I felt foolish.

Then Black summoned me for my pose, and told me how to cradle the puck and stare at the camera. I stole a glance at the stands.

And up there I saw … outsiders.

However gracelessly, however ineptly, I was *on the ice*, stared at, rather than staring. I felt, for a moment, what the players must feel all the time at camp, stared at, surveyed, measured, commented on, their every move noted, their every mistake written down, their every characteristic immutably rated from one to nine.

They are like show animals, I thought, always on parade and always separate from their judges. The game they play is the game all of us played, but the game of our lives is the business of theirs, and they are a long, long way from Dickson Park.

## 8

*… Sather went to his home in Banff to celebrate the New Year and lick his wounds*

With Bryan Watson gone, Glen Sather moved quickly behind the Oilers' bench, taking complete and vigorous control where only his influence had been felt before. Billy Harris, the gentlemanly assistant who had survived all the turmoil over Watson, continued to do what he had been doing all along, teaching during practices, acting as a kind of consultant—a coaches' coach—during games, relaying his insights by walkie-talkie from the pressbox.

Harris was a favourite of almost everyone who had spent time around hockey. As a tall, slight centre—"Hinky" he was called—he played some of the Leafs' prettiest hockey of the 1950s and 1960s, although his style didn't fit the grinding play that pleased so many coaches of his day. He was a play-maker, a dipsy-doodler. He left the Leafs in 1965 and drifted around with a few other NHL clubs, then moved on to coaching. He ran the Toronto Toros in their brief stint in the WHA, and coached several international teams, including the WHA's Team Canada in 1974 and the Swedish team that came to Canada in 1976. Everywhere he went he made friends, and newspapermen constantly sought him out for his stringent analysis. There were those who thought, though, that for all his knowledge of the game he lacked the fire to be a successful coach; it was as if the thoughtful distance he kept from the wars and the great pleasure he drew from recounting their lore (he is one of the great trivia players of the world) made it impossible for him to lead the troops over the battlements. In the late 1970s he had retired to academe, setting up and running a department of sports administration at Laurentian University in Sudbury, and enjoying his growing family. He made only occasional forays into the hockey world; most of them, as in 1979, when CBC radio sent him to the Moscow world tournament, to act as a commentator.

In the summer of 1980, Sather lured him back to work with the young Oilers, and his presence on the team became an important part of its chemistry. At forty-five, he had a splendid head of white hair and a scholarly air. In tense situations, the players sought him out for counsel, and at practice sessions they listened attentively to his soft-spoken comment. Now, everyone around the team hoped, he would make a perfect foil to Sather's chippy zeal.

If the new brain trust was to be the answer to the Oilers' woes, however, it wasn't yet showing in the results. The Oilers won their first game under Sather's control, beating Buffalo at home, then lost to Colorado in Colorado. In a repeat of their mastery of Chicago, they whipped the Black Hawks at home 10–3. Then the wheels fell off. They lost eight of their next nine, eleven of their next fourteen. About the only pleasant interruption came during a televised game against Montreal in which Dave Hunter, so used to playing a defensive role, got the puck in the dying seconds, seemed for a moment to be frozen in puzzlement while the fans and his teammates yelled "shoot," and finally did, to bring off a 4–3 victory with just two seconds left on the clock.

Much of this dismal history arose from circumstances no coach could have avoided. The injury toll continued to mount. On November 29, Dave Lumley was blindsided in Boston by the Bruins' robust forward Stan Jonathan and sprained his shoulder. On December 10, Charlie Huddy, the defenceman who had been playing capably in place of the injured Doug Hicks, sprained *his* shoulder against the Islanders. On December 17 came what appeared to be the most devastating injury of all. Ron Low, reaching out to catch a shot by the Washington Capital rookie Tim Tookey, felt a sudden pain at the base of his thumb. Low thought at first it was a sprain, but the pain continued. X-rays showed a break. Doctors ordered a cast until after Christmas. "After that," said Low, "I'm going to get them to make a playing cast." But he would be out until at least mid-January.

In desperation, the Oilers, who had flirted with two other minor-league goalies over the year, called up a baby-faced twenty-year-old named Andy Moog. Moog had good breeding. His father, Don, had been a backup goaltender with the Penticton Vees in 1955, when the Vees went to the world championships, one of the last times a Canadian team won that tournament. But Andy had been the 132nd player chosen in the junior draft; the Oilers had taken him from a junior team in Billings, Montana. More than almost any of their other young draft choices, he was a Barry Fraser special. On the forms Fraser had designed to rate goaltenders, where "use of stick," "control of rebounds," "use of hands," and "durability" replaced the skating and checking characteristics of the forwards and defencemen, he had ranked high, although in practice at training camp he had frequently looked dreadful. He was not a practice goalie, he insisted to the few people who listened to him at camp; he saved his skills for games. Fraser endorsed this contention, and said he had seen Moog play brilliantly in Billings. Relying largely on Fraser's word, the Oilers had signed Moog to a contract and sent him to Wichita, from where he was now summoned, and quickly pressed into service.

On December 23, Eddie Mio took a hard shot on the collarbone in a game against Los Angeles, and Moog went in to replace him. On the first play after Mio's injury, Mike Murphy of the Kings grabbed a loose puck, scooted in on Moog, and put past him the first shot the young goalie had faced in the NHL. When Mio came back into the game two minutes later, Moog left with a goals-against average of thirty per sixty minutes of play.

Although that December 23 game marked the return—at last—of a fully sighted Brett Callighen, it also saw the departure of yet another of the important young players. Glenn Anderson, whose skating had been laboured for some time, pulled up lame in the warm-up. Doctors found a bone chip floating in his knee, and surgery was prescribed. And the next night, in Quebec City, the Nordique enforcer John Wensink slashed B.J. MacDonald across the hand and broke a finger. For B.J., leaving the lineup marked the end of a consecutive game streak that stretched back almost 400 professional games.

As the year turned, the Oilers were in twentieth place, saved from the league's absolute basement only by the Winnipeg Jets, who were on their way to having the worst season in the history of the NHL. On December 23, the Jets had beaten Colorado 5–4, "bringing springtime to the prairie city" as the *Hockey News* reported, "when the outside temperature was 55 below Fahrenheit." The reason for the jubilation was that before their victory over the Rockies, Winnipeg had played thirty games in a row without a win, a streak that had broken by three games a record once held by a team called the Kansas City Scouts. A lot of hockey men, though, while rolling in Winnipeg jokes, thought the Jets, a team almost as young as the Oilers but lacking a Gretzky, would nevertheless have a solid future.

More dismaying was the fall from respectability of such good old teams as Detroit, the New York Rangers, Boston, and Toronto, all of whom were struggling along in the bottom half of the league. The Islanders, to no one's surprise, were in front, but chasing them boldly—to almost everyone's surprise—were the St. Louis Blues, a team without a notable scoring star. What St. Louis did have was a collection of very solid players, many of them of the new, quick style, and all of them superbly coached by Red Berenson, a veteran player who had been the foundation of earlier St. Louis teams. Even more important was the goaltending of Mike Liut. Liut's was a name that had crept up on everyone who followed hockey. St. Louis had drafted him in 1976 out of Bowling Green University, taking him fifty-sixth on the list of draft choices. He opted to play a couple of years at Cincinnati in the WHA, returning to St. Louis only when that franchise folded. He was tall—six-two—and lanky, at 185 pounds. In his stand-up, solid game he reminded many people of Ken Dryden. In other ways, too, he was like Dryden—articulate and studious. Statistically, he was not impressive; he led the league in neither games won (Mario Lessard of Los Angeles did that) nor goals-against average (a squadron of Montreal goalies held that mark). But he won all the big games, and time after time, as the Blues came up against teams that in another year would have eaten them alive, staved off the scorers until his own team of *inconnu* could rally. By the new year, Liut was being talked of as a candidate for the league's most valuable player award. Even that talk served to underline the Oilers' frustrations; in the previous season, Gretzky had walked away with the MVP trophy, and many people had figured that if he continued to play up to his potential he would own it for as long as he played in the NHL.

On December 30, the Oilers lost again, this time to Calgary, 5–3. With a grimace, Peter Pocklington wrote a cheque to Skalbania for the same amount he had collected after Edmonton's earlier win and had spent on the players' gifts of frozen meat. Pocklington was at a loss as to what to do. The Omega instructor had been unable to come to Edmonton in the fall, and Pocklington sometimes thought he should bring one or two of the players into his office to give them a shot of positive inspiration. Maybe Semenko could be his executive assistant for a few days, he had suggested once. For Christmas he had given the whole team Morlands sheepskin jackets, on the linings of which were sewn the words *Edmonton Oilers, Stanley Cup Champions, 198–*, but the team had not won a game since.

The next day Sather went to his home in Banff to celebrate the New Year and to lick his wounds in the surroundings he liked best. There, he talked mournfully of his injury list. Anderson's leg had been operated on that afternoon and he would be out for a month. MacDonald's injured hand could keep him out just as long. Lumley and Huddy were still incapacitated. Ron Low? He'd play right now if he could get his cast inside his glove, but there was no way he could do that. Mio, however, had emerged as a major-league goalie. At one gathering of the veterans he'd said that he didn't mind playing backup to Ron Low, but there was no way he'd be second string to Andy Moog. And Moog himself, whom Sather had tested under real fire in Philadelphia, had played strongly in a 2–1 loss.

Don Murdoch was still not playing well. Sather couldn't understand what it was. When someone hinted at Murdoch's old problem, Sather leaped to his defence. "Listen," he said, "I'd know. There's just no way in this league you can carry on with dope and not have it show while you're travelling as much as we are. No, he's clean." Stan Weir was struggling, he said, and Pat Price was taking far too many penalties, especially in the first period. But there were a lot of good points, too. Paul Coffey was blossoming. And many of the other defencemen were playing solidly: Kevin Lowe, Fogie, and Risto—Risto should be an all-star.

Gretzky, of course, was Gretzky, but "I've got to get him someone to play with." Right now, Jari Kurri was playing in B.J.'s spot on Wayne's right, and maybe he'd develop, but ...

Was he thinking of making trades?

"I'm always *thinking* of it," he said. "And talking. I'm on the phone every day. It's part of the business. You call someone just to rap for a while, and then you say, 'By the way, would you be interested in so-and-so?' and he says, 'No, but I'd sure like so-and-so-else,' and then you dicker for a while. But I can't get anywhere. Everybody wants the kids. Toronto wants a young defenceman, and they'd give me practically anyone I would name, or so they say. But when I name someone it just seems to break down. I could have Turnbull, I guess, but I'm not sure I want him. Buffalo right now, why I could pick up the phone to Scotty and have Jim Schoenfeld and Rick Martin. Schoenfeld's just the kind of defenceman we need, and Martin has scored fifty goals twice; he's been an all-star. But they're—what?—twenty-eight and twenty-nine, and what Scotty wants in return are Hunter and Coffey. I could do that and, sure, we'd move up about four places this year, just with that trade, but in three or four years, why, they'd kill me. Coffey's going to be one of the best defencemen in this league. That's all they want: the kids. I'm going to stick with these kids even if it means finishing last. Well, maybe not last."

Meanwhile, what of the replacements he'd been flying in from Wichita? For a while, he'd brought up Tom Roulston, a laughing redhead from Winnipeg with a gift for scoring goals and spreading goodwill—he was an all-night disc jockey in the summertime—but he hadn't worked out. Now, he was going with Peter Driscoll, a big, tough schoolteacher's son from northern Ontario who had played thirty-nine games for the Oilers the year before. Driscoll had given away the winning goal in Calgary, but at least, Sather said, he was knocking some people around, and he would make a useful addition to the Swat team. After all, Sather said, as he poured himself another New Year's rum, Brack couldn't carry that part of the team's needs alone.

Brack. Curt Brackenbury. John Curtis Brackenbury, if you wanted to be formal, as Brack seldom was, unless there were ladies around, in which case he was capable of the most extraordinarily winning manners. Born, Kapuskasing, Ontario, January 31, 1952. Right wing. Shoots right. 5'10". 197 pounds. Last amateur club: Jersey Devils (EHL). Professional clubs: Des Moines (IHL), Long Island (NAHL), Chicago (WHA), Hampton (SHL), Minnesota (WHA), and, for five happy years, Quebec (WHA and NHL). Total goals in seven years: 75. Total minutes in penalties: 1,218. Total enemies: zero, if you didn't count the fans who objected to his exuberantly bashing style of play. Total number of friends: nearly everyone who met him. As his mother had once written to a journalist who had published an admiring portrait: "Curt is a very special person, which has nothing to do with hockey … Appearances notwithstanding, he is very private. He seldom speaks of his feelings, doesn't know he is funny, nor that he possesses the faculty of making others interested or happy. But he does in fact add spice to life."

By the end of December, the spice that Brackenbury was adding to the Oilers' daily lives was one of the few bright elements in their unsatisfying year. As Sather had hoped, Brackenbury had taken over the emotional leadership of the team, and both on and off the ice he was a constant illumination. He had enormous physical presence: pale blue eyes that were squeezed by his high cheekbones into an appearance that was close to Oriental; a head of tight, curly blond hair; a thick neck; and a chest that bulged up under his chin and threatened to burst through his clothes. The first time I had a private conversation with him, he was wearing a white shirt, a subdued grey tie and red suspenders. That morning at practice, Dave Hunter asked him why he always wore red suspenders. "To keep my pants up," Brack replied—and I still don't know if he knew or cared that that was an old joke.

He bought me a beer and asked me about my work. Did I have an agent? How much royalty do you make on a book? Was the work hard? In the couple of months I had been hanging around hockey players this was the first time I had ever felt one of them was interviewing *me*. I couldn't help remembering a remark made by Gary Ronberg, a fact that had finally sunk into him after more than a decade as a sportswriter. "If you ever want to sum up hockey players," he said, "just try to remember the last one who ever asked you how you were."

Inevitably, with Brack the talk turned to hockey. It was all very well to hang out with a team for a year, Brack said, but did I have any sense of the game itself? "I'm not sure," I said, and I told him a story.

One year in Galt, I said, when I was about ten, there was a set of meteorological circumstances that I had not seen before and have not seen since: snow followed by rain, followed by a snap freeze. The Scots, I learned much later, had a name for the condition that resulted: *verglas*, the hard surface of ice that is formed by precisely the right heaviness of rain falling on precisely the right bed of snow. After half an hour or so of playing our usual pick-up game, somebody accidentally shot the puck over the boards. Instead of burying itself, the puck slithered across the frozen surface, the *verglas*. Someone else went to chase it and, miraculously, his skates held too. We followed the leader out into the park, skimming across the snow, firing infinitely long passes to each other. At the park's end, yelling excitedly to each other, we flung our sticks over the fence and headed for the open country. The snow held again, and off we went, soaring across roads and frozen lawns, like skiers who never had to climb their hills, and out, out into the country, by this time followed by every boy from our side of town who had skates—forty of us, fifty of us, gliding across farmers' fields, inventing new rules for our unending game, allowing for fences in the middle of a rush, or goals that might be half a mile apart. I didn't know if that had anything to do with hockey, I said to Brack, but I know I'd never been happier.

By this time, there were a few other people listening to us, and our talk turned to boyhood. Ken Brown, the former goalie who worked with Roddy Phillips on the radio broadcasts, told a yarn from his own childhood on the prairie when, one Saturday morning, a milk truck had overturned in a dairy yard and the milk had frozen. That afternoon the boys of the town had had a rousing game of shinny on the whitest ice they'd ever seen.

And Brack said: "Fishing. I did it fishing. Up near Williams Lake, where my family lives now, there's this salmon river that gets black as night when it freezes over, but the fish keep swimming under it. You can see them, just sliding along like dark submarines, and one time I went chasing them. Just went out on the river, the way I think the Indians used to do—although I guess they didn't have skates—but I put my skates on and I followed one salmon for—it must have been miles. I don't know, I just sort of lost track of time. It was great."

When he practised, which he did harder than anybody, he would come to the bench, throw his curly head back, and squeeze the water bottle into his face, then shake himself until the water splashed over anyone who was standing near. He would drive himself into extra laps, pushing himself into head-down sprints between the bluelines, then rising to coast behind the goal, then spring full-out again, blueline to blueline, getting everything from his body that he could, throwing off a spray of sweat. After practice, he would go into the dressing room and work on the Nautilus machine, or on a special wheel, about the size of a lawnmower wheel, through which there was a steel axle; he would grasp the axle with one hand on each side of the wheel, do a push-up and then roll the wheel out till his arms were fully extended, then pull it back under him again. He had made some special push-up blocks, each with a handle on it like that of a large carrying case. He would place two of these blocks on the floor the width of his shoulders apart, then grasp the handles and do still more push-ups, reaching down below the level of the blocks to touch his chin to the floor. He could do fifty of these without stopping. In contests of sheer strength, Lee Fogolin could out pull him with his greater weight. And often he and Fogolin would work together on Brack's special devices. But even Fogolin could never outlast him, and sometimes, in fear for Brack's health, the coaches would order him to stop.

Once, after a particularly tough practice, Brack and Brett Callighen played extra games. First, they stood near the boards, one on either side of the ice, about even with the face-off circles. Then they fired pucks around the end of the ice at each other, banking them from corner to corner and out again; if you got the puck past your opponent you won a point. Callighen won. Then they lined up in front of the net and had a contest to see who could hit the crossbar most often. Brack won. Then they stood, one in each corner, and tried to bank shots cross-rink into the empty goal at the other end. Callighen won again, and Brack, as loser, had to pick up all the practice pucks in a bucket. Callighen, laughing, skated off, and said, "Jeez, you're lovely to play with, Brack."

Brack had a brother, a bad seed. On parole from one conviction, he had run wild with a group of other ex-cons in Edmonton, and one of them had sawed through a woman's windpipe with a serrated knife. Curt's brother was doing life in Stoney Mountain Penitentiary. At Christmas, Curt quietly left the team party to visit him. But, to my knowledge, he never spoke of him, and the subject was off limits even for the often tactless teasing of his teammates. His parents were a remarkable couple. Stuart and Nancy. Stuart was a forester when they lived in Kapuskasing, but when he was forty-nine, and Curt was fifteen, he decided to take up a second career, so he packed the family up and moved to British Columbia where he enrolled in law school at the University of British Columbia. He wore a lumberjack shirt to classes. Before they'd moved, Curt recalls, his dad had been very strict about things like long hair, but at school he came to understand. Sometimes, at night, the phone would ring and one of his fellow students would ask to speak to "Tex." When Curt himself went to university for a couple of years, he found his father was still a hero. He was very proud of his father, as his mother and his sister were proud of him. The family were all close, and in the summers, they would gather at the Brackenbury homestead near Williams Lake, hand-built by Stuart, with no phone—"my clients can reach me at the office"—and an Old Macdonald-size menagerie of ducks and geese and turkeys.

Brack was not a superior hockey player. On the ice, he looked, as Jim Matheson of the Edmonton *Journal* once wrote, "more like a linebacker than a right winger." Passes seemed to be repelled by his stick as if it and the puck had been magnetized to the same pole. His shots rattled glass more than they bulged twine. His choppy skating style often left him outdistanced by the play, no matter how hard he dug. But there was no one on the team who wasn't glad he was there.

His humour, which mostly consisted of unfailing good spirits and personal—though never cruel—remarks, was hard to reproduce. Wherever the team travelled, Brack was at its centre. When he was dressed for a game, as he was regularly during the rash of injuries, he was always a part of it, even if that part might just be his intense cheer-leading from the bench. Loosing him on the ice involved a calculated risk that he would cause an injury—to a member of the opposition or to himself—or add to his impressive penalty total. He just ran over people and sent them flying.

There was no viciousness in him, and once when I asked an executive of the Quebec Nordiques how they could ever have let go a player who was such an obvious spiritual leader of his team, the executive simply said, "He wouldn't fight. Guys like that have to fight."

A few days after Christmas, Brack at practice asked Billy Harris if Billy was going out New Year's Eve.

"Oh, I don't think so," Harris replied. "At our age, my wife and I just put another log on the fire and sit back to watch Lombardo on the television."

Then, on New Year's Eve morning, Brack approached Harris again.

"You can't stay home tonight," he said.

"Why not?"

"Because Vince Lombardi's dead."

On January 2, the Oilers beat Boston, 7–4, at home, but the win was only their ninth of the year, and Sather's fifth. Under Watson, they had won only four, but tied nine, for a total of thirteen points in the standings after eighteen games. Under Sather, along with the five wins had come one tie, so that after eighteen games under his direction, their record was actually worse: eleven points. In the new year, with a new round of road trips on the schedule, the team would face an awesome set of challenges.

## 9

*… the sense of team was rampant*

The Quebec Nordiques, whom the Oilers visited early in January, were one of the most interesting teams in the NHL, not only because of the mixture of French- and English-speaking players on their team—a mixture that occasionally exploded under the pressure of their Québécois environment—but because of the presence of yet a third cultural strain, Slovakian. This strain was represented by two extraordinary young brothers, Peter and Anton Stastny, who, besides being excellent hockey players, represented the league's new emphasis on European stars and the lengths to which some of its members would go to import them.

Before their arrival in Quebec, the Stastnys, playing on a line with their older brother Marian, had been mainstays of a Czechoslovakian national team that, among other accomplishments, had once knocked off the Russians for the championship of the world. The first member of a Czech national team to defect, Vaclav Nedomansky, had been thirty years old when he'd fled his homeland—old by the standards of European hockey, where players were discarded younger than in the NHL. The Stastnys were in their prime in 1980: Peter was twenty-four, Anton twenty-one. Their departure for the West had been an international incident.

The central figure in that incident was an Eastern European

businessman then living in Toronto, to whom, for reasons of his own safety, it is best to refer only as K. K had a murky past. At one time, he told various acquaintances, he had been arrested over a matter of drugs, but had "bought his way out of that one." He had been involved in the Nedomansky affair, and over the years had approached various general managers around the league about the possibility of further defections.

One who listened with more than casual interest was Gilles Léger, the director of player personnel for the Nordiques. Léger was an unorthodox hockey man, a casual dresser who wore thick-lensed glasses and enjoyed smoking cigars down to their butts. After a coaching career in college hockey in the Maritimes, he had been one of the senior officials of the Toros and had assisted in their transfer to Birmingham, first luring the biggest names he could find from the NHL—Frank Mahovlich had played briefly for him, as had Carl Brewer and Paul Henderson—and, over another period, assembling the biggest collection of goons he could find. He had also been involved in harvesting Nedomansky. The idea of acquiring the Stastnys excited him. Not only would the quick, clever, deceptive style of their Czech-bred hockey appeal to the Nordiques' fans, but the defection of two of the major stars of a champion European hockey team would yield him huge returns of publicity in a province where, all too often, the Nordiques were overshadowed by the Montreal Canadiens.

With K's connivance, Léger began to woo the brothers. At first, he concentrated on Marian, the oldest. But Marian was married and had young children. He was sure he would be unable to get them out. "Take Peter and Anton," he had said. "I'll try to come later." By the summer of 1980, after a pursuit that had led Léger through many of the Western European countries into which the Czech national team ventured and to the Olympics at Lake Placid in the spring, Léger had contracts signed by Peter and Anton in his pocket. In August he and Marcel Aubut, a Quebec City lawyer with high political connections who was the president of the Nordiques, checked into the Inter-Continental Hotel in Vienna. At Innsbruck, some 400 kilometres to the east, the Czechs were playing their final game in an international tournament.

That night in Innsbruck, K, with his rented red Mercedes' headlights dim, pulled up beside the Czech team bus. In the car's trunk were four battered suitcases, holding all the transportable worldly possessions of Peter and Anton. When the team had left its hotel for the Innsbruck arena, K had stealthily made his way past their security guards and carried the suitcases, one by one, to the car. It was not the first time he had been inside a hotel where the Czech team was staying. Once, in West Germany, he had been talking to the Stastnys in their room when security had launched a last-minute, lights-out check, and the Stastnys had had to hide him in their closet. Tonight, the plan was for the brothers to finish their game, change to street clothes, and then join a party of Czech fans who had come to Austria for the tournament. The party of fans included Peter's pregnant wife, Darina. After a suitable stay, Peter, Anton, and Darina would leave the party, make their way toward the team bus, bolt for the Mercedes, and be gone.

Now, however, there was no sign of them, and K was worried. The factors that had finally convinced the Stastnys to defect had included more than money, although money had played a part. In Czechoslovakia they received only the equivalent of $230 for a win and less for a loss. They had also, for some time now, been unhappy with the coaching they'd been getting and had felt they were taken for granted. They were, moreover, Slovaks on a team that was known around the world as Czech, and the national label had never rested comfortably on their shoulders. But the Czechs would not let them go easily. The Stastny forward line had meant more than international hockey awards to the Czechs; their presence had helped to draw fans, paying hard currency, wherever the team travelled.

At last, Peter and Darina came out of the gloom, holding hands. They sauntered first toward the bus and then, in its shadow, moved briskly to the Mercedes.

"Where's Anton?" K demanded.

"He must have gone back to the hotel," Peter said. "He's already left the reception."

Cursing, K spun the Mercedes to retrace the route he'd already followed. The hotel had been the point from which they had intended to take off. At the last minute, they had devised the plan to meet at the bus. Anton must have forgotten. As they neared the hotel, they saw him, standing in the light of a street lamp, his coat collar turned up in the chill summer night. He climbed into the Mercedes' back seat, and K headed off for Vienna.

They drove all night, arriving in Vienna at 8 a.m. At the Inter-Continental, Léger and Aubut had reserved two suites, one in their own names, one in the name of a fictitious German family. They had also alerted Canadian embassy officials, but, fearful of the slightest leak, had declined to give the names of their two potential refugees. Besides, they recalled, there had been false alarms before, in Sweden, in Amsterdam, and at Lake Placid. Now, they shunted K, the Stastny brothers, and Darina to the dummy suite and told them to rest while they went to the embassy. As their elevator arrived at the main floor, they were dismayed to find the lobby swarming with Czech agents. "If you've spent as much time as I had chasing European hockey players," Léger said later, "you know who the agents are."

In anticipation of this turn of events, the Canadians had rented three cars, the Mercedes, another that Léger and Aubut had driven ostentatiously around Vienna, and an extra one that now sat parked on the street. Knowing the red Mercedes would be watched and fearful that the car they had been driving would also be known to the Czechs, they walked boldly past them both, then began to run toward the parked alternate. They jumped in and sped off, only to realize that, after all their preparation, they were unsure of the route to the Canadian embassy. In heavy traffic, they deserted their rented car and hailed a taxi.

At the embassy, Léger and Aubut were treated coolly—until the arrival of a female agent whose identity, like K's, Léger would like kept secret. "All I can tell you," he had said, "is that she was perfect for the part—long hair, long legs, and a cigarette holder. I think Jane Fonda could play her in the movie." Jane Fonda, it turned out, spoke with a Viennese accent and was available for special work for the Canadians and other Western embassies.

"You've got who?" she said now.

"Peter and Anton Stastny."

"Let's go."

In the agent's car, Léger related their adventures up to that moment. "We'll need help," their benefactress said, and pulled into a police station, where she enlisted a posse of two carloads of Viennese policemen. Sirens yodelling, the caravan dashed back to the Inter-Continental.

The agents were still evident in the lobby. Frantically, the Canadians led a rush to the elevators. As they arrived at the door of the suite registered to the non-existent German family, they could hear the telephone ringing. Snatching the key from Léger's hands, the Viennese Jane Fonda led her rescue party through the door. She ran to the telephone receiver while a white-faced K looked on. A male voice, speaking Czech, asked to speak to Peter or Anton Stastny.

Meantime, in Canada, diplomatic wires were buzzing. Aubut had called both his wife and a Toronto lawyer named Michael Bukovac, whom the Nordiques had retained for the occasion. Mrs. Aubut called an old family friend, Gilles Lamontagne, former mayor of Quebec City, now Canadian minister of defence. Bukovac called an official of Hockey Canada who, in turn, placed a call to the Winnipeg home of Lloyd Axworthy, minister of citizenship and immigration. Axworthy agreed to fly east for a series of special hearings at the Toronto airport. Finally, and in spite of advice from some members of his department that other nationals of Eastern European countries would raise a furor if the hockey players were given special status, the minister ruled that the Stastnys were in immediate danger and should be allowed to enter Canada on minister's permits, issued through orders-in-council of the cabinet.

After one last dash through the Vienna traffic, with their long-legged agent ordering police to let them through the worst jams, the Canadians and the Stastnys caught KLM's last flight of the day to Amsterdam, while K, as unobtrusively as he could, took a train for Berlin. At Amsterdam, the Nordique party switched to a Canadian Pacific flight to Montreal. After take-off, a stewardess brought them their first-class champagne. "It was," Léger says, "the first moment the Stastnys knew they had done the right thing."

By the time the Oilers arrived in Quebec, the Stastnys had become comfortably ensconced Canadian residents. Peter and Darina's daughter, born in Quebec in the autumn and named Alexandria, was a healthy North American consumer of Pampers. Darina, shy and not yet comfortable in either of her two new languages, nevertheless made her way regularly through the aisles of the supermarkets of St. Nicholas, across the St. Lawrence from Quebec. And back and forth from practices and games, the brothers drove matching Toyota Celica Supras, Peter's brown, Anton's white. About the only NHL luxury in which they had not yet begun to indulge themselves was the wearing of well-tailored clothes; in spite of their quarter-million-dollar salaries, the Stastnys still owned only one North American-style suit each.

On the ice, they had more than lived up to their promise; with sixteen goals and thirty-three assists, more points than any other first-year player in the league, Peter was leading the Nordiques in scoring; Anton, with seventeen and twenty, was not far behind. They had established themselves in other ways, too. In Philadelphia one night, Peter, outraged by the close checking he was receiving from Mel Bridgman, one of the more aggressive Flyers, had set out after Bridgman with revenge in his eye and chased him nearly out of the rink. "I thought he was going to choke me," a shocked Bridgman told the press after the game. And, on the night before they were to entertain the Oilers at home, Peter had scored a breakaway against Montreal, outskating, as he headed for the Montreal goal, none other than Guy Lafleur, widely regarded as one of the fastest in the league.

Most of the Oilers watched that game on television in the Quebec Hilton hotel. The evening was a reminder of how much hockey dominated their lives. Since September, when they had checked into training camp, they had had virtually no time away from the game, no weekends to themselves, no breaks from the steady grind of travel, practice, and play. The life was easy in that the time they spent actually working, or on the ice, was limited to a few hours a day, but there was no surcease from it, no time when they could, like ordinary workers, pack things up for a few days and get away. Win or lose, there was always a practice the next morning, and when there wasn't, they were off once again for the airport.

Partly as a result of this super-saturation, their moods were tre-

mendously affected by the results of their work. When they were winning, they would be as playful as puppies the next day at practice or
on the airplane; when they were losing, they would sulk. In contrast to
life in the real world outside hockey, their work could be measured in
black and white: "we won" or "we lost." However any of them might feel
about his own individual accomplishments, the score for or against the
team was the only measure that counted. Indeed, it was unseemly even
for those who had played well to be smiling after a loss; the fortunes
of the team were something they all held in common, and which were
reflected, inevitably, in their common emotions.

In the first two weeks of January, things had been going well. They
were responding to the challenge of the new year. While they were still
in the bottom third of the league, and well away from a spot that would
have put them in the playoffs—and while MacDonald, Anderson, and
Low were still on the injured list—they had won three and tied one of
their last four games. Furthermore, Gretzky was scoring at a rate that
bode well for them all. In the eight games before Quebec, he had seven
goals and seventeen assists, so that while the league scoring statistics
showed him still well behind Dionne and Bossy and a few others, he
was moving up. With sixty-five points in his first thirty-nine games, he
was well ahead of the pace of his first season.

On the flight into Quebec City, the Oilers' mood was close to carefree. The Toronto Maple Leafs had just fired their coach, Joe Crozier,
leaving the announcement of his successor until just before the nation-
ally televised game they would play the next night. On the plane, the
Oilers organized a pool on who Crozier's successor would be, laughing
as they expanded the number of names that would go into the draw to
include such unlikely candidates as Bobby Hull, whose name had been
in the papers because of an ugly divorce action, and Hull's old nemesis,
their own departed Bryan Watson. At the Quebec airport, there was
yet another pool, this one for whose luggage would come down the
conveyor belt first, and they crowded around the luggage area like chattering schoolboys. When Donny Murdoch won, they applauded as if
he'd been named the *Hockey News* player of the week. The sense of team
was rampant.

THE COLISEUM, QUEBEC CITY, QUEBEC, SUNDAY, JANUARY 11, 1981: This is familiar country to at least three of the Oilers—Brackenbury, Peter Driscoll, and Matti Hagman were Nordiques for a while. This morning, Brackenbury was running around shaking hands with everyone from the Zamboni driver to some of his former teammates, who practised before the Oilers. He speaks a workable street French, and uses it at every opportunity, blasting his way past grammatical obstacles as he blasts his way past opposing defencemen, not always successfully. Driscoll, too, looked at home, although at breakfast this morning he was talking grimly about how he would never go down to the minors again. Only Matti, of the ex-Quebeckers, seems to have no feel for the place. Kevin Lowe played his junior here; in 1978–79, he was the captain of the Remparts, a rare honour for a player with an English name and a tribute to his own Quebec-bred bilingualism. This morning, he insisted on giving everyone a tour of the various dressing rooms. For several of the others, the Coliseum holds memories of the Quebec Peewee Tournament.

As the game unfolds tonight, however, they are all business, playing with confidence and poise. Right off the opening face-off, Brackenbury, as if aware of his reputation among the Nordique brass, picks a fight with the toughest of their players, a vicious young defence man named Kim Clackson, and both go off for high sticking with the clock reading eight seconds. With both teams short-handed, Gretzky and Brett Callighen combine to set up Pat Price for his sixth goal of the season. At 8:37, Jacques Richard ties it up, but before the period is over Gretzky has set up Jari Kurri, who seems to fit well in B.J.'s old spot, to make it 2–1 for Edmonton. Just before the intermission, Price continues his unfortunate habit of first-period penalties by getting caught for holding.

The rough play continues through the second period. The Hunter brothers—Dave for Edmonton and Dale for Quebec—are banging away at each other in fraternal glee; the others just look mean. Even the normally mild-mannered Kurri at one point trips Anton Stastny, who, along with his brother, is living up to all advance billings. With Kurri off, however, Gretzky scores the kind of goal that wins games. In the midst of killing the penalty, he knocks the puck off a Nordique stick and prances in alone to score short-handed and unassisted. At 11:13, Risto Siltanen makes it 4–1.

Then, at 16:05, there is a curious and discomfiting incident. Gretzky, once again bothered by tight checking, and this time run from behind by yet another of the more belligerent Nordiques, John Wensink, turns and punches Wensink. Wensink whirls to retaliate, but before he can close with Gretzky, Pat Price intercedes. Suddenly, all the bad feelings of the game bubble up around them, and the Oilers line up to do battle: Callighen, Lowe, and Kurri all pick partners for the fray and begin the half-waltz, half-shoving match that indicates a willingness to fight. Gretzky, however, skates over to the designated neutral zone beside the Oiler bench. He is following the letter of the anti-fighting rule, and as the heart of the Oiler attack, he is right to keep himself distant from the possibility of a misconduct penalty. But his punch at Wensink is what started it all.

The Quebec fans boo him as he stands in peaceful solitude. Wensink and Price each get double minors—once again the referees are unwilling to call a fight a fight—and, for good measure, misconducts. No one else gets anything, and the booing of Gretzky continues.

If the crowd's displeasure has bothered him, though, he responds by playing another superlative period. In the third, Anton Stastny scores to bring the Nordiques within two, but Gretzky again sets up Kurri. When Alain Coté makes it 5–3, Gretzky sets up Kurri for a third time, and the game ends 6–3 for Edmonton. Kurri's hat trick is cause for celebration, but there has been an even more significant statistical event. With his goal and four assists, Gretzky has brought his scoring total to seventy points. The game is the Oilers' fortieth, marking the halfway point in the season. Next morning, the papers will show Marcel Dionne still well ahead in the league's scoring race. But, because of the vagaries of scheduling, Los Angeles has played three more games. After his fortieth game, Dionne, too, had seventy points. Halfway through the season, in other words, Gretzky is tied for the scoring lead. All along, as he did last year, he has been gaining momentum. If he keeps his pace, he stands a chance of winning the title all alone this year, and if he does *that*, there will be little doubt about his place in the pantheon of players who have, over the years, dominated the game.

*... the tradition to which Wayne Gretzky was now the apparent heir*

The bus trip to Montreal, where the Oilers were due to play the Canadiens, was a happy ride. The trainers laid on a supply of fried chicken and cold beer, and while Sather insisted that they ditch one of the cases of beer before take-off, he was not annoyed. He had enjoyed playing in Montreal himself, not only for the élan of the city and the sophistication of its fans, but for the air of history that hung over every hockey game that was played there.

The game had been played in the city since well back into the nineteenth century, and there were claims that it had been invented there. While these claims were disputed—and still are—by such other Canadian cities as Kingston, Ontario, and Dartmouth, Nova Scotia, there was no doubt about Montreal's importance in the development of the professional game. The first Stanley Cup was won by the Montreal Amateur Athletic Association in 1893. Twenty-four years later, when the NHL was formed out of a number of attempts to maintain a professional league, the Montreal Canadiens were already nine years old.

From the beginning, too, the Canadiens had helped to establish the tradition to which Wayne Gretzky was now the apparent heir. As the Oilers' bus rattled through the January night, the talk among the coaches and the writers turned to some of the men who had worn the mantle to which Gretzky was aspiring.

In the first NHL game ever played, Joe Malone of the Canadiens scored five goals against the Ottawa Senators. Malone was twenty-six that year, a big, handsome, dark-haired man who had been born in Quebec City and had played most of his hockey there. He was scarcely an unknown quantity to the men who had put together the new league. In the previous four years, playing seventy-two games—less than one season in modern hockey—he had scored 107 goals, including nine in one game, and helped the Bulldogs win two Stanley Cups. From his blazing start in Montreal, he continued scoring at a rate no one in the NHL has ever matched, finishing the twenty-two games of that first season, two of which he missed because of injury (or, as he once told a reporter with characteristic candour, "maybe I was drunk for one of them"), with the magnificent total of forty-four goals.

Malone's manner of play, from all accounts, was careful and deliberate. Men old enough to have seen them both compare his style more to Gordie Howe's than to that of any of the flashier players, except that Malone, unlike Howe, had no penchant for cruelty. In 1950, Charles G. Power, MP, or Chubby Power as he was more commonly known in political circles, wrote to the Hockey Hall of Fame in support of Malone's nomination and described him as "chivalrous." Indeed, reading through contemporary reports of his skills quickly one is led to believe that he would have won the Lady Byng trophy for gentlemanliness, except, of course, that his hockey career predated Lady Byng's arrival in Ottawa. Much of the memorabilia that survives him indicates the same kind of demeanour off the ice: modest rejoinders over the years when reporters called him to ask about some new scoring record— "Mahovlich or Richard wouldn't put in as much time on the ice as I did," he once told Jim Proudfoot of the *Toronto Star*— and an elegantly written thank-you note to the Hall of Fame for sending him a copy of a photo. But on the ice he was a scoring terror, racking up a total of 338 goals in the 271 professional games he played. In 1920, in a record that still stood in the NHL record book sixty years after he set it, Malone scored seven goals in one game, against the Toronto St. Patricks.

Malone spent time with a couple of other teams in the fledgling NHL before showing up for a final training camp with the Canadiens in

1923 when he was in his early thirties. At that camp, which was held in Grimsby, Ontario, it was as if he had seen the future himself. "I took a look at a new kid and I knew right then I was ready for the easy chair," he later told the Toronto reporter Vern DeGeer. "In practice he moved past me so fast I thought I was standing still. The kid was Howie Morenz."

Morenz, the Stratford Streak, was born in Mitchell, Ontario, on September 21, 1902, the youngest boy among the six children of a railroad man. His mother wanted him to take piano lessons. On Saturday mornings, he'd go across the bridge over the Thames to Miss Ida Holman's and on weekday afternoons he'd practice. The practice, though, always seemed to be just one piece, "One Fingered Joe," over and over again. One day, when Mrs. Morenz went up to Miss Holman's place to find out why, Miss Holman said she hadn't seen young Howarth for weeks. He had, it turned out, been stashing his skates at a friend's house on Friday afternoons and on Saturday when he'd started out across the Thames he'd never got any farther, just stayed there to play hockey with the bigger boys.

When Howie was fourteen, his dad got a better job in the CNR yards at Stratford, and the family moved. Howie, who had long since given up on "One Fingered Joe," joined the Stratford Midgets. He started work at the Canadian National Railways, too. As often as he could, he'd play one game for the Midgets in the afternoon and another for the CN team at night. Sometimes, at the yards, they'd find him in the morning, sleeping behind one of the locomotives. He didn't like shop work; it was too dirty.

He soon became the most celebrated hockey player in town, moving up quickly to the junior team. In Stratford, they still tell stories about him—the time he swooped around behind the goal on an outdoor rink, turning so suddenly that he sliced the toes out of the goal judge's rubbers; the time he dropped a piece of steel on his foot at the yards and his foot swelled up so badly he couldn't get his shoe on, but he covered his sock with one of his galoshes and limped to the rink. Somehow he managed to get his skate on, but after the game, he had to have it cut off his foot.

With Morenz at centre, the Stratford team became a provincial power, going to the finals once and the next year beating Queen's University to win the Ontario junior championship. The pros all wanted him. He had offers from Toronto and Saskatoon and Victoria. But in 1922 the Stratford juniors played a game in Montreal in which he scored nine goals—some accounts say eleven—and the Canadiens decided they had to have him. Leo Dandurand sent an emissary to Stratford with orders to pay him $2,300 a season and, because the word was that he'd run up some debts around town—including $45 to the local tailor, to lay some cash on the table first. Morenz signed, but even after the training camp at Grimsby where Malone saw him, Morenz didn't really want to join the NHL. Besides, one of the local ministers had started a write-in campaign to keep him playing for Stratford. Reluctantly, the Canadiens threatened to make public the fact that long before they had approached him, he had been paid to play amateur hockey in Stratford, and he agreed to stay with Montreal.

In his first year with the Canadiens, centring a line between Aurel Joliat and Billy Boucher, Morenz scored thirteen goals in twenty-four games, tying for seventh in league scoring; the next he got twenty-four. For the next fourteen seasons the statistics piled up: 270 goals and 197 assists. Twice he led the league in scoring; three times he won the Hart trophy as the most valuable player. Although he had been playing in the NHL seven years before an all-star team was named, he made that team three times. Once he scored thirty goals in thirty games, and in 1928–29, he got forty in forty-four.

Even more impressive than the number of his goals was the way he scored them. With rules that discouraged forward passes, he would often carry the puck end to end, adding his most exciting touches as he crossed into his opponents' zone; he would fake to the outside, flip the puck between the defending players and leap between them to retrieve it. He was unsurpassed at feinting on the fly, and defenceman after defenceman was left gasping at the whir that had just gone by them. "He was the best," King Clancy, who played against him, once said. "He could stop on a dime and leave you nine cents change. He was in a class by himself. And when he couldn't skate around you, he'd go right over you." Jim Coleman, the veteran newspaper columnist, described his style as "fire dancing on ice." In the golden age of sport, which gave the world Babe Ruth, Jack Dempsey, and Big Bill Tilden, Morenz was hockey's brightest jewel. It was seeing him play in Montreal that convinced Tex Rickard he could make hockey pay in New York in 1924, and many historians are convinced that Morenz was responsible for the crowds that kept the NHL in Detroit and Boston and Chicago, too.

A fierce, dark man, with a high hairline and a frequent heavy stubble on his chin, Morenz loved hockey and kids and the racetrack. When the Canadiens lost, he would sometimes pace the streets all night, and when he went to nightclubs, as he often did, he would sit at a table for hours, moving salt and pepper shakers around to show anyone who would listen—and dozens would—how the game had gone that night. Lou Hill, one of Morenz's favourite nightclub entrepreneurs, would send over a tray of salt and pepper just for props. Whenever the car in which he was travelling would pass a pickup game of kids' hockey, Morenz would jump out and join in, and sometimes on Saturday afternoon he would just go downtown and shake hands. Once, on the way home from a bad day at the racetrack, he threw his last fifty-cent piece into a stream, and when his companions asked him why, he said, "So some kid will find it, and have the best day of his life." Another time, when he heard that the horse that had finished ahead of his selection had been disqualified, he dragged his companions back to Blue Bonnets Raceway at night, leaped the fence, and, laughing, scrounged through the discarded tickets until he found his own pair of hundred-dollar wins.

As he travelled, Miss Ida Holman's early musical training was put to use on the ukulele. In railroad cars he would sit and plunk "If I Had A Girl Like You," with more élan than he had ever shown on "One Fingered Joe." All his life, he dressed with taste and splendour, sporting spats, and changing his clothes two and three times a day. He was the definitive figure of the Roaring Twenties, pleased by the company of the fast and famous. There are pictures of him on visits to Chicago waving from Al Capone's roadster, though no breath of gambling scandal ever touched his life.

Whatever else, hockey was fun for Morenz—as it was for all his contemporaries—and the laughter seemed as if it would last forever. One Saturday afternoon in Montreal, writes Stan Fischler in *Those Were The Days*, he showed up at the house of his good friend Elmer Ferguson, where

> he sipped beer and mixed Limburger cheese with onions. Having devoured all the onions, Morenz switched to garlic and finally polished off a turkey leg before leaving for the match that night. He scored a three-goal hat trick and explained after the game that he had used a secret weapon. "First I breathed on their goalkeeper," said Howie, "and then I shot her in."

In 1934, Morenz seemed to be slowing down. He heard boos in the Forum. To his dismay he was traded to Chicago. With the Black Hawks, whose strengths were defensive, he was ineffectual. The next season he was traded again, this time to the New York Rangers for a forward named Glenn Brydson, who has never been remembered for anything else. The greatest career in the NHL's history seemed over. In Montreal, however, the regime was changing. After the departure of Morenz, crowds had dropped to 3,000 a game. Leo Dandurand, who had signed Morenz, sold his interest in the club and left for New Orleans. Cecil Hart, the son of the man after whom the league's most-valuable-player trophy had been named, was asked to move back in as coach. As a condition of accepting the job, Hart asked for the return of Morenz, and management complied. He was reunited with Aurel Joliat on one wing and, this time, Johnny "Black Cat" Gagnon on the other. For a while at least, his fortunes seemed to be turning up again. The Canadiens climbed to first place in the Canadian division of the NHL.

On January 28, 1937, Morenz played his last game. The scene was the Montreal Forum. The Canadiens' opponents were the Chicago Black Hawks. The man who hit Morenz was the Hawks' defenceman Earl Siebert, although no one who saw it blamed Siebert for what happened. Morenz went awkwardly into the boards and caught his skate, and Siebert, apparently without malice, fell over him. There was a resounding crack. Morenz's leg was broken in five places. He was rushed to St. Luke's hospital.

In the hospital, forty days later, he died. Of all the dozens of accounts of his death that have been written since, no two agree on the cause. Heart attack? Embolism? Too many parties in the room? No one seems to know, and the records at St. Luke's have long since become inaccessible. For a while, the reports had been optimistic, although, because of the severity of the fractures to his leg, there was always doubt that Morenz would ever again play the game he loved. A week after he had been admitted, he wrote to his family in Stratford: "I sure would like to have finished the season but fate gave me quite a blow. You can bet it's not going to get me down." But, according to Dean Robinson, a one-time sports editor of the Stratford *Beacon Herald* who has made a vocation of collecting Morenz lore, the situation did get him down, to the point that, on March 8, he suffered a nervous breakdown. There is also little doubt that, at least before the breakdown, his hospital room was the scene of unusual revelry. "It looks like Grand Central Station in there," one visitor reported. On March 11, Morenz rose to visit the bathroom. He took two steps and collapsed. Whatever the physiological causes—and his death might well have been postponed by modern hospital techniques—there are still men who believe that what killed him was a broken heart. Years later, Mrs. Gertrude Bushfield, Morenz's sister, told Dean Robinson: "My father was at home, laid off by the railroad. Howie called one day and asked where he was. 'Come on down,' he said. Dad said he was waiting until Howie got home [from the hospital] but Howie said, 'No, I want you to come now.' So he did. And that night Howie died."

The funeral was the greatest outpouring of public grief the nation had ever expressed. The body lay in state at centre ice in the Forum, while Presbyterian ministers conducted the services. Outside, 200,000 people stood in mourning as the coffin was borne through the streets of Montreal.

Only one player in the NHL's history of superstars ever really approached Morenz's magnetism, and that was the man who succeeded him in Montreal: Maurice Richard. The image that most people who saw Richard play still carry of him is how he looked after he scored a goal, something he did 544 times in regular season play. He would circle under the clock. His stocky body would still be quivering with excitement, and it would not have surprised anyone to see steam coming from his nostrils. From time to time he would glance upward, and even in the least expensive seats in the arena you could see the fire blazing in his eyes. His eyes were his most noticeable feature. They were as dark as coal, and they shone with fissionable power. In conversation they were mesmerizing; when he played they would light up even more fiercely. Glenn Hall, one of the several master goalies of whom Richard in his heyday made dupes, used to say that when Richard broke toward the goal he could see the eyes flashing "like a pinball machine."

Unbelievably in view of the records he was to establish, Richard was thought too fragile to last when he first broke into the NHL. He was the oldest son of a machinist from the north end of Montreal. At night, as a boy, he used to listen to the French radio broadcasts of the Canadien games and dream of someday filling the skates of such stars as Joliat, whom he was later to befriend, or Morenz, who was his idol but died when Richard was sixteen. In each of his last two seasons as an amateur he broke bones and, in his first year as a Canadien, he did it again—an ankle this time—after just sixteen games. But in his next year, playing on a line with Elmer Lach and Toe Blake, he scored thirty-two goals; the next season, 1944–45, he scored fifty in fifty games, an accomplishment that was as meaningful as Babe Ruth's sixty home runs in 1927.

Although many hockey purists insisted that Richard's record was tainted by the wartime absence of too many other premier players— Richard was kept out of the service by his brittle bones—he continued to score at almost as significant a pace throughout his career. From the opponents' blueline to the goal, there has never been anyone to match him; on the attack, he was a man possessed, and some of his most dramatic goals were scored with opponents draped over him like drunks at the end of a party—he would simply carry them home. He seemed to have a special affinity for the Stanley Cup, which the Canadiens won seven times when he played for them. Eighteen times in playoff games he scored the winning goal, six of them in overtime. Seven times he scored three goals in a Stanley Cup game, twice he scored four, and in one unforgettable game in 1944 the score was Maurice Richard 5, the Toronto Maple Leafs 1. But, playoffs or not, there was an intensity to his play that transcended statistics. Everything he did he did with incomparable flair; he lifted us from our seats and brought our hearts to our mouths. When Maple Leaf Gardens installed shatterproof glass to protect the well-tailored customers in the front rows, Richard—or the Rocket, as he was by then universally known—shattered it, cartwheeling up against the boards and sending the "impenetrable" barrier onto the ice in a shower of shards and slivers.

He was a national hero in Quebec, bigger than his team, bigger than the game. In "The Hockey Sweater," a story about growing up with hockey in Sainte-Justine-de-Dorchester, Roch Carrier wrote:

> We all wore the same uniform as he, the red, white and blue uniform of the Montreal Canadiens, the best hockey team in the world; we all combed our hair in the same style as Maurice Richard, and to keep it in place we used a sort of glue—a great deal of glue. We laced our skates like Maurice Richard, we taped our sticks like Maurice Richard. We cut all his pictures out of the papers. Truly, we knew everything about him.

In 1955, an ugly series of events illustrated how deeply the people of Quebec felt toward him. These events began in Boston, on March 13, when the Canadiens played the Bruins in the fourth-to-last game of the schedule. The game was a rough one; tempers and sticks were both high. Late in the third period, Richard was hit across the forehead by the stick of Hal Laycoe, a Bruin defenceman. The hit drew blood. Richard went berserk, charging at Laycoe, taking dead aim and giving him a two-hander over the head. When a linesman wrestled Richard's stick away, Richard picked up another that was lying on the ice—by this time nearly everyone was in the fracas—and then broke *that* across Laycoe's back, too. In the midst of it all, he also struck the linesman.

This was not, unfortunately, Richard's first run-in with officials; just after Christmas of the same season he had slapped another linesman across the face with his glove. This time, President Clarence Campbell ruled decisively. Richard, who had been leading the league in scoring at the time of the Laycoe incident, would be suspended not only for the remainder of the season but for the playoffs as well.

That Thursday, St. Patrick's Day, when the Rocket-less Canadiens lined up at the Forum against Detroit, with whom they were now tied for first place, the crowd was seething. Richard took a seat near the Canadiens' bench. In a gesture that seems in retrospect both brave and foolhardy, Campbell showed up too, sitting in his regular box seat, along with his secretary, whom he was later to marry. Throughout the first period, the crowd continued to rumble; someone threw a smoke bomb and the game was delayed. Raw eggs splattered the ice. Somehow, the teams got through the first period. But when it ended, someone got past the policemen who were hovering near Campbell's box and hit him in the face while his horrified fiancée looked on. Pushing and shoving broke out everywhere. The authorities cancelled the remainder of the game, and an announcement to that effect went out over the PA system.

The troubles spilled out of the Forum with the crowd, and through much of the night people went on a rampage in downtown Montreal, hurling bricks through windows, overturning streetcars, setting bonfires; more than $100,000 in goods were looted from stores on Ste. Catherine Street. The city boiled with anger until Richard himself went on the air and asked people to calm down. "I will take my punishment," he said, his eyes burning out of the television screen. "I would ask everyone to get behind the team."

The Richard Riot, as the events of March 1955 came to be called, was, if not the beginning of the Quiet Revolution that was to change Quebec society in the 1960s and 1970s, then at least an important event in its development. Like the Asbestos Strike, which brought together such political figures as Gerard Pelletier and Pierre Elliott Trudeau, then a professor of law at the University of Montreal, or like the bitter strike of radio and television producers against the CBC, the Richard Riot seemed, to its participants at least, to set the French *people*— represented in this case by fiery Maurice—against the hated English bosses, as symbolized by the elegant anglophone Campbell. And, later, when the Parti Québécois came to move the Quiet Revolution toward Quebec independence, there was more than one reference to the bitterness of that St. Patrick's night at the Forum.

But if there was a historical significance to the events, it did not interest the man at their middle, the Rocket. He was a hockey player. He was as gifted and dedicated as anyone who had ever played the game, but he used his gifts and dedication to score goals, not political points. However others might see him, during the riots of 1955 or the *indépendantiste* campaigns of 1970s, this was how he saw himself, no more but certainly no less.

*... the five men who are on the ice when the winner is scored will put
their names in a hat ...*

At 10:30 sharp on the morning of Monday, January 12, I reported for work at the Montreal Forum. My head was long cleared of history. I had a job. Taking advantage of Sather's mellow mood on the bus from Quebec, I had said I wanted to follow a game from the dressing room. The dressing room was the *sanctum sanctorum*, off limits to the press except during practices or, following a ten-minute waiting period, after games.

"Sure," Sather had said. "But I'm not letting you in as some kind of observer. You're going to have to work."

"You mean like a trainer?"

"I mean like a stick-boy," he had said. "Trainers have skills."

Peter Millar, who would be my boss for the day, was indeed an alert young professional, college trained and studious of manner. He guarded his pharmacy, whose contents were subject to a surprise check by NHL security men at any time, with the benevolent stinginess of a candy-store proprietor, and took obvious pride in his ability to wrap bandages over aching limbs or dispense first aid in the heat of action. The day before, he had been named one of the trainers for the league's all-star game the next month in Los Angeles, and the morning I showed up to work with him he was trying hard not to gloat.

There are few rewards in a trainer's life. For all their technical expertise and the responsibility they hold over the players' well-being, they are paid less than a quarter of the salary of a journeyman player. Their hours are brutal. With the Oilers' equipment manager, Kelly Pruden—christened "the vagon-burner" by Risto Siltanen, because of his Indian blood—Millar would be at any arena the team played in long before the players, unpacking bags and laying out clean underwear, towels, and uniforms in each stall. Long after the players had left to test the social climate, the trainers would remain, picking up the dirty laundry and packing the bags yet again. When I arrived at the Forum, Millar and Pruden had already been at work for six hours, having risen at four to oversee the arrival of the team's equipment from the bus. As always, Lee Fogolin was the first Oiler at the rink. He had brought coffee for the trainers, a small ritual that was also typical of Fogolin's thoughtfulness; some players treated the trainers as if they were valets.

"Here, put these on," said Millar. "You'll be moving pretty fast." He handed me a grey Oiler T-shirt, the blue and orange top of one of their sweatsuits, and a pair of sneakers. In the outer dressing room, I changed from my street clothes, hanging my sports shirt and jacket on a hook that Millar had carefully marked with my name, and shoving my boots under the bench.

The players, arriving from the hotel in small groups, seemed tense and preoccupied. The high spirits of the bus trip had faded with the morning, and now they were aware of the twenty-two Stanley Cup banners that hung from the Forum's rafters and, perhaps, of the ghost of Joe Malone.

Although the practice was optional, everyone showed up, most of them early and still rubbing the sleep from their eyes. There was some talk of plans to invade the bars and discos of Crescent Street after the game that night, but everyone, obviously, had gone straight to bed when the bus arrived last night.

"Got any gum?" Dave Semenko asked me, and several of the others took up the cry. Ostensibly, the stick-boy is in the dressing room to look after the team's weapons, to keep the various piles of Kohos, Diamonds, Titans, Sherwoods, and Victoriavilles separate, and to be ready with a substitute if any should break. In fact, because of the players' devotion to their own sticks, this job is secondary to having a pocket full of the small artifacts of hockey life: gum, lozenges, scissors, Band-Aids, and the ever-ready towel or water-bottle.

Although the practice was light, I found myself constantly running back and forth from the dressing room to the bench to replenish my supplies.

"Hang in there, stick-boy," Sather called to me once. "You're keeping them loose."

Shortly after noon, all the players were back in the dressing room, to shower and change for the pre-game meal back at the hotel, and to attend a brief meeting Sather had called in the inner dressing room. I puttered about, keeping busy until the door to the inner room closed for the meeting. Then I padded over in my sneakers to overhear as much of the day's strategy as I could. "I don't care what you listen to," Sather had said the night before, "I just don't want to notice you around that room." Now, ear cupped to the door, I heard few secrets.

"Dougie Risebrough has been the key to this team recently," Sather told his troops. "He's a gutsy player who doesn't make many headlines, but if you can slow him down you can slow a lot of them down. I don't want to say too much, but he's got a bad shoulder. Lafleur is out for tonight, hurt, but they're going pretty good without him. They were really strong in the third period against Quebec the other night, so you've just got to stay with them."

I heard the shuffle of feet and returned to sit near my own hook.

Sather came out first and settled near me in the outer room. He seemed in an inordinately expansive mood, and we chatted for awhile about his own playing days in Montreal. Gradually, as our talk continued, the players filed out of the inner room. Several of them gathered around us, some joining in the talk. A few seemed impatient to get back for the pre-game meal, but others would shush them, and urge them to be patient.

"Aren't you going to change?" Sather said to me at one point.

I began to slip my sports shirt on over the Oiler grey. I reached under the bench for my boots, and slipped off the borrowed sneakers. As I began to pull my left boot on, a hush fell over the assembled players. Something was wrong. And then I felt it: warm, gooey, shaving soap was squishing up from the boot, oozing over the top. My foot felt as if I had stepped into a swamp. For a moment, I wondered whether I could just slip my boots on and slurp my way out of the building as if nothing had happened. But the players were already cackling around me, pointing with glee at my sopping foot.

"Welcome to the Oilers," said Brett Callighen.

THE FORUM, MONTREAL, QUEBEC, MONDAY, JANUARY 12: The game has two different dimensions from the perspective of the team's bench. The first is the tension. You can *feel* it down here. It started well before the game. Fogolin, of course, was the first man in the dressing room, arriving shortly after 4:30, three and a half hours before game time, changing to his underwear and beginning his ritual of stick-taping and checking his equipment. Peter Millar worked for a while on one of Fogie's leg muscles, which has been cramping. Brack was next, working out on his push-up blocks even before the game. Then Mark Messier, still suffering from a groin that was pulled in Toronto last week. Messier put on a special girdle Millar has given him, then spent much of the pre-game time limbering up in the outer dressing room practising sprinter's starts, hoping he looked better than he felt. There is such animal grace to him, even when he's hurt. Several of the others had made a trip to one of the league's most popular tailors. Doug Hicks reported he'd had a dozen pairs of trousers altered to fit the season's new style, and Kevin Lowe was sporting a snappy new tweed jacket. But the sartorial standout was Semenko, who appeared in a purple jacket, white shirt, and black tie, ready to conquer Crescent Street.

At first, conversation was light and bantering. Linda Ronstadt's picture was on the front page of the *Gazette* this morning, and the players were making much sport of the weight she had gained. "I see the trouble," said Don Murdoch. "It's in her right hand." In the picture she was holding a fork.

The first ripple of tension hit about 5:30, when everyone was at the rink and it was time to start suiting up. It washed over the room, stopping the banter and turning faces grim. It receded, then rose again, receded and came again, faster each time, like waves on a rising tide. By

7:30, when it was time for the pre-game skate, no one was saying anything. Breaking sweat out on the ice failed to help. Not speaking, they clumped back up the aisle to the dressing room. Millar, in what must be the worst of all his unpleasant chores, had the assignment of telling Semenko he would be sitting out tonight. In front of his silent teammates, big Dave stripped off his uniform, had an unnecessary shower, and made his way past their drooping heads, the purple splendour of his attire now looking somehow ridiculous.

The other dimension that changes from behind the bench is the speed and violence of the game. Here, you get an extraordinary sense of how fast the players on the ice are moving and how hard they are hitting each other. Early in the first period, Bob Gainey, the Canadiens' stalwart defensive forward, ran Stan Weir into the boards right at the bench. Weir's face was clenched in pain and concentration. The collision was as hard as if a car had run into the boards; I was sure I could hear bones crunch. Yet for Weir and Gainey the crash was part of the routine. Eighty nights a year they do this, all of them, thrashing their bodies about at inhuman speeds, trying to focus on a bouncing puck while some of the best and toughest athletes in the world hack and pound away at them, and they, in turn, hack and pound back. Perched above the action, the fans view it from an angle that slows it to a comprehensible speed. But down here, the speed and the force spill over the boards. Eyes bulge, throats sweat, mouths suck for wind.

There is an awesome, rushing beauty to this game. Even from this perspective, patterns emerge, fade, shift, change, fade, and form again. A rhythm sets in, as the play flows back and forth, eases off, gets broken, and picks up. For an immeasurable instant, a gap appears, a pathway down the ice, and suddenly a player moves into it, or sends a pass skittering down its length, and other openings appear around it. Then they close. The play stops, hangs in balance as one man controls the puck, feints. Then the action pulses again. Fresh bodies leap over the boards.

Combining so many skills, played at such speeds, hockey is, surely, the most difficult of games, and the men who play it are the finest athletes now playing any sport in the world. They are fast, strong, balanced, brave, and quick. And unlike the other men who play fast and violent games for a living—notably football and basketball—hockey players are men of normal physical proportions, selected not for their eccentric physiques, but for their skills and talent. It is possible to think of any of them playing golf, or baseball, or even fighting for a living—and, indeed, Gordie Howe came close to doing all of those—but it is *im*possible to think of Jack Nicklaus or Johnny Bench or Muhammad Ali playing hockey.

Tonight, the Canadiens are roaring up and down the ice in the fire-wagon style that has characterized Montreal teams since Morenz's day, whipping crisp, short passes to one another, blazing past the defence. They pour in on Mio as if he were alone, blasting thirteen shots at him in the first period alone and scoring on three of them, while holding the Oilers to four shots and no goals. At the intermission, Sather has little to say, allowing the players to sit in silence for nearly all of the fifteen minutes. From the inner room, I hear a few shouts of encouragement— "Come on, guys, it's not over yet"—but on the bench, as the second period begins, the feeling is that it is over. The Canadiens simply keep coming at them, and in response the Oilers appear flat and overawed. It is 4–0 before the period ends.

In the third period, disaster strikes. A blistering shot by Réjean Houle hits Mio flush on the mask, and Eddie goes down as if injected with curare. Before he even hits the ice, it seems, Peter Millar is over the boards, and shortly after there is a call for a doctor. Finally, a stretcher is wheeled out, and Mio is whisked away through a gate at the opposite side of the ice. Spared the sight of their fallen comrade, the Oilers are nevertheless shaken.

As Andy Moog skates out to replace Mio—his first day in Montreal and, aged twenty, about to face the guns of hockey's greatest dynasty—word passes along the bench to try to give him extra protection. For a few minutes they seem able to. But, almost inevitably, the Canadiens score on Moog, and the game ends 5–0.

There are no jokes in the dressing room afterward. Peter Millar is still at the hospital with Mio. As unobtrusively as possible, I help Kelly Pruden pick up the towels and dry the skate blades. "God *damn*," says Sather despondently, "were they ever flying tonight."

For some time after the others leave, Andy Moog sits quietly by himself. In spite of the goal he allowed, which was scored on a power play, he played steadily. He is pleased with himself. I ask him if he found a difference between the NHL game and the game he has been playing in Wichita. He cocks an eye at me to see if there is anything behind the question.

"It's still hockey," he says. "They just go a little faster here."

MAPLE LEAF GARDENS, TORONTO, WEDNESDAY, JANUARY 14: Mike Nykoluk, who was doing radio broadcasts when the Leafs fired Joe Crozier, is the new Toronto coach, which won Stan Weir the pool collected among the Oilers in Quebec City and has the fans here alive with anticipation. Nykoluk has the Leafs playing well, although he has not made any dramatic changes. Tonight, he told the papers confidently, he will not designate a player to the Gretzky patrol. "I don't believe in that," he said. "It detracts from the game."

Gretzky will be on his mettle anyway. His parents are here, as they always are when he plays in this part of the world, and he likes to play well in front of them. But more than that, the Toronto media, which he has followed since he was a boy, seem to care only about how well a player does in the Gardens, and are, many of the Oilers feel, unconcerned about what happens in the Canadian west. When the Leafs got trimmed by Winnipeg 8–2 this year, the Toronto-based telecasters spent all of their post-game show probing what was wrong with the Leafs, and paid not a whit of attention to the Jets, who had played the game of their careers to beat them. Last March, Gretzky came here breathing down Dionne's neck in the scoring race. *Maclean's* magazine published a story on Dionne that week, and pointed out that he was sixteen points ahead of Guy Lafleur, without mentioning Gretzky at all. It was only after he put on a show here in that same March game, scoring two goals and four assists, that the pundits of *Hockey Night in Canada* recognized him at all.

"He's for real," said Gary Dornhoefer in the broadcast booth to Bill Hewitt.

I saw my own first NHL game here, sitting in the Gondola, just down the way from Foster Hewitt, Bill's father. I was eleven. A favourite uncle, newly returned from the war, had a job in the advertising department of Imperial Oil, sponsors of *Hockey Night* on radio, and he took me up to where all the broadcasts of my Saturday nights came from. Someone gave me earphones. I was more excited than I had ever been before, and I came perilously close to whoopsing my supper thirty-four feet below onto the balding pate of Sweeney Schriner. As it was, I tore my earphones off during a Leaf rally and banged them against the ledge. The bang echoed over Foster's microphones, to hockey fans in Canada and Newfoundland and on the ships at sea.

I know what it is to be a Leaf fan, and for much of my life was convinced I could no more change my loyalty to them than I could change the colour of my eyes. But tonight my heart is with the Oilers.

For the first period and a half, whatever Nykoluk has done seems right. The Leafs jump to a 3–0 lead. Eddie Mio, miraculously recovered from what everyone was sure was a broken jaw, plays steadily, but gets little support. In the first period, the Oilers achieved only two shots on the Toronto goalie, Jim Rutherford, and the figures are not much better for the second.

Then, just before the period ends, Gretzky's line pulls off a pretty passing play, Callighen over to Kurri, who quickly whips it across to Gretzky at the open side of the Toronto net, and the teams go into the dressing room at 3–1. I make my way down to the bar of the Hot Stove Lounge, where I have arranged to meet Pocklington for a drink.

Pocklington is late. When he finally arrives, striding through the crowd and sitting to order champagne among the rye drinkers, he tells me he is confident the Oilers will win.

"They haven't done well when they haven't scored the first goal," I point out. (They have won only two of the twenty games in which they have been scored on first.)

"Ah, but I've been to the dressing room," Pocklington says. "I spoke to Wayne, and I told him if they could bring this one off, I'd give him …"

"What, Peter?"

"It's our secret, Wayne's and mine."

This practice is a favourite Pocklington device. He thinks it gets the Oilers going, and on occasion, it apparently has. When he goes into the dressing room between periods (a habit Sather disapproves of but is unwilling, or unable, to stop), he likes to invent new incentives. Sometimes it will be a bonus for the player who scores the winning goal, but more often it will be a special production: the five men who are on the ice when the winner is scored will put their names into a hat and draw for a trip to Rome; once, he offered to put *everyone's* name into a hat if the team won and send the winner and a friend to Hawaii.

Not all the players are enthralled by these displays of generosity. "It's kind of humiliating," B.J. MacDonald said once. "As if you weren't going to put out unless you got a trip somewhere. We're professionals, you know. We take some pride in what we do."

"But the trips themselves," I had replied. "They're good."

"If you collect on them," B.J. said.

"What does that mean?"

"Oh, you know, you sometimes wonder if he remembers. There was one game early in the year when he came in and said if we won everyone could put their names in a hat and the winner would get a trip to Paris. You know the one, when Wayne was kidding around and said if he drew Kevin's name he'd go as Kevin's guest. Well, you know who won that draw? Pete LoPresti, the goalie they'd brought up from Wichita. He hadn't even played in the game, so how do you think he felt? And the next day he was back on the plane to the bushes. Do you think he's going to come up at the end of the year and say, 'Hey, Mr. Pocklington, how about my trip to Paris?'"

In the last period, the Oilers take total control of the game. Almost as soon as the teams are back on the ice, Dave Lumley gets his fourth goal of the year to bring them within a goal. Will Paiement of the Leafs makes it 4–2, but less than a minute later, Kurri finishes off a snappy passing play from Price and Callighen. 4–3. Then Doug Hicks breaks up a Toronto play and flips the puck to Gretzky, who is off on his own, bonus bound and thinking. Coming in alone on Rutherford, he fakes from his forehand, draws the puck across in front of himself, and tosses a backhand into the now-open net. 4–4. Four minutes later,

Gretzky sets up Lee Fogolin, and then, with three minutes left, Stan Weir pops one in from a scramble in front of the net, 6–4. Assists go to Fogolin and Brackenbury, who has been working his heart out through the game. And finally, and with just nine seconds left on the clock, Stan Weir scores again, to finish 7–4.

In the dressing room, Gretzky stands naked and laughing.

"I guess that's as big a thrill as I've ever had," he says. "Coming from behind like that."

Pocklington comes in to ask him for an autographed stick for some friends he has been sitting with.

"Will you tell me now what you promised him if they won?" I ask.

"I'll just tell you it was something big," he says. "Something very big."

**12**

*Banishment to the minor leagues had always been a fate professional hockey players feared*

In the month that followed their victory in Toronto and led up to the all-star break in February, the Oilers lost the momentum that had begun in early January, and returned to the unpredictable pattern that had confounded their fans and their coaches all season. Of their next eleven games, they won only four and tied one. Many of their losses were to teams they ought to have beaten: Chicago, the Rangers, Washington. In the midst of this discouraging run, however, and right after having been soundly defeated by Minnesota, they rose up and smote Montreal 9–1. No one could explain this extraordinary event; it was the worst loss anyone could remember a Montreal team having suffered, and it was inflicted on essentially the same personnel who had skated so dynamically through the Oilers less than a month before. After the game, the Edmonton police quietly passed the word that a bomb threat had been phoned in to the Coliseum, but since the players had known nothing about it at the time, even that couldn't account for the Canadiens' collapse. They had simply stopped skating, and the Oilers had started.

The Oilers were as astounded by their one-sided victory as anyone else, but it reinforced their view that when they were playing well there was no team—even the Montreal Canadiens—they could not beat. By February 1, however, they had returned to their losing ways. When, after fifty-three games of the schedule, all play stopped to allow the all-stars to appear for an exhibition game in Los Angeles, the Oilers were in seventeenth place.

Over the course of their gloomy month, the Oilers' luck continued to run sour. Just before the all-star break, Ron Low appeared ready to return to action. Because he had been inactive so long, Low asked if he could go down to Wichita for a game or two to prepare himself for his return to the NHL. In the warm-up for his first game there, he took a shot on the same hand that had been broken, felt pain, and, to his and the team's dismay, discovered that he had broken another bone. He would be out for the season. In cold fury, Low, the supreme competitor, and the man who had been at the heart of their surge for the playoffs last year, shaved off his pirate's beard— "no bloody luck left in that"—and went home to his farm at Foxwarren, Manitoba, to await the spring.

Sather, in the meantime, had come tantalizingly close to solving his goaltending problems. Throughout the season, the Calgary Flames had been sitting on a goaltender of proven NHL calibre, Dan Bouchard. Bouchard had been a mainstay of the Flames in Atlanta, but with the emergence of two younger goaltenders, Pat Riggin and Réjean Lemelin, the Calgary team had declared him excess baggage. Bouchard, a cantankerous young man, had made no secret of his unhappiness, and by the turn of the year word around the league was that he wasn't speaking to his teammates. Desperately, Sather tried to trade for him, at one point offering B.J. MacDonald, man for man. The Flames said no, claiming MacDonald was too old, then turned around and dealt Bouchard to Quebec for a forward named Jamie Hislop, who was two months and three days younger than MacDonald and had scored a hundred fewer goals.

When Sather next met Cliff Fletcher, the Flames' general manager, Fletcher told him he was sorry; the Calgary-Edmonton rivalry was too intense for him to risk giving up someone who would come back to haunt him. By then, Bouchard had started five games for the Nordiques; the Nordiques had won all five and had shot up past Edmonton in the standings. It was precisely the kind of lift the Oilers needed and were not getting.

Now, with Low gone, the situation was doubly drastic. Sather turned to an old friend, Lou Nanne, the general manager of the Minnesota North Stars, with whom he had roomed as a player. While old friendships count for nothing in hockey—Bryan Watson, idle at his family's home in the Haliburton region of Ontario, would have testified to that—old favours sometimes do. The year before, when Nanne was as desperate for goaltending help as Sather was now, Sather had lent him a promising minor-leaguer named Jim Corsi. This year, Nanne had two brilliant young goalies, Don Beaupre and Gilles Meloche, and an extra veteran in the person of Gary Edwards. Edwards, a thirty-three-year-old journeyman, had not played a game for Minnesota all year. Nanne said Sather could have him for a third-round draft choice in 1982, and Sather accepted.

The situation, however, was still not resolved. Since the days of Georges Vezina, the Chicoutimi Cucumber who learned the game without skates and wrote inspirational poetry during his time with the early Montreal teams, goaltenders were noted for their individual ways. Jacques Plante, the man who brought masks to the league in the 1950s, used to knit toques. Glenn Hall was sick before every game. And the legends of the position included everyone from wild alcoholics to the reflective Ken Dryden. Edwards, an almost non-stop conversationalist who sported a Franciscan beard, proved to have his own mind, too. He would not come to Canada because the taxes were higher. Although his salary would automatically go from $70,000 u.s. to $84,000 Canadian in Edmonton, he would not be able to deduct the expenses of driving his car or of playing golf to stay in condition over the summer. The tax structure was a common problem for Canadian teams dealing with players on u.s. rosters, but in the Edwards case, with the Oilers down to Mio and the unproven Andy Moog, Sather was particularly distressed. Finally, he cajoled Edwards into moving—the team would help relocate his family—and Edwards showed up in time to play part of a game against Calgary, which the Oilers lost 10–4. While the goals scored against him were not Edwards's fault, the score was still a bitter reminder of *l'affaire Bouchard*.

Up front, the problems were of a different nature. Sather had finally decided that Don Murdoch was not helping the team. Playing irregularly, Murdoch had lost his touch and his confidence. The blithe spirit that had been so evident at training camp and on his return to

New York had long since turned to depression and self-doubt. In forty games, he had ten goals, not far from the number that, as a rookie sensation, he had knocked off in a week. He looked tired. His once chubby cheeks were wan. Down on himself, he had asked Sather to trade him. No one wanted him—not even his beloved Rangers. When Sather put his name on the league's waiver list—meaning anyone could have had him for $25,000 cash—no one took him. It was a crushing blow. The Oilers assigned him to Wichita. There was some question whether he would report. He had not yet reached his twenty-fifth birthday.

Dave Semenko, too, had gone down. Sather, as he had from the beginning, had confidence in Semenko's ability and his value to the team. But since his scoring explosion in October, he had only three more goals; on the ice he looked clumsy. There was, the coaches knew, a catch to Semenko's situation. Much more than the smaller, quicker men, a player of Semenko's size and role on the team needed regular assignments to stay sharp and limber. The less he played, the more out of place he looked. Perhaps more ice time in the minors would get him back on track.

Saddest of all, John Hughes had also been assigned to Wichita. With the defensive corps playing at full strength, and with young Charlie Huddy continuing to show promise, there was no place for him on the roster. Once more, Hughes packed up his wife and baby daughter to move, trading houses this time with Peter Driscoll, who so far had lived up to the resolve he had expressed in Quebec never to go back to the bushes.

Banishment to the minor leagues had always been a fate professional hockey players feared, but in the expanded NHL, with its emphasis on youth, it was an especially serious blow; once down, many players feared, they would not be able to fight their way back up, as Driscoll had done. In the season of 1980–81, moreover, nearly everyone in the league had been touched by one case that had dramatized the fate of the minor leaguer in a particularly tragic way. The case was that of Billy Heindl, a thirty-three-year-old journeyman who, out of hockey and facing a bleak future, had jumped off the Winnipeg Perimeter Bridge in September of 1979, barely failing to kill himself.

Heindl had been a promising junior. After a successful debut in Winnipeg he had gambled his education against a chance at the big time. He had been a good student, with marks that were in the high 80s in grade ten and that fell off only slightly as his hockey grew more demanding. He had signed a Boston c-form, a document of indenture that has since been discarded. When the Bruins invited him to Oshawa for a season or two of major Junior A, he had to decide whether to head east, to continue his education in civil technology at Red River Community College, or to accept one of the three scholarship offers he had received from American colleges. "If I was one of the best in Manitoba," he said, "I could be one of the best out east." He went to Oshawa. Bobby Orr, the celebrated young phenomenon from Parry Sound, was the heart of that Oshawa team, and Billy was one of its legs. The year that Orr wore the captain's c on his sweater, Billy wore the assistant's A, and in the 1965–66 team picture, they sit next to each other, grinning under their brush cuts.

After junior, Orr's career went into orbit. Billy's plummeted to reality. Boston sent him to Clinton, New York, in the Eastern League—for a $4,000 bonus and a salary of $10,000. "I guess I should have realized where I was," he says now. "Better players than I in the Bruins organization—Wayne Cashman, Jean Pronovost, Jean-Paul Parisé—were playing in Oklahoma City. But I was too young." That year, Billy, twenty, got married.

He never did make it to the Apple, which is what he called the NHL, to stay. Minnesota owned him for a while, and Atlanta and New York. He played in Providence and Cleveland. For two happy years— the international game seemed to suit his style—he played for Father David Bauer's national team, based in Winnipeg. Then the team folded and it was back to the minors. When the WHA raised the ante for marginal players, Billy settled for $22,500. He got shots at both Minnesota and the New York Rangers, but couldn't stay up. At last, in Cape Cod and the North American Hockey League, scoring well but ignored, wearing the A again as a "steadying influence on younger players," Billy faced the facts.

For a while, he played in Europe, but the strains of foreign life wore at his marriage. He came home, but his marriage broke up anyway.

For a year he coached the Steinbach Huskies, a senior team, earning $400 a month, a far cry from the $35,000 he had drawn in his best years as a pro. To supplement his income he tried selling insurance. But no one, he would say with rueful humour, would phone him up to say they needed a policy. He was drinking heavily. On the morning he jumped, he had not eaten for a day and a half.

While Billy was still unconscious in hospital, someone called Don Baizley, a Winnipeg lawyer who had known him as a youngster, and who now acts as an agent for a number of NHL players, including, on the Oilers, the three Finns. By the time he could go to see Billy in the hospital, Bobby Orr had already been in touch. Together, Baizley and Orr worked on Heindl's behalf.

Through the winter of 1979–80, while Billy lay partially paralyzed, in Winnipeg General Hospital, they rallied the hockey world. Over the signatures of Ted Irvine and Ted Green, both former pros and now successful businessmen in Winnipeg, a letter went out to the hockey world. The response was overwhelming: money, phonecalls, offers of help. A benefit game for Billy was held in Winnipeg in April. Veterans of the National Team, many of them successful in civilian careers that varied from law and academe to the retail business, played a team of former NHLers. Gump Worsely was there. So was Ken Dryden. And Orr, of course. Wayne Gretzky flew back from Hawaii for perhaps the only time he and Orr would ever be seen together on the ice. Ron Low drove down from Foxwarren. Net proceeds for the Billy Heindl Fund were more than $80,000.

The hockey men felt good about more than the money they had raised. They felt relief. Billy's story, many of them knew, was only one turn of fate's wheel away from their own.

One more of the Oilers regulars was almost sent down to Wichita during Sather's February purge: Mark Messier. His groin pull now healed, Messier was still showing spurts of impressive speed, and from time to time he would electrify both the crowd and his teammates with a scintillating rush or a devastating bodycheck. But on other shifts he would drift aimlessly, circling deep into his own zone, failing to move onto the attack with his wingers. His mind did not appear to be on the game. In spite of a shortage of players who could play with Messier's natural skill, Sather took him aside and threatened him with summary demotion. If he wanted to stay with the Oilers, Sather told him, he would have to get his head back into the game, and cool down his social life. He was to be home at night, subject to bed checks.

Messier, newly turned twenty, did not react as quickly to this lecture as Sather might have hoped. In fact, as he was to say later, he gave very serious thought to shoving the whole business, and devoting his youth to enjoying himself. But as he thought his situation through, he realized how much he had to gain from hockey. He resolved to mend his ways, and in February his play began to reflect his decision.

With Messier entrenched, the forward lines were now at full strength. MacDonald, unaware of how close he had been to becoming a Calgary Flame, was healthy again, waging competition with the improving Jari Kurri for his old spot on Gretzky's right wing. Glenn Anderson, too, had returned to the lineup, and was skating with even more energy than he had at the season's outset.

Best of all was Gretzky's performance. Through January, the Kid had continued to score at a pace even more furious than that of the previous year, picking up ten goals and thirty-five assists. On February 6, in a 10–4 Oiler romp over the unhappy Winnipeg Jets, he had three goals and three assists, moving him past the 100-point mark for the year and putting him, for the first time, ahead of Dionne and everyone else in the scoring race. In the voting for all-star positions, he led all centres handily, although Mike Liut, the goaltender who had meant so much to St. Louis's continuing good fortune (the Blues had passed the Islanders and were in first place when the break occurred), drew more votes for his position than Gretzky did for his.

The all-star game, held in Los Angeles, was billed as a showdown between Liut and Gretzky, who lined up on opposite sides. Insofar as it was, Liut won. Gretzky was held to one assist, and Liut was named the most valuable player in the game. But the Oilers, at least, took the game lightly. The party that went to California to represent Edmonton— Pocklington, Sather, Peter Millar, and Gretzky, who also took along his parents and his girlfriend, a vivacious young singer named Vickie Moss—came back talking more of the NHL's attempts at glamour than of the game. Their most memorable event had taken place not at the rink but at their table during the elaborate black-tie dinner on the evening before the game, when the husband of the movie starlet who had been assigned to their party fell face forward into the soup.

NORTHLANDS COLISEUM, EDMONTON, FRIDAY, FEBRUARY 13: The Quebec Nordiques are here, and so is Krazy George. He wears rolled-up jeans, an Oiler sweater with *Krazy George* written across the back, and a rubber mask that makes him look bald and wild. Underneath he is bald. His name is Henderson; the George is real, if not the Krazy. He lives in Colorado. The Oilers, along with other professional sports teams around the continent, bring him in at $500 a night to whoop up their crowds. He carries a drum and a stick, and sprints around the upper rows of seats, leading cheers. He has some theatrical tricks: He will start a cheer in one corner and then roll it around the arena, with each section rising from its seats as it yells. The players find it more distracting than encouraging.

Hockey has been in Edmonton a long time. Eddie Shore played here. In 1924, the Edmonton Eskimos—a team that became the nucleus of the Chicago Black Hawks—won the championship of the professional Western Canada Hockey League, and in 1937, when the Gardens, which now stands next door to this new palace, laid down artificial ice, there was an exhibition game between the New York Rangers and the New York Americans. Edmonton fans know their hockey, but they are not demonstrative, and some players refer to this place as the Library. Krazy George has his work cut out for him.

So do the Oilers. They get off to a quick lead as Gretzky tucks one in from behind the net, his thirty-third of the year, but Quebec retaliates on a power play. Briefly, Callighen puts the Oilers ahead again. Then Peter Stastny scores a pretty goal and the first period ends 2–2. As both defences play tightly, it remains that way through the second.

Early in the third period there is a moment that could mean the season to the Oilers. This is the only game in the NHL tonight, so that any points they pick up could move them up in the standings. In the few games other teams have played since the all-star break, everyone struggling for the last playoff spot has moved up, and the Oilers are now twentieth; Quebec, one of the teams they will probably have to beat out, is fourteenth. The race is so close, though, that an Oiler win would put them right back in the thick of things. Now Gretzky, killing a penalty, intercepts a break and heads toward the Nordiques' goal. Breakaways are not the Kid's specialty. He gets a lot of them, but he is rarely able to score. He practises them in the summer, going one-on-one in the driveway in Brantford against whichever of his brothers wants to play. His problem may be that he tries too hard.

Tonight, the role of the brother is played by Dan Bouchard, and Gretzky is alone on him. He shifts, feints, lifts one shoulder, then fires toward the open upper corner. With a last-instant reflex, Bouchard flings up his arm; the puck catches the edge of his glove, glances off the crossbar and goes over the net.

Not long after Bouchard's save of the goal that would have put the Oilers ahead, the Stastny brothers combine, Anton from Peter, to make it 3–2 for Quebec. Then, with time running out, the Nordiques get the clincher. The Oilers stay in twentieth place.

"And here," said Glen Sather, laughing, "I brought *you* one of these." He tossed me a small package across his living room. He was late. He had invited me for dinner, but I had arrived before him. Remembering at the last moment that it was Valentine's Day, he had rushed out to buy his wife candy and flowers. She had bought him a watch. I opened my package. It was a tiny ashtray, the kind you can stick against a bedpost. "When that's full," Sather said, "you quit smoking." He was always the coach.

Sather was a different man on his own turf, surrounded by his family. He has an attractive blonde wife, Ann—called Annie universally—and two perky, handsome young sons, Shanon, aged nine, and Justin, six. That morning at practice Shanon had bet me he could shoot a roll of adhesive tape through a small hole in a plywood barrier. If the hole had been any bigger, he would have won. In their presence, Sather was relaxed and expansive. But the competitive edge, the need to keep even his guests on their toes, never left him.

Among Sather's most attractive qualities is the value he places on simply doing things—hunting, fishing, training his dogs, taking photographs, reading, talking, collecting experiences. In the summers, he lives in Banff, and he loves to talk of the mountains, to show pictures of the wildlife that surrounds him and about which he is impressively expert. When things are slow around him he will launch one of his infinite supply of competitive games, and when they aren't slow he will keep them moving by drawing on his own supply of energy. He has opinions about everything, and is constantly seeking new information to reinforce them. About hockey, he brooks no arguments; in his own view at least, he is never wrong.

"In this job," he said once to me, "I can't afford to be."

Over dinner, I asked him about the firing of Bryan Watson.

"Yes," he said, "that was the toughest thing I've ever had to do in my life."

"You were pretty good friends."

"Brothers. We were like brothers."

"And you didn't have any doubts about what you were doing."

"Everything I do is for the good of the team."

"And you didn't make a mistake with Bugsy?"

"Maybe in bringing him here. Not in letting him go. It just wasn't working out."

"Can I ask you about Dave Archambault?" I said.

"Sure. What about him?"

Archambault was the rookie Sather had sent down to Milwaukee from training camp, the young man who had broken his hand in a fight and then been told he lacked aggressiveness. He was a graduate in criminal justice, aged twenty-four. The salary he had signed for, $10,000 plus a $4,000 bonus, was exactly what Billy Heindl had signed for.

"He could have been a lawyer," I said.

"I wasn't stopping him."

"Sure you were."

"How?"

"You could have told him he'd be in Milwaukee forever."

"I didn't tell him he'd be anywhere else."

"You could have said, 'Look, kid, you haven't got what it takes to make the big league. You should get out of all this right now and go back to school.'"

"He still can, can't he?"

"Oh, come on, Slats. Do you think he will?"

"If a kid wants to play a year or two of minor-league hockey, that's not my problem, is it? It's a pretty good life."

NORTHLANDS COLISEUM, SUNDAY, FEBRUARY 15: "It's Buffalo tonight," Peter Pocklington explains to his guests in the six seats he holds for his own use. "Surely we can beat Buffalo."

Except for the disappointing play of his hockey team, Pocklington is having a good year. His business empire has grown to include the Swift Canadian Company Limited. With Swift's, an $800 million company, his enterprises now gross $1 billion a year. For years, as he says, he has "rolled it all," ploughing the profits of each deal back into more deals, wheeling and grinding, taking chances. Now, those days are over; he is too big to be hurt by gambling. Furthermore, the Swift's deal has included a yacht—"worth a mill by itself"—that has come as a pleasant surprise. It is a new toy for him, and he loves his toys.

He has had a pleasant day. One of the men he has brought to the game with him tonight is a piano player, who spent the afternoon at Pocklington's house playing the ivory-coloured grand that sits in his living room under the Picasso. For nearly two hours Pocklington sat on a couch with Eva, crooning, in his pleasant, lilting baritone, some of the music he loves best: the score of *South Pacific*, old Frank Sinatra hits, songs from *Pajama Game*. When he ran out of popular tunes he requested, and was given, accompaniment for some of the songs he used to sing at campfires, and when he ran out of those he sang a medley of anthems: "La Marseillaise," "The Battle Hymn of the Republic," and in a stirring climax, the national anthem of the Union of Soviet Socialist Republics.

As a hockey fan, Pocklington makes up in enthusiasm for any lack of expertise. When Edmonton scores, he nudges his elbow forcefully into the ribs of whoever is sitting next to him. Edmonton is not scoring much now; as usual, Buffalo has gone into its defensive shell.

Buffalo goes ahead early. B.J. MacDonald, playing on a line with Stan Weir and Dave Hunter (Kurri seems to have the lead in the competition to play with Gretzky), evens it up. Until the third period, that is that, with Gary Edwards playing solidly in the Edmonton goal.

I have an extra stake in tonight's game. In Friday's edition of the Coliseum program I wrote about the damage done to my boots in Montreal. I suggested their worth.

"Are *those* the 'handmade calfskin boots'?" said B.J. MacDonald, when I showed up at practice Saturday morning.

"I think we'd better get them," said Peter Driscoll.

"For the dressing room," added Lee Fogolin.

"If you beat Buffalo," I said, "I'll donate them." In the third period, the teams exchange goals, and the game ends in a tie. In the dressing room, the Oilers are in a mixed mood. The tie is better than the losses they have been suffering, but they need to start winning.

"Where are those boots?" says Fogolin.

"I said a *win*," I reply. "I'll give you one boot."

"Hand it over."

Kelly Pruden, the equipment manager, goes into the trainers' room and emerges with some cotton batting.

"What's that for?" I ask.

"To stuff your boot," he says. "We're going to burn it."

"Not in here," says Fogolin. "We have to dress in here."

"Give it to me," says Driscoll, who, playing regularly now, has become something of a social leader. He ceremoniously nails my boot to the dressing-room wall.

"What's that?" says Pocklington, who has been over in the corner getting Gretzky to sign a stick for the piano player. I tell him the story.

"That's good," he says. "They enjoy that sort of thing."

Then, handing the signed Gretzky Titan to his guest, he says: "You'll treasure this some day. The Kid is really going to be one of the immortals."

*… if Michael Gobuty had been a better backgammon player …*

Whether or not Gordie Howe, the man who first moved up along-side Maurice Richard at the pinnacle of professional hockey and then went on, in the most remarkable case of durability in sports history, to surpass him, was actually a better hockey player than Richard is a question that can still keep hockey fans waging arguments late into the winter nights. In 1951, when Richard was thirty years old and Howe, who had broken into the NHL in 1946, was twenty-three, Lloyd Percival, then the game's most technically oriented student, and the proprietor of an institute called Sports College, ran the two of them through a series of seventeen competitive tests of basic skills. Howe won sixteen; of the basic skills, Richard did better only at acceleration. Still, as Percival noted, there were attributes of the game no stopwatch could measure at which the Rocket excelled: he attempted, completed, and received passes better than Howe, although Howe, who carried the puck five times as often, had a better interception record.

About one aspect of comparison there was never any argument. Howe lacked star quality. On the ice, he was the complete player, skating only as fast as the play allowed, always cruising, looking, waiting, controlling the game. But his art concealed art; he *looked* unspectacular. As Richard's supporters used to say, put them in arenas across the street from one another and see who would draw the fans. Off the ice, too, Howe was unassuming and modest to the point of being bland.

As a boy, he had been agonizingly shy. He was the sixth of nine children of a family that suffered acute Depression poverty in Floral, Saskatchewan, and later in Saskatoon. They sometimes ate only oatmeal and they walked fifty yards across the bald prairie to visit the outhouse. Howe was exceptionally strong—he could lift a ninety-pound grain sack with each arm when he was thirteen—but not academically gifted; he repeated grade three. As a youngster, listening to Foster Hewitt, he used to practise his signature, *Gord Howe, Gordie Howe, best wishes G. Howe*, before settling on the careful, legible loops and swirls that were to embellish so many autograph books later on. He shared his first pair of skates with a sister, but rapidly emerged as a player of promise, being invited first to a training camp of the New York Rangers at Winnipeg and, when they wouldn't give him a jacket, going home.

The next year, Detroit coaxed him east again and signed him to a junior team in Galt, although as a transferred westerner he would be ineligible to play. His first fall in Galt, he loped up Water Street hill to enrol at the collegiate, stood for a while on its manicured lawn, shuffling his feet, in awe of the number of city dwellers who would be inside, and loped back downtown to get a job at Galt Metal Industries. The next year, the Red Wings sent him to their minor-league team in Omaha, Nebraska, but within a season he was in the NHL to stay, a tall, slope-shouldered man who marked not only the game but any opponents who tried to cross him. There was a mean streak to his play that intimidated his opponents, although, as far as anyone could tell, the vicious jabs he dealt out in the corners, or the lacerations he imposed on the back of the legs of anyone who tried to stick too close to him, were distributed with no malice. Cruelty was simply part of the game he understood.

Howe may well have been the most gifted athlete ever to play the game. He managed his strength with almost superhuman co-ordination. Not long after he came into the league he was absolved of the necessity to fight; there was simply no one who wanted to take him on. In the season of 1958–59, one man, Lou Fontinato of the New York Rangers, tried to, and *Life* magazine the next week carried a picture of Fontinato in a hospital room, his nose squashed like a tomato, his eyes swollen and bruised. The Rangers finished last that year and there were those who thought the reason was Howe's demolition of Fontinato. (In a demonstration of how hockey players were able to keep this sort of punishment separate from their social relationships, Fontinato later shook hands with Howe at a sports banquet, laughingly adding that he was not sure he wanted to lower his hands to do so.) There were boxing men who were convinced Howe could have been the heavyweight champion of the world if he had wanted to be. Bucky Harris, the manager of the Detroit Tigers, with whom Howe used to work out, said he could have played major-league baseball. He was a scratch-handicap golfer. But his most remarkable feats came on the hockey rink—even at practice. I can remember watching him working out with the Red Wings one day in Detroit, lofting wrist shots from one end of the rink to the other on the fly and, in another session, standing in front of the net while other players fired at him, calmly batting the pucks out of the air like baseballs and sending them into the stands. He was such a student of the game that with his linemate Ted Lindsay he used to work on sending apparently harmless shots into the opponents' zone—but aiming them in such a way that the rebounds became accurate passes.

By the middle 1960s, Howe was one of the most famous men in Canada. A CTV poll showed him to be more recognizable than the Governor General or the premier of Quebec, and some commercial enterprises approached him for endorsements. Supported, now, by a garrulous and businesslike wife, he accepted some of these invitations. The shyness was still with him, but in his thirties he was better able to conquer it, offering easy and often self-mocking after-dinner anecdotes or simply hanging out, shaking hands and accepting adulation with an apparently natural grace. A near-fatal head injury in the early 1950s had left him with a chronic blink, and somehow that added to his aw-shucks appeal. Although he had none of the Rocket's flair, people liked him. They enjoyed the reflected glow of his company. He was one of the first hockey players to supplement his NHL income by something other than a summer construction job or delivering beer. But he was a long way from being wealthy. Not until long after he had established himself in the league's record books did he discover how much his fame might have been worth. But even before he retired for the first time, in 1971, he had become the stuff of history. He had played more games than any-one ever had, scored more goals, collected more assists, been given more honours. He had set records for setting records.

One by one, three other players came along during Howe's career to ascend to the plateau of supremacy. The three were Jean Béliveau, who joined the Canadiens full-time in 1953; Bobby Hull, who came to the Black Hawks in 1957; and Bobby Orr, who became a Boston Bruin in 1966. While only Orr among them managed to carve out an era for him-self, a time when the game belonged to him alone, each of them brought such special qualities to the NHL that there was no question that they belonged on the same list as the earlier titans.

Béliveau was born in 1931 in Trois-Rivières, but when he was three his father, a lineman for Shawinigan Power, moved the family to Victoriaville, where they lived next door to a church. Jean became an altar boy. As he told Hugh Hood, the Quebec writer who took time out from his career as a novelist in 1970 to write an adulatory book about Béliveau:

> In the winter especially the boys wouldn't turn up on time and the sacristan would go next door to our house and ask for me. I was on the altar almost every morning. I served at weddings and funerals too. The families would always tip the altar boys. I served High Mass often. As I got taller I would be censer, then Master.

Later, as he played in the NHL, the influence of those early years showed. "Nobody's sense of good conduct is innate," Hood wrote, "but his comes about as close to that as possible. He learned how to behave when he was young and it shows in everything he does."

Christian or not, Béliveau's play was marked by a grace that set him apart from his peers, an elegance, a nobility. He was a marvellous passer, and such a dedicated team man that the Canadiens rapidly elected him captain. He had not come to the team easily, however. As an "amateur"—his religious convictions, apparently, did not include vows of poverty—he had virtually taken over Quebec City, becoming so much a part of the town that he could not, as word had it, afford to turn pro. To acquire him, the Canadiens bought out the whole league he played in, declared it professional (La Ligue Senior Professionelle du Quebec), and, with a burst of publicity, signed him up for $20,000 a year. At first, and in spite of his size—he was six foot three and weighed 205, he seemed so meek that the NHL's intimidators went after him with glee. But after a couple of years of turning the other cheek, he began retaliating, and the intimidation stopped. Yet however fiercely he was prepared to play, he continued to show the same qualities that had characterized his career. "He reminded one," wrote Herbert Warren Wind in *The New Yorker*, "of one of the characters Gary Cooper played and just as Cooper in real life was as honest and decent as he seemed on the screen, so was Béliveau off the ice." By the time he retired, he had recorded more scoring points than any centre-man in history, and he had led the Canadiens to ten Stanley Cups in eighteen years.

On the Christmas that fell just a week before his third birthday, Bobby Hull, one of eleven children of a cement-plant worker in Point Anne, Ontario, got his first pair of skates and set out immediately for the nearest ice. "As young Bobby toddled out the door," Jim Hunt wrote years later in an authorized biography, "his mother said: 'Remember, now, no crying or the skates go back to Santa Claus.'" Hunt went on:

> Young Bobby just grinned and, supported by two older sisters, went across the road to the Bay of Quinte, fifty yards from the front door of their home. His mother needn't have worried. Mrs. Hull, who can recall in considerable detail most of the moments in the boyhood of her eldest son, said, "I looked out the window a couple of hours later and I could hardly believe it. Here was this little gaffer skating by himself. He fell down often but he would always get up, brush off the snow and keep on skating. It was almost dark when I finally called him in for his Christmas dinner and by this time he could skate by himself without any help from his sisters."

The ability to skate stayed with him, of course—in full flight, he was clocked at nearly thirty miles an hour, making him certainly the fastest skater of his day, and so did the grin. He left Point Anne when he was fourteen, played junior in St. Catharines, dropped out of school, got hurriedly married and just as hurriedly divorced before he turned pro, and drew fans wherever he went. He was a Black Hawk at eighteen, a star at twenty. When he reached maturity, and fame, the grin would start on the left side of his mouth and spread slowly across his handsome face, expanding like the sunrise. His eyes would crinkle and a dimple would appear in his left cheek. His tongue would curl playfully under his upper lip. At the peak of his career, the smile was everywhere; where Gordie Howe had ventured, Hull rushed in. Trent Frayne wrote:

> On television he was a dimpled pitchman for hair tonic, rubbing his head with Vitalis and advising you to try it, too … In *Esquire* his muscles bulged from swimsuits and sweaters and even from socks. In four colour displays for practically suitless swimsuits, there he was in Hawaii on the sands of Waikiki with other big athletes from other big sports, his tawny pelt glistening, his grin caressing some delicious doll wearing delicious skin and a Jantzen that just did make the picture. While in work-clothes he extolled a Ford tractor and on radio plugged the firm's sedan. Or, back on television between periods, there he was being interviewed after firing three goals past some hapless goaltender telling the interviewer with a nice warm gratifying smile and a nice warm gratifying touch of humility that it was fine to score.

He scored in clusters: fifty goals or more in each of five years, in each of seven years more than anyone else in the year, and, finally, in total more even than the Rocket. But, like Morenz or Richard, it was the way he scored them that stuck with us longer than the numbers. He was the Golden Jet, whose slapshots seemed to be detonated by explosives, and who could soar down the wing, his blond hair flying, and lift our hearts. When his hair began to fall out he got a transplant to replace it, and when he grew tired of his Black Hawks sweater he exchanged it for a uniform of the WHA's Winnipeg Jets and a million dollars in cash. But always he was grinning, laughing, playing the game and living his life with what seemed untramelled joy.

He was, perhaps, the best ambassador the game ever had, as exuberant as Howe was shy or Richard intense. He seemed always to have time for children—he had four of his own from his second marriage to a stunning former figure skater—and wherever he went he was besieged by young fans. He would, invariably, stop to talk with them, sign their autograph books, and ruffle their hair. When he finally left Winnipeg in 1979, someone wrote in the paper that they should erect a statue to him there, showing him with his coat draped over one shoulder, surrounded by kids, signing autographs, grinning.

The first time Gordie Howe saw Bobby Orr play was in the season of 1965–66. Orr was still a junior. He had been discovered by the pros when he was twelve, and had gone with a team of fourteen-year-olds from his hometown of Parry Sound, Ontario, to play in Gananoque, near Kingston. He was already something of a celebrity in Parry Sound, the son of a man who packed munitions for Canadian Industries Limited and the best little hockey player in town. The pro scouts who saw him, including Wren Blair, who later helped to bring Minnesota into the NHL but who was then in the Boston organization, and Lynn Patrick, the general manager of the Bruins, had actually gone to the game to see a promising youngster from Gananoque, but the young Orr instantly turned their heads. For much of the next few years, the Bruins invested their energies in seeing to it that Bobby would end up as their property. As part of their campaign, they had him play for a Boston-controlled junior team in Oshawa, just a half-day's drive from Parry Sound, so that, unlike Bobby Hull, he could commute. He was an outstanding junior at fifteen, and by the time Howe saw him, when he was seventeen, he was famous. The game Howe saw was ostensibly between a travelling team of young Russians and the Toronto Marlboros, but to equalize things the Marlies had been allowed to stack their lineup with some other Ontario players, one of whom was Orr. The game was fast and furious and excellently played. The Russians won, 3–2, but by far the most exciting player in the rink was Orr. Whenever he was on the ice, which was about two-thirds of the time, he dominated the game, anticipating patterns, blocking shots, carrying the puck up the ice himself, feeding his barely familiar teammates or shooting from the point with remarkable accuracy. "What do you think?" someone asked Howe after one particularly spectacular rush. "I think he's everything people say he is," Howe said in his Saskatchewan drawl. "When he gets to the NHL next year, he's going to tear the league apart."

Tear it apart, of course, he did, not only setting records for every scoring aspect of the position he played, defence, but changing our understanding of what that position could mean. No defenceman had ever scored twenty goals in a season before he arrived. Orr did it seven times in a row, and each time was named the outstanding defenceman in the league. Playing defence, he twice led the league in total scoring points. When he joined the Bruins they were the worst team in the NHL. Under his helmsmanship they became one of the best, winning Stanley Cups in 1970 and 1972, and packing in fans wherever they went. And it was Orr they went to see. Three years in a row he was named the most valuable player in regular season play and twice the most valuable in the Stanley Cup playoffs. Time and again, he would do seemingly impossible things with the puck, whirling 360 degrees at the blueline and keeping control through his spin, gathering momentum behind his own end and carrying the puck through a maze of opponents, batting a puck out of mid-air—as, in a moment that is burned in all our memories forever, he did once while he was diving across the St. Louis goal mouth, in a play that won a Stanley Cup. He had everything: speed, size, stamina, skill, savvy. He seemed the perfect hockey machine, except there was nothing mechanical about anything he did.

From the beginning, there were signs of the physical flaw that would end his career so early. On December 7, 1966, his first year in the league, he sat out the first of what would be eight consecutive games with a knee injury. As the years rolled on, and his list of absences grew, it became more and more evident that he was playing on borrowed time. Reports on his knees dwelled in gruesome detail on the swelling and discolouration. Almost from the outset, he played in constant pain. He sought specialists around the continent, but no one could offer permanent relief. By 1972, knee trouble prevented him from playing for Team Canada in a series that ought to have been the high point of his career. Even crippled, as he sometimes played, he continued to dominate every game he took part in, but by the late 1970s he—and we—had come to accept the fact that his knees were gone. The Bruins dealt him, as Montreal had dealt Morenz, to Chicago. In one last gallant effort he tried to help the Black Hawks. It was no use. In January of 1979, the Bruins, with whom he would be forever identified, retired his number 4, while the fans, many of them weeping, stood and roared their appreciation of his years on the ice.

His retirement ceremony, though, was one of the few times Orr touched our hearts. Throughout his playing career, as glorious as it was, he had somehow failed to reach out and touch us the way Morenz had touched our fathers or Richard or Howe or Béliveau or Hull had touched us. Orr was (and is) an admirable young man, modest, well-spoken, polite. It may have been that he just lacked soul, or that he was too perfect, too far above us all. A more likely explanation, though, is that he came along during one of the NHL's least attractive eras, when instant expansion—he was in his second year when the league doubled—reminded us how commercial our game had become. Orr, indeed, was the pioneer of super-salaries, having acquired a lawyer, Alan Eagleson, before he even entered into negotiation with the Bruins and having signed, early in his career, hockey's first million-dollar contract. Somehow, for a while at least, the romance had gone, and Orr, who brought as many skills to the game as anyone we had ever seen, never quite became the hero he might have been in another time. But, like all his predecessors at the top of hockey, he had enlarged the stage to which, it was evident in the season of 1980–81, Wayne Gretzky would one day ascend.

Even compared to Orr, who made the cover of *Maclean's* Magazine when he was sixteen, Gretzky had a precocious hockey childhood. When he was six, in his first year of organized competition, he scored only one goal—a moment Walter Gretzky, an amateur photographer, caught in a snapshot—but he was named to the Brantford novice all-stars, most of whom were four years older. He got twenty-seven goals the next year, and 104 in forty games the year after that. By his final year in novice he was an established phenomenon.

"The scoring feats of ten-year-old Wayne Gretzky of Brantford," began a Canadian Press story out of Brampton, Ontario, in 1972, "are posing a pleasant problem for the organizers of the novice tournament. The four-foot-four, seventy-pound dynamo has been turning them away at the doors here and didn't disappoint his fans again Wednesday night, scoring nine goals and assisting on two others in Brantford's 12–2 win over Sault Ste. Marie." That was the year he scored 378 in sixty-eight games, some of them in clusters that would have done credit to a combination of Billy Batson and Frank Merriwell: three in forty-five seconds in the third period of a game Brantford had been trailing 3–0; six in a row against Oshawa, which had been leading 5–0; fifty in one six-game tournament; eleven in a single game. He was interviewed on national television and featured in the *Toronto Telegram*, and was a regular post-game interviewee on the hockey telecasts on CKBC, Brantford. The Gretzkys' living-room began to fill with trophies and plaques.

In 1974, when he was thirteen, Wayne went with the Brantford team to the Quebec Peewee Tournament, the world's largest event for players of that age. Although Brantford didn't win, Wayne was the centre of attention, for both the media and the fans, who are connoisseurs of prepubescent stars. One minor-hockey executive who went there especially to see him was able to get a seat only in the aisle, as more than 13,000 people crowded into a stadium built for 10,000. People jammed into Wayne's dressing room after games, sought him out for autographs in his childish hand, and stole his sticks for souvenirs.

"When the team went out to shake hands with the crowd after they lost the semi-final," remembers Ron St. Amond, the coach of that Brantford team, "I had to tell Wayne to take his gloves off first. Someone might have grabbed them."

I met Wayne the year after, when he showed up on *This Country in the Morning*, a CBC radio program I worked on. His lifetime total of goals, scrupulously kept by his father, was 988 when we met. My most vivid impression was of how small he was, five-two, and how unspoiled. Because of my involvement with minor hockey, and my casual acquaintance with adult hockey stars, I suppose I was expecting a kind of pocket edition of Phil Esposito, brash and self-aware. (It was about this time, incidentally, that Esposito, who had set an all-time scoring record in 1970–71 with seventy-six goals and seventy-six assists, was told by *his* father that the youngster who would someday break that record was Gretzky.) Instead, I found a youngster who, while scarcely what broadcasters call "a good interview," even then had a disarming ability to put people around him at ease. He had already lost three of his teeth— "not babies," he told me with the slightly exasperated manner of kids to whom you've posed a dumb question, "seconds"—when someone smashed a stick across his mouth. The three pegged replacements gave a slightly buck-toothed cast to his thin features. He looked not unlike a solemn squirrel. Already, he had an impressive ability to talk about specific plays and situations, and to recall, without bragging, his own goals. I remember in particular his praise for the team that had put Brantford out at Quebec.

I asked him if the other kids at school razzed him. "Ah, no," he said, "they just tell jokes about that. They tell me what people are saying—as if I didn't know." Then he laughed.

Did other teams lie in wait for him?

"Not really."

But he must have been meeting some rough stuff.

"Oh, some butt ends and that."

What did he do in return?

"Just try to hit them fair."

Life may not have been quite as smooth for him as he led me to believe then. "To tell you the truth," one young man who played against Gretzky in tournaments told me later, "I used to think he was a prick. There were always adults around him, treating him like he was something special. And on the ice, too, he was always protected. You knew if you took a run at him, someone else would flatten you. I guess I was just jealous."

Some of the worst moments came from within the Brantford organization—not from the players, most of whom were content to count
the victories their special young teammate was helping them reap, but
from their parents. "I remember one game in particular," Walter said one
day. "It was in Burlington, and we were playing a very strong team. A lot
of people made a point of coming to see us. It was a terrific game. We
lost, 5–4, but it was really something to see. Wayne got all our goals. But
on the way out I heard one of the other parents—I won't say who—say,
'Sure, he might have scored four, but he cost us five.'"

Wayne: "The season I scored all the goals, the 378, well, after that
I had a coach who told me, 'We don't want no hot dogs on this team.'
Well, I had 120 assists, too. A little kid, and I got 120 assists, and this
guy was telling me I was a hot dog. That was the year Gordie Howe had
retired—for the first time—and my idol was Gilbert Perreault. And
you know what this coach told me? He said, 'We don't want no Gilbert
Perreaults on this team.' And I said, 'What are you saying? Gilbert
Perreault's a hot dog or something?' 'Yeah,' he says. And I say, 'Well, if
Gilbert Perreault's such a hot dog, why is he playing in the NHL and on
Team Canada while you're coaching in this league?'"

But such outbursts, apparently, were so rare as to be almost un-
noticeable. According to all accounts, including theirs, Wayne remained
popular among his teammates. In *The Great Gretzky*, Terry Jones went
to considerable pains to track down young men who had played with
Gretzky throughout the minor ranks. Without exception, they sang his
praises. They had liked him then, and many had remained his friends.
Yet people who saw him play, and marvelled at the way he could dominate a game, expected him to be objectionable off the ice, as if he had a
right to be. When he wasn't, when he presented the same modest, shy
poise that I saw in the CBC radio studio, it was as if they were disappointed; a young man—a boy, really—with every reason to be spoiled
to the soul, had remained exactly as they would have liked their own
sons to be, yet somehow doubted they would.

Questioned about this remarkable quality, both Wayne and
Walter refer to one tournament, and one moment. The tournament
was in Kingston, Ontario, and, as was nearly always the case, the local

paper had run a story about the prodigious young Brantford player who would be its major attraction. Wayne was reading the story and nodding his approval. And Walter, who fixes teletype machines for the Bell Telephone Company and is quiet to the point of taciturnity, spoke to him firmly about the future he was then almost certainly facing.

"You're a very special person," Walter told his son. "Wherever you go, probably all your life, people are going to make a fuss over you. You've got to remember that, and you've got to behave right. They're going to be watching for every mistake. Remember that. You're very special and you're on display."

In 1975, when Wayne was fourteen, the Gretzky family came to a difficult decision. They were worried that the attention Wayne was getting was making it difficult for him to have a normal boyhood. Futhermore, Wayne was running out of competition. While he still enjoyed the game, the pressure was outweighing the rewards. Toronto beckoned. In Toronto he would be relatively anonymous, and would stand a better chance of meeting players closer to his own ability. There was one organization on the tournament circuit that they admired, the Young Nats. The Nats were among the elite of the highly competitive Metropolitan Toronto Hockey League, and the MTHL, with 100,000 boys registered, had produced over the years such hockey luminaries as Charlie and Lionel Conacher, Red Kelly, and Frank Mahovlich. A call to Toronto quickly established that the Nats wanted Wayne.

The Gretzkys had met a couple they liked, the Cornishes, at various tournaments. Among the pleasant aspects of minor hockey is the camaraderie it occasionally fosters in the stands. The Cornishes, who had a boy in the Nats' organization, invited Wayne to move into their home in the Rexdale area of Toronto and play for the Nats' bantams, a team of boys his own age.

The Nats' competitors in the MTHL were not amused. "Import," someone cried, and Wayne became an even greater *cause célèbre* than he had been in Brantford. To qualify him for the MTHL's Toronto-boys-only rule, the Cornishes, with the Gretzkys' agreement, made him their legal ward. The league was still not satisfied. The Ontario Minor

Hockey Association, under whose jurisdiction he'd played in Brantford, claimed the transfer had been illegal. Wayne could not play. The families appealed to the courts. The ruling, in *Gretzky et al. vs. the Ontario Minor Hockey Association et al.*, upheld the hockey bureaucracy. Wayne, already established in Toronto, and out of hockey for five weeks while the authorities wrangled, decided to stay in Toronto and play for the Young Nats Junior Bs. The team was open to boys as old as twenty, and could draw players from anywhere it wanted. In his first game he scored two goals, and went on to win the league's rookie-of-the-year award.

For a while, in his second year of Junior B, Wayne just couldn't get going. On the bench, he often looked exhausted. "I thought he might have mono," Walter remembers. In the Christmas ranking of players of midget age eligible to be drafted to a higher league, he was 184th in the country. During this time, Bill Cornish recalls, Wayne was constantly in touch with his parents in Brantford. Walter, and sometimes Phyllis, Wayne's mother, and even the younger children, would drive to as many of the Young Nats Junior B games as they could. Wayne called home every night.

Shortly after Christmas, as inexplicably as he had slumped, he began to come around. His ranking in the draft shot up. He finished second in the league scoring. In the spring of his sixteenth year, he was drafted third in the nation to play Junior A for the Sault Ste. Marie Greyhounds. In his first game with the Greyhounds, he scored three goals, ending the season with seventy, along with 112 assists, and he won trophies as the league's best rookie and most gentlemanly player.

While in the Sault, Wayne stayed with Jim and Sylvia Bodner, friends of his parents who had moved to the Sault from Brantford. He continued to call home as often as he could, and to impress both the Bodner family and his teammates, as he had impressed so many people, with his modesty and politeness. The pressures of Junior A hockey, however, which is big time in scheduling if not in salaries, began to erode his school work; he struggled to keep up with grade eleven.

The fans were ecstatic about him; average attendance in the Sault doubled, to 2,500 a game, and at arenas from Ottawa to Hamilton, the Greyhounds set records for attendance. The team remained at the bottom of the league, but people flocked to see what Harry Wolfe, the Greyhounds' radio announcer, called "The Wayne Gretzky Show."

If there was a weakness in that show, it was in Wayne's inability to play down to the level of some of his teammates. Like a bridge master bidding so expertly that he confuses his own less experienced partner, Gretzky would sometimes make passes that would have been wonderful if they'd been made to him. As it was, they often went to open ice. Even so, his linemates on the Greyhounds, neither of whom had made it to professional ranks, scored sixty goals each the year he played with them. The ability to score, which had carried him to so many records and attracted so much attention through his boyhood, was now broadened and embellished by an even greater ability to set up goals for other people. He had developed techniques for passing the puck that some hockey men said were already the equal of that of anyone in the game, and he had a marvellous sense of patterns and flow. E.M. Swift, a writer for *Sports Illustrated*, ventured north to seek him out and came away in wonder. "Gretzky' s talent is all in his head," he wrote. He "knows not only where everyone is on the ice, but he also knows where they're *going*. Uncanny anticipation."

To those of us who had grown up on the outdoor rinks, Wayne's accomplishments were especially pleasing. He was a throwback. He played the game of our lives. We cheered his rise to stardom.

Two changes occurred during the Sault years. The first was his sweater number. He had always worn 9, emulating Howe, but with the Greyhounds 9 was not available. He tried 14 and 19, but, he told a reporter in mock seriousness, the numeral 1 didn't feel right on his back. The Greyhound coach, Muzz MacPherson, wanting something distinctive, suggested a number that might offend hockey traditionalists but would certainly set him apart: 99.

The second change was that he developed a mild but troubling case of acne.

Of all the overlapping of careers that have marked the history of hockey's dominant players—Malone being discouraged by the young Morenz; Howe watching Orr play his remarkable game against the

Russians—no two have ever dovetailed quite so neatly as those of Howe and Gretzky. The relationship between the man who wore the mantle longer than anyone else and his young heir apparent is an extraordinary one, as if the young Mozart had had a chance to visit and talk shop with the elderly J.S. Bach. The first hockey book Wayne ever read was Jim Vipond's *Gordie Howe, Number 9*, published in 1968. In 1972, Howe presented the awards at a hockey banquet in Brantford, where the principal recipient was Wayne. (The prescient Walter took a photograph of that occasion, too.) Later, Wayne made a pilgrimage to New York after he'd signed his first contract, and Howe took him about the town, introducing him to such celebrities as Muhammad Ali, Bobby Hull, and Debbie Boone. Few hockey fans lucky enough to see either game were not moved by their appearance together in Gretzky's first and Howe's last all-star games in both the WHA and the NHL. In all these encounters, Howe was generous with guidance and advice, although much of his influence on Gretzky was by example; as they skated out for their first mutual all-star appearance—at the time Howe had been in more all-star games than Gretzky had in *league* games—Howe made a laughing remark about his own nervousness, calming Gretzky down. But no link between their careers has had a more direct effect on Gretzky's fortunes than the one that led to his introduction to Gus Badali.

Badali first saw Wayne play with the Junior B Nats. Badali was employed by Famous Players Theatres as an auditor in the confections division, but at heart he was a hockey man. He had played Junior B himself, and later coached it in Markham, Ontario. He is a soft-spoken man, with an easy manner and a bright smile that transforms his sombre features. Kids like him. Through hockey he had become friends with two of Gordie Howe's sons, Mark and Marty, who were then playing for the Junior A Toronto Marlboros, and even closer to a third son, Murray, who was with the Junior B Nats. Murray boarded with the Badalis. It was while watching Murray's games that Badali first saw Gretzky play. In the stands, he struck up an acquaintance with Walter Gretzky. They got on.

"Actually," Badali had said since, "that was during Wayne's bad period, and he wasn't too impressive when I first saw him. He seemed to be struggling. But there was something about him that made you realize someday he'd be great."

This was at a time when the WHA was fighting to gain recognition. The Houston Aeros had managed not only to entice Mark and Marty Howe away from the Marlboros but to lure their father back from what was turning out to be a frustrating retirement. One of the other Marlboros, Wayne Dillon, who had known Badali over the years, indicated he'd like a slice of the WHA pie as well. As a favour, Badali called Buck Houle, the manager of Johnny F. Bassett's Toronto Toros. Houle expressed interest. Badali agreed to sit in on a meeting between the Toros and the Dillon family. Shortly afterward, Dillon signed a professional contract.

More prominent Junior A players began seeking out Badali. For the next year or so he found himself in interminable meetings, dealing with a complex set of regulations that governed the acquisition of young Canadians for big dollars by the still precarious WHA clubs. Through all these negotiations, he kept his amateur status as an agent, doing intricate contractual work at night and counting popcorn receipts by day. Finally, Wayne Dillon had had enough of the WHA. He asked Badali to represent him formally, and Badali negotiated a contract for him with the New York Rangers of the NHL.

In the meantime, Badali's generosity with his time and advice had not gone unnoticed around the Young Nats organization, especially among the parents. One night, Walter Gretzky asked Badali if he would be interested in handling Wayne's affairs. Badali said he would. Their first agreement was a handshake—"a gentlemen's agreement," Badali has said—and it turned out splendidly for all. Badali, not long afterward, left Famous Players, and by the fall of 1980 had more than forty players in his stable, including the Oilers' first draft choice, Paul Coffey. Badali takes only five percent of hockey income, although he gets fifteen of the remainder, which, he says, is harder to negotiate.

The first approach for Wayne's professional services came from Johnny Bassett, who had had his eye on him since Wayne was eight. Badali named a figure. Bassett said it was too high for him, but he knew of another owner in the WHA, Nelson Skalbania, who might be interested. At the time Skalbania had a WHA franchise in Indianapolis. Attendance was meagre, and he was in need of a name that would make some impact.

SKALBANIA: "I'd never seen Gretzky play, but I'd heard about him. When John told me about him, we were at a WHA meeting in the Hotel Toronto. And when I went down to the lobby, who should I see but Badali?"

BADALI: "He walked up to me and gave me a thousand dollars for plane fare, and told me to get Walter and Phyllis and Wayne out to Vancouver. I said Walter is a working man, you know, but we'd be there as soon as we could. That was how we got our *Fantasy Island* weekend."

WAYNE: "What a place he had out there. Not just one of those big houses, but two lots. Jeez, was it ever nice!"

BADALI: "He seemed willing to meet all our conditions, and I thought I'd try for something extra—one of the paintings he had on the wall. I can't remember what they were called, but I asked him to choose one that was worth fifty thousand dollars and we'd take it as part of the signing bonus."

SKALBANIA: "In my living room there was a van Ruisdale, a Utrillo, and a what's-his-name, A.Y. Jackson. There was no way I was going to give them one of those."

Wayne signed. The bonus, without a painting, was $250,000, with $50,000 cash. The remainder of a total of $875,000 was to be paid over four years. Skalbania, anxious to get as much publicity as possible at the expense of the NHL, which still ruled out the signing of players as young as Wayne, and would be holding its annual meeting that weekend, and perhaps to enjoy a moment of one-upmanship over his former partner Pocklington, swept his new prize and the family off in his private jet to Edmonton to hold a press conference before proceeding on to Indianapolis.

Gretzky, at the time, was seventeen.

If Michael Gobuty had been a bolder backgammon player, Gretzky might have been a Winnipeg Jet. Gobuty, who owns Victoria Leather in Winnipeg, is another of the free-wheeling money men who have moved into the ownership of hockey in the Canadian west; he is one of the owners of the Jets.

Skalbania's Indianapolis franchise had not worked out. Even with his celebrated rookie, his crowds could sometimes be counted in three figures—Indianapolites preferring to watch cars zoom around a brick oval—and he appeared headed for a loss of as much as a million dollars in the 1978–79 season. Worse, the city wasn't included in plans for a merger between the WHA and the NHL. If Skalbania wanted to bail out, Gretzky's contract, which had seemed an extravagance, would be his greatest asset. Skalbania called Gobuty. They met. Gretzky went to Winnipeg and was a guest in Gobuty's home.

Not all Gobuty's advisors were sold on the *wunderkind*. One of them—Gobuty will not say who, although a fair guess (in spite of his denials) is Rudy Pilous, one of the NHL's better coaches and, usually, one of its better judges of talent—said the kid was too scrawny. Besides, Skalbania wanted too much money. There was a final meeting, on board Gobuty's private plane.

"Tell you what," said Skalbania. "We'll play one game of backgammon. If you win, you can have him at your figure. If I win, I get a piece of the Jets."

"I'm not that good a backgammon player," said Gobuty.

Skalbania called Peter Pocklington. Pocklington instantly agreed to fulfil Gretzky's contractual needs and to pay Skalbania's asking price, except that most of it would have to come from writing off the half-million dollars that Pocklington had agreed to owe his former partner when the Edmonton franchise was absorbed by the NHL. He said he'd give Skalbania, who was cash short in his sporting adventures because of the drain in Indianapolis, $300,000 on the spot, but Skalbania would also have to accept a $250,000 note to settle the half-million dollar debt. Skalbania agreed. Later, with Skalbania again cash short, Pocklington was able to redeem the $250,000 note for $100,000 cash, which meant, in effect, that Pocklington had acquired Gretzky's rights for less cash, $400,000, than the value of his old debt to Skalbania.

The following January, on Wayne's eighteenth birthday, Pocklington held a ceremony at centre ice. With a baby-sized bottle of champagne and a birthday cake in the shape of a 99, he announced to the world that he had signed Gretzky to a twenty-one-year contract, the longest in the history of professional sports. This time, Walter was in the picture, as were Phyllis and all three of Wayne's younger brothers, Keith, Brent, and Glen.

"The contract," Pocklington told the press, "is for personal service. There's no way anyone's going to touch him when we join the NHL."

To no one's surprise, Gretzky—or Brinks, as his teammates occasionally called him—had a productive year for the Oilers. He finished third in WHA scoring with forty-six goals and sixty-four assists, and was named rookie of the year.

Furthermore, his acne cleared up.

## 14

*Even before he got on skates, Wayne seemed to have an almost spiritual
attraction to hockey*

On the evening of February 18, Gretzky put on one of the most
remarkable demonstrations anyone in the NHL had ever seen.
Watching it was what it must have been like to see Nijinksy dance in
his prime, or hear Caruso sing. Throughout the season, Billy Harris
had been saying that one night, when all Gretzky's perfect passes were
received perfectly by his teammates, and all his perfect shots went in,
he would score fifteen points. In his February display, he didn't quite do
that. Some of his passes were missed (he made some bad ones, too), and
some of his shots were blocked. But he accumulated as many points in
one game as all but five players in league history, scored as many *goals* in
one game as all but an historic few, and, in one period, scored as many
goals as anyone, ever.

At lunch the day before, he had looked tired. After practice, we
had ridden in his four-wheel-drive Jeep downtown to Walden's, one of
Edmonton's smarter restaurants, which has more ferns than Guatemala,
but was one of the few places where he felt we might not be bothered
by his fans. He was enjoying the adulation that had now become part of
his life. When it became too much for him, he would remind himself of
his own boyhood worship of hockey stars—Gordie Howe in particular—and the grace with which they had treated him (or, in some cases,
the lack of grace) and he would be patient and outgoing. For all the

shyness he still retained from his boyhood, he did not like to be alone, as indeed he almost never had been. He was raised in a large family, and all the homes he lived in during his hockey travels had had other children present. Rooming with Kevin Lowe was good for him, since Kevin was as good at cooking as Wayne was bored by it—although never with eating—and as neat as Wayne was inclined to be sloppy. By the middle of his second season, however, there were places in Edmonton where he could not go. On the way to lunch, he told a charming story about this part of his life, which was also a measure of Vickie Moss, the young woman who had become his steady companion.

"Vickie sometimes forgets," he said. "Last night we went to dinner at the Edmonton Plaza"—he had been there to receive one of the endless array of plaques and trophies he was collecting, this one as Edmonton's athlete of the year—"and we could hear music coming from the convention room next door. It was that Edmonton group, you know, the Emeralds, that Vickie had sung with last year. When she heard them she wanted to go and say hello, and maybe sing with them for part of a set. 'Let's go,' she said, and grabbed me by the arm. Well, outside the door I saw a sign saying it was some kind of business gathering, Imperial Oil, I think. 'I can't go in there,' I said, 'but she just grabbed me and dragged me, and when I looked up there were about a thousand pencils coming at me. Sometimes on Saturday afternoons she'll say, 'Let's go to McDonald's and have a hamburger.' Well, I can't go to McDonald's on a Saturday afternoon. I couldn't get near the counter. She just seems to forget."

"Stick with her," I said.

"I'm going to," he said. "She's one of thirteen children, and when I go over there it's just like I'm one of the family."

"One of her brothers is, well, mentally challenged, isn't he?"

"Yes. Joey. He's terrific. When I go to visit he puts on an Oiler sweater and he grins at me and says my name. Last week there was a Leaf game on TV, and he spelled Toronto. I got a real kick out of that."

"I wonder if people know why you put so much effort into your work for the mentally challenged."

"My dad's sister, you mean?"

"Yes."

"Well, I was very fond of her. I was really close to my grandparents, you know. I used to go down there and visit every weekend. They had a great place on the Nith River, not far from Brantford, all trees and that. I'd like to have a place like that someday. My aunt used to be there, and, yes, I guess that's why I do the work I do."

"Some people think you're getting overexposed."

"Oh. Who?" He looked up to challenge me.

"I don't know. Just some people. Do you ever worry about that?"

"I guess I'd worry if they stopped asking for me. Gus is pretty good about handling requests."

"You're having a good time, aren't you?"

"Jeez." He laughed. "I must be about the luckiest guy in the world. Can you imagine getting paid as much as I do for playing hockey? I've only had one real job in my life, you know. One summer I had to haul myself out of bed at six-thirty and go shovel gravel off a truck, for the highway department. I hated it. Later on, when I didn't want to practise hockey very hard, my dad would say, 'Do you want to get up every morning at six-thirty?' and I'd sure go and practise. You hear guys complain about the schedule and that. But for me this is just the perfect life. I'm having, well, you know, I just can't think of anything better than this."

"Are you ever embarrassed by the amount of money you're making?"

"No. Why should I be? There are guys making a lot more, and I'm supposed to be the biggest draw in hockey. It must be worth it for somebody."

"Pocklington says he wants to make you rich."

Wayne laughed. "Yeah. I don't know what that would be like. Right now, we're just trying to make sure the family will be okay." Most of the money he was earning was going into annuities for his siblings. It was something that Walter Gretzky had wanted from the beginning—although he had asked nothing for himself.

I told him I thought he looked tired.

"Do I?" he said. "I can't be too worn out. I'm gaining weight. I started the season at 166 and I'm 172 now. I've been gaining five pounds a year. Anyway, after lunch I'll go get some sleep." Making a confident U-turn, he pulled the Jeep into a parking spot near Walden's.

Wayne Gretzky is as unaffected by his fame as it is possible to be. He has kept in touch with boyhood friends, and still regularly calls the various families with whom he boarded on his way to maturity. He is diffident and polite with his elders and considerate of the children who crowd around him as if Edmonton were Hamelin and he the Pied Piper. Through the season I tailed around after him, he would amaze me off the ice nearly as often as he would on it. He has a capacity for making people feel welcome around him, of sharing even the pleasure of his accomplishments. When friends would ask me what he was like, for in the season of 1980–81 he became as celebrated as any Canadian alive, I would tell them, and they would be skeptical of my enthusiasm.

We are not good with our heroes, we Canadians. Starved for figures of national interest, we, or our media, seek out anyone who shows a flicker of fame, and shove them onto the nearest available pedestal. We leave them up there for a while, and then we begin to throw things at them. When Anne Murray first stepped out of the chorus of a maritime television program called *Singalong Jubilee* in the mid-1960s, magazines raced to put her on the cover. You could scarcely turn on a television set without seeing her pretty blonde head. Then came the rebound. The same writers and producers who had put her there in the first place began questioning their own judgement; a spate of articles appeared belittling her talents, and as suddenly as she had blossomed on television, she disappeared from it. Years later, as she kept plugging away, the media began honouring her again, when she (and to some extent they) had grown up. Her singing, which had brought her to our attention, was no better than it had been in 1965, although certainly no worse, but this time she seemed less open to the press and even—at least in Canada—television. When Pierre Trudeau came out of Quebec, he was a national saviour; when he turned out after all to be only a brilliant politician, the people who had once hailed him savaged him. Pierre Berton, among the best journalists the country has produced (in a nation without movie stars, journalists sometimes have to do as celebrities), has gone through as many cycles of adulation and vilification as he has written books. I expounded a bit of all this to Wayne over lunch, trying to prepare him for what would, inevitably, happen to him.

"Pierre Berton?" said Wayne Gretzky. "Is he a Canadian?"

And I remembered, as I would often forget, how young he was. In fact, the beginnings of an anti-Gretzky press had already begun to appear. In a December issue of the *Hockey News*, Stan Fischler had devoted most of a column to debunking him. "I wonder," Fischler had written, "whether Gretzky is suffering from the too-much-too-soon syndrome. I wonder why a kid who is slurping up money from Skalbania's mint [I think he meant Pocklington's mint] had to spend the summer of 1980 hyping himself and being hyped like there's no tomorrow. Couldn't Wealthy Wayne have relaxed, saved himself for the 80-game NHL push that was to come?" Wayne had been hurt by Fischler's comments; like so many other people who are written about, he took criticism much more seriously than praise. Even being teased in public by his friends would sometimes set him back. He worked hard at holding his poise, and he was uncomfortable when it was challenged. But rather than sulk, he had accepted an invitation to appear on television with Fischler on his next trip to New York; they had a frank talk. As the season wore on, Fischler, too, joined the cheerleaders.

At Walden's he ordered a quiche and a wine cooler with 7-UP (one of his sponsors) instead of ginger ale. The waitress brought a mix called Bubble-Up. "You're getting closer," he said, laughing. I told him I wanted to ask a favour of him. I said that to help with some work I had been doing about how he thought when he was on the ice, I would like him to make a tape for me. We would select, together, one of his goals on videotape, and he would look at it several times, dictating notes about what had been going through his mind as he made his moves. He responded with enthusiasm.

"When can you do it?" I said.

"Well, I'm going home right after lunch," he said. "And tomorrow after practice I've got some interviews I have to do. But I'll do it before the game. I'll get there early."

"Gretz," I protested, "there are a million things you do well. But one of them is not getting to places on time, never mind early. You've never been early for anything in your life."

"I'll do it," he said. "We'll choose the goal tomorrow morning and I'll do your tape before the game."

NORTHLANDS: The display begins early. The Oilers are playing St. Louis, who are still in first place, and have lost only three of their last twenty-seven games. Tonight could be another showdown between Liut and the Kid. In the first period, Gretzky is concentrating on setting other people up. At 2:25, he takes a pass from Paul Coffey in the middle of the St. Louis zone, fakes a shot, and sends a backhand pass to Callighen, who makes a smart move to score. At 12:30, on a power play, he is an intermediary again, this time between Siltanen and Kurri, who pops his twenty-first of the year. With Pat Price off for his usual first-period penalty, Bernie Federko scores for St. Louis; a minute later, Wayne Babych adds another, and the period ends 2–2.

I have my tape. Wayne did not arrive early at the rink, but when he did, he went right to the video machine, my tape recorder in hand, and sat down to work. This morning we chose one of the goals he had scored in the 9–1 romp over Montreal. This afternoon he played it through once at regular speed and once at slow motion, recording his comments. When Sather arrived in the coaches' room, where the video machine sits, he found Wayne still in street clothes. "We have a hockey game tonight," he said.

At 4:44 of the second period, he sets up Brackenbury, who is out to create some action. Brackenbury shoots, Liut saves, and Wayne pokes in the rebound. 3–2. At 7:03, Mark Messier, who is playing with the abandon we have expected from him all along, combines with Glenn Anderson to make it 4–2.

Stan Weir wins the opening face-off of the third period, and passes to B.J. MacDonald. B.J. drops it back for Paul Coffey. Coffey carries it to the blueline, feints twice, appears indecisive, and then swerves to his backhand to beat Liut again. 5–2.

And then the deluge starts. At 5:49, with Pat Price and Perry

Turnbull off for roughing, Gretzky picks up a loose puck, cuts to his left, and drifts a shot along the ice back across in front of Liut and into the furthermost corner of the net.

Bill Tuele, the Oilers' publicity man, begins an announcement in the press box that this is Gretzky's thirteenth goal and thirty-eighth scoring point in the last sixteen games, when ...

He does it again. Nine seconds after the unassisted goal, he takes a pass from Coffey and moves in alone toward the goal. Liut comes out. Gretzky moves to his left again and shoots with the same motion as for his last goal, but this time aims it instead for the closest corner, and Liut misses.

The crowd, without Krazy George, gives Gretzky a standing ovation. With the hat trick, Liut publicly acknowledges his loss of tonight's showdown, and takes himself out of the game. In his place comes Ed Staniowski, who has been doing yeoman service all year as his more celebrated colleague's back-up.

At 8:17, with the Oilers short-handed, Gretzky scores again. Stealing the puck, he cuts yet again to his left, and this time, as Staniowski tries to outguess him, he repeats the low, short, cross-corner shot that first beat Liut. There is no power to these shots that are going in, but they are as accurate as a surgeon's needle, and there is something about their timing that is keeping the goalies off-balance.

The pressbox is buzzing. The three consecutive goals are among the fastest ever scored by one player, although Jean Béliveau once got three in 44 seconds. The crowd stands again, this time mixing their applause with merriment. The Oilers are whipping the first-place Blues 8–2. Tuele is chattering statistics into the pressbox PA.

And then Gretzky does it again. He is standing in the attacking zone when Doug Hicks, taking a pass at the blueline from Siltanen, rips an apparently harmless slapshot in the vague direction of the goal. As the puck is about to whistle by Gretzky, he flicks his stick in the air and directs it into an open corner of the goal.

Are these the fastest *four* goals ever scored? No one in the pressbox knows. But the record he has tied—four in one period—goes back to 1934, when Busher Jackson did it for Toronto against a team called the

St. Louis Eagles. And what about Gretzky's five goals in one game? In all the NHL's history, only seventeen men have scored five goals in one game; one was Maurice Richard, one was Howie Morenz, and five of them were Joe Malone.

There is an unhurried grace to everything Gretzky does on the ice. Winding up for a slapshot, he will stop for an almost imperceptible moment at the top of his arc, like a golfer with a rhythmic swing. Often the difference between what Wayne does with the puck and what a less accomplished player would have done with it is simply a *pause*, as if, as time freezes, he is enjoying an extra handful of milliseconds. Time seems to slow down for him, and indeed, it may actually do so. Dr. Adrian R.M. Upton, the head neurologist at McMaster University in Hamilton, Ontario, has done some fascinating experiments with elite sprinters that suggest (the reservations about the work are that it is very hard to get a sufficiently large sample to test) that their motor neurons fire faster than those of mere mortals; the quicker their reaction times were to even simple tap tests, the faster they were liable to run. If this is true, it may account for much of what we see among the champions of a lot of sports. When Bjorn Borg, playing tennis as fast as any human can play it, appears to have the same control the rest of us would have in a casual Sunday morning knockup, it may well be that for him the pace *is* slower; his neurological motor is running with such efficiency that his response to his opponent's actions is as deliberate as ours would be at a more turgid pace. Dr. Upton, who has published several technical papers about his work with athletes, compares the difference between the neurological systems of the superstars and those of the rest of us to the difference between a highly tuned sports car and the family sedan. The sports car is simply capable of firing faster. When George Brett claims that he can see the stitches on a baseball spinning toward his hitting zone, he may be telling us something about his motoneurological capacity. Wayne, too, if Dr. Upton's suppositions are correct (and from neurological evidence alone he was able to predict the 1976 Olympic sprint victory of Hasely Crawford of Trinidad), is reacting to the situations of the games he plays as if it were being played for him in slow-motion film.

In the fall of 1980, John Jerome, a former editor of *Skiing* magazine, brought out a book called *The Sweet Spot in Time*, in which he examined much of the most recent exploration of athletic anatomy. His title was an echo of one of his central observations, that just as there is a physical "sweet spot" on a tennis racquet or a baseball bat, so is there, for the exceptional athlete, an almost immeasurably brief moment in time that is precisely right for performing his action. In explaining this thesis, Jerome cited a musical analogy. He wrote:

> I happened to hear violinist Isaac Stern discuss his art one night, and a jazz musician (whose name escapes me) the next. Both of these immensely talented individuals would sing wordless snatches—"dum dum ti dum," and so on—to illustrate points about their very different forms of music. I am not a musician, and could barely catch the significant differences they were demonstrating so effortlessly. I could discern, but I'm sure I did not fully comprehend, these differences—in emphasis and tone, but mostly just in timing. Each man would illustrate one way to play a phrase, then an alternate, varying the timing of the notes subtly without violating the form, changing in major ways the emotional content of the music without changing a note. I suddenly realized that for musicians—and for athletes—there must be a great deal more *room*, in effect, in the flow of time than there is for the rest of us.

Gretzky uses this room to insert an extra beat into his actions. In front of the net, eyeball to eyeball with the goaltender, he will ... hold the puck one ... extra instant, upsetting the anticipated rhythm of the game, extending his moment, as he did against Liut and Staniowski, the way a ballet dancer extends the time of his leap. He distorts time, and not always by slowing it down. Sometimes he will release the puck before he appears to be ready, threading a pass through a maze of players precisely to the blade of a teammate's stick, or finding a chink in a goaltender's armour and slipping the puck into it before the goaltender is ready to react. Because of hockey's speed, the differences between his actions and those of anyone else are invisible from the stands (as they often are, for that matter, from a position next to him on the ice). If he did not repeat their results so many times it would be possible to dismiss many of them as luck. If there is such a thing as sleight of body, he performs it.

On top of his neurological advantages, Gretzky seems to bring certain special qualities of metabolism to the game. With Gordie Howe, he shares an exceptional capacity to renew his energy resources quickly. Even when Howe had been out on the ice longer than any of his teammates he would be the first man on the bench to lift his head. Similarly with Gretzky, who often, as against St. Louis, or in the turnaround of the game in Toronto in November, has his best moments in the third period. When Dave Smith, a University of Alberta exercise physiologist who tested all the Oilers in the spring of 1980, first saw the results of Gretzky's test of recuperative abilities, he thought the machine had broken.

In the simplest terms, Gretzky is an exceptional pure athlete. Bearing out Dr. Upton's suppositions, he is a runner fast enough to compete at respectable levels. (His sister, Kim, was a provincial champion.) In baseball, he batted .492 for the Brantford CKCP Braves in the summer of 1980, and he was offered—seriously—a contract by the Toronto Blue Jays. But he is hardly a superman. Smith's tests also showed him to be the weakest of the Oilers. ("Am I stronger than my Mom?" he asked when he saw the results.)

His physical gifts, in any case, are not enough to account for Gretzky's supremacy. Each year in Canada alone, some hundred thousand boys totter out on the ice for their first game of organized hockey. By the time they reached puberty, about half of them will have dropped out. Some of those who leave will have done so for reasons that have little to do with ability: girls, school, their parents' unwillingness to continue the Saturday dawn drive to the rink, or simply because they don't like playing hockey. At about the age of twelve, however, those who are playing at the most competitive levels will include a high percentage of gifted and ambitious athletes. As with my own contemporaries from Galt, all that will keep most of them from professional hockey is that somehow they are not good enough. I asked various sports physiologists how many of, say, a hundred elite Canadian peewees they could eliminate from potential stardom in the NHL through physical measurement alone. The highest guess was twenty, which came at the University of Alberta; the lowest was none, which came at Waterloo, in Ontario. Given a certain minimum standard of size-for-age, in other words, and a general aptitude for sports, there is almost nothing in the human body—unless Dr. Upton's sophisticated tests are someday made universal—that can separate the potential million-dollar hockey player from the potential weekend racquetballer.

Much of the most interesting recent work in sports physiology has been done with muscle fibres. Researchers have taken painful biopsies of athletes to see what they could learn. While much of this work has been of value in understanding how muscles work—what fast-twitch fibres (the dark meat) do, as opposed to slow-twitch fibres—it has not been of much predictive use. "Little, if any, of the information has been of any value to the athletes studied," wrote the authors of an overview of their work in *The Physician and Sportsmedicine* in January 1980. For an even more exhaustive view of "Physiological and anthropometric characteristics of elite Canadian ice hockey players" published in *The Journal of Sports Medicine and Physical Fitness*, Drs. William Houston and Howard Green of the Waterloo department of kinesiology studied various characteristics of two teams of different levels. They concluded: "The absence of significant physiological differences emphasizes the fact that physiological criteria were not differentiating factors."

And yet by the time the hundred thousand boys who started hockey reach an eligible age, perhaps fifty of them—in a very good year—will win places in the NHL, making the odds against a young hockey player reaching the pinnacle of that profession higher than they are against a random student in grade one becoming a university teacher. What has winnowed them out, finally, is not their ability but the way they are able to apply it, to put together the various small components of hockey that are so painstakingly measured on the Oilers' scouting chart. As Drs. Houston and Green concluded: "In the absence of a fundamental understanding of the physiological systems involved, coaches tend to differentiate between hockey players on that aspect with which they are most familiar, skill."

Even skill, however, is not a sufficient standard by which to measure

Gretzky's mastery. At many of the skating techniques the Oilers' scouts would rate, he would be, perhaps, seven out of nine; at shooting less. And yet scrawled across his reports are only the words "can't miss." What separates him from his peers in the end, the quality that has led him to the very point of the pyramid, may well have nothing to do with physical characteristics at all, but instead be a matter of perception, not so much of what he sees—he does not have exceptional vision—but of *how* he sees it and how he absorbs it. Here, some work in fields that at first glance seem a long way from hockey yield some enlightening clues.

Much of this work is recent, but it is an extension of experiments carried out in the late 1930s by the Dutch psychologist Adrian de Groot. De Groot worked with chess players, whom he divided into groups according to their level of play: grandmasters, experts, and club players. In one experiment he had each player look for a limited time at a number of chess pieces arranged on a board in a fairly complex middle-game position. Then he asked his subjects to reconstruct that position. Perhaps not surprisingly, the grandmasters did much better than the experts, and the experts much better than the club players. Then, however, de Groot exposed all three groups to yet another set of positions, only this time the pieces were arranged not in game situations but at random. This time, there was no measurable difference in the participants' ability to recall the arrangement. What the better players had remembered, in other words, was not so much the positions of the chess pieces but the overall situations. Later experiments confirmed these findings; the more highly gifted the chess player was, the more likely he was to see on a board not individual pieces, but the combinations they formed, the forces in play. In the 1970s, Neil Charness, a professor of psychology at the University of Waterloo, himself a chess player who had carried on work in the de Groot tradition, extended these explorations to the field of bridge. Charness found—to oversimplify—that expert bridge players could remember bridge hands much better than beginners, but at remembering combinations of cards that had no relationship to bridge they were no better at all. And in a recent PhD thesis, an Ontario psychologist named Lynne Beal showed that the same principle held for music: accomplished musicians could recall and repeat sets of chords better than non-accomplished musicians could, but when notes were assembled in random clusters, the experts fared no better than their less well-trained partners in the experiment.

The more we are trained in a given field, then, the more we tend to understand that field in combinations of familiar information, or what the psychologists call "chunks." A chunk, to use one of Neil Charness's examples, might be a telephone number. If you are familiar with a telephone number—your own—you can summon it up at will. If you're learning a new one, you will stumble over it as you begin to dial. Given two new numbers at once, you will almost certainly get them confused. This is the difference between short-term memory and long-term memory. Short term is what you pick up and use instantly. Long term is what has become part of your bank account of information. When a *chunk* of information becomes part of your long-term memory, it can be summoned up as a single piece. The chess player can react to a combination he has seen before, and expert chess players carry around as many as 50,000 combinations in their memory bank. A concert pianist tends to practise longer phrases from his musical repertoire, and recall them as longer phrases, than a Sunday thumper.

In the 1970s a sociologist named David Sudnow set out to teach himself to play jazz piano like a professional. When he had progressed to the state he was happy with, he wrote a book called *Ways of the Hand.* At the beginning of his experiments, Sudnow wrote: "I wrote down the names of the notes under each finger, then went home and duplicated the songs. I gained a little repertoire of tunes this way, but I didn't know what I was doing." At the end, he concluded, he had absorbed a new language. "I learned this language through five years of overhearing it spoken. I had come to learn it in a terrain ... of hands and keyboard whose respective surfaces had become known as the respective surfaces of my tongue and teeth and palate are known to each other."

In 1965, the American journalist John McPhee set out to discover some of the secrets that at the time appeared to set the basketball player Bill Bradley (now a u.s. senator) as far apart from his peers as Gretzky now appears from his. McPhee found that Bradley, who, like Wayne, had an impressive ability to articulate his own performance, had an

almost mystical sense of the shape and situation of the basketball
court. McPhee wrote:

> All shots in basketball are supposed to have names—the set, the
> hook, the layup, the jump shot, and so on—and one weekend last
> July, while Bradley was in Princeton working on his senior thesis
> and putting in some time in the Princeton gymnasium to keep
> himself in form for the Olympics, I asked him what he called his
> over-the-shoulder shot. He said he had never heard a name for it,
> but that he had seen Oscar Robertson, of the Cincinnati Royals,
> and Jerry West, of the Los Angeles Lakers, do it, and had worked
> it out for himself. He went on to say that it is a much simpler shot
> than it appears to be and, to illustrate, he tossed the ball over his
> shoulder and into the basket while he was talking and looking me
> in the eye. I retrieved the ball and handed it back to him. "When
> you have played basketball for awhile, you don't need to look at the
> basket for awhile when you are in close like this," he said, throw-
> ing it over his shoulder again and right through the hoop. "You
> develop a sense of where you are."

In 1980, Fran Allard, a colleague of Neil Charness's at Waterloo,
did some tests whose results seem to bring together both the conclu-
sions of the work done on chess, bridge, and music, and the "court
sense"—a phrase Allard used in the publication of her work—that
Bill Bradley had exhibited for McPhee. First, Allard exposed basketball
players of various levels of accomplishment to photographs of basketball situations that were both structured and unstructured—real game
positions or arbitrary ones. As with the more exotic disciplines, she
found the better the basketball player the more likely he was to be able
to recall a real situation; with the unstructured positions there was no
difference. Elite basketball players, Allard and her fellows wrote in *The
Journal of Sports Psychology*, "as do chess and bridge players, encode structured information more deeply."

With volleyball players, however, Allard at first seemed to have
found an exception. Exposed for a short time to slides of players on a

volleyball court, expert players seemed no better able than non-players to answer questions about whether or not there was a ball in the picture. Puzzled, Allard and her partner, Janet Starkes of McMaster, began running the same test with a timer. Now, there was a difference. The good players were able to figure out the situation more *quickly* than the rest of their group. The principle had held.

Elite athletes, then, like chess masters or artists of the jazz piano, may not so much think differently as perceive differently. Moreover, because they can quickly recall chunks of information from their long-term memories, they can react to those perceptions more efficiently. What Gretzky perceives on a hockey rink is, in a curious way, more simple than what a less accomplished player perceives. He sees not so much a set of moving players as a number of situations—chunks. Moving in on the Montreal blueline, as he was able to recall while he watched a videotape of himself, he was aware of the position of all the other players on the ice. The pattern they formed was, to him, one fact, and he reacted to that fact. When he sends a pass to what to the rest of us appears an empty space on the ice, and when a teammate magically appears in that space to collect the puck, he has in reality simply summoned up from his bank account of knowledge the fact that in a particular situation, someone is likely to be in a particular spot, and if he is not there now he will be there presently.

The corollary, of course, is that Gretzky has seen all these situations before, and that what we take to be creative genius is in fact a reaction to a situation that he has stored in his brain as deeply and firmly as his own telephone number. When I put this possibility to him, he agreed.

"Absolutely," he said. "That's a hundred percent right. It's all practice. I got it from my dad. Nine out of ten people think it's instinct, and it isn't. Nobody would ever say a doctor had learned his profession by instinct; yet in my own way I've put in almost as much time studying hockey as a medical student puts in studying medicine."

Even before he got on skates, Wayne seemed to have an almost spiritual attraction to hockey. Once, when Walter and Phyllis were both working,

Wayne, not yet two, was staying with his grandparents at their home on the Nith River. His grandmother had a Saturday afternoon hockey game on television. Wayne imitated the players, sliding back and forth on the linoleum. When the game was over, he cried, thinking his grandmother had turned it off to punish him.

He started skating before he was three years old; there are films of him on the ice, taken by his father, when he was two and a half. Walter built a rink in the backyard. He couldn't flood it with a hose; a hose might have made it too lumpy. He got out his lawn sprinkler, and laid on coat after coat. Every night, when he got home from his job as a technician with the telephone company, he would turn on the sprinkler and lay down another smooth coat. One year, the sprinkler broke, and Walter asked Phyllis to get him another one. When she got home from the store, she told him that was the last time for that. The clerks had thought she was crazy, buying a lawn sprinkler in February.

Walter had played Junior B himself, but he had been too small, they said, to make it to the pros. He was determined to give his children every chance. Wayne's first skates were single-bladed, not the bobskates so many kids wasted time on. When Walter couldn't find a hockey stick small enough for Wayne, he bought the lightest he could find, then shaved it down with a plane. Even today, the Titan stick Wayne uses is shaved thin.

Walter had a lot of ideas. He got some tin cans, and Wayne would skate patterns through them. He'd set sticks down on the ice and Wayne would hop over them while Walter sent him passes. There were balance drills and target shooting. Walter would put targets up on the net he had bought for the backyard rink, and Wayne would fire at them for hours, going in for supper and coming back out again under the lights Walter strung, and practising again until bedtime. Walter put a picnic table on edge so that it blocked all but the outer edges of the net. Wayne would shoot for the corners.

"When the Russians came over here in 1972 and '73," Wayne once said, "people said, 'Wow, this is something incredible.' Not to me it wasn't. I'd been doing those drills since I was three years old. My dad was very smart."

When Wayne was five, Walter drove him all around the Brantford area, looking for an organized team that would take him. No one would let him play until he was six. Walter coached him anyway, and when Wayne was finally old enough, Walter took over his team.

"People say you can't teach anticipation," Walter says now. "I'm not so sure. I used to get them out on the ice and I'd shoot the puck down the boards toward a corner and I'd say, 'Chase that.' Well, they'd all go right into the end after it. Then I'd say, 'Wait, watch me.' I'd shoot it in again, and let it roll around the net. Instead of following it around the boards, I'd cut across to where it was rolling. 'There,' I'd say. 'You've got to know where it's *going* to go.'"

The concentration, the dedication, has never relaxed. From training camp on, none of the Oilers, not even the labouring Brackenbury, practised skills with more single-mindedness than Gretzky. At training camp, long after everyone else had headed for the showers, he would still be out on the ice. Sometimes, he would lay a stick down beside the net and take a bucket of pucks behind it, and practise flipping them just high enough to clear the stick and lie in the goal-crease. Often Glenn Anderson would work on this drill with him. But sometimes Wayne would just stand alone and shoot at a crossbar or a goalpost. The trick he does in the 7-UP commercial—the one that he pretends to let his little brother, Keith, teach him—is one he does at practice all the time, hoisting a puck in the air with the blade of his stick and then bouncing it as long as he can. In the summers, when he cannot skate, he still works for hours in his driveway, honing his stick-handling skills or trying to figure out, as he did in the summer of 1980, what he was doing wrong on breakaways.

The practice alone, of course, has not made him what he is, nor even the early beginnings. Although all the superstars whose boyhood stories we know, from Morenz to Orr, started skating at amazingly early ages, so did millions of other boys who never made it past peewee. It is a combination of things, the neurology, the metabolism, the father, the coaches, the Kid's own determination to succeed, and the gift of mind he has. In various permutations, these elements have combined in modern hockey's brief history to give us all our superstars, and if Gretzky is unique in the pantheon it is in his knack of articulating his skills. Today, the ability he showed as a young teenager to recreate game situations has become uncanny. There is scarcely a goal he has scored, or a chance he has missed, which, if asked, he cannot recreate in detail, setting each teammate and opponent into place with the precision of a chess master replaying a game. The joy of it all is that we have found him, that the game is so much a part of our lives that when a Wayne Gretzky is born we will find him. The sorrow is that there may also be Wayne Gretzkys of the piano or the paintbrush who, because we expose our young to hockey so much more than to the arts, we will never know about.

In the dressing room after the St. Louis game, the Oilers crowded around a television set. The Kid had gone down to the ITV studio under the stands, to accept his praises as the game's star, and to look at replays of his goals. The other players were shaking their heads in wonder. "Jeez," they were saying. "Look at *that*. How did he ever put it *there?*"

I remembered I was supposed to appear on the post-game show myself. I left the dressing room and headed for the studio. Along the barriers that separate the paying customers from the participants and the press, fans were lined up four and five deep, waiting to catch a glimpse of Gretzky as he went back to shower. As I approached the studio, he emerged, still in skates and uniform. He was keeping his head down, trying to avoid the eye contact with his fans that would have kept him there, acknowledging their applause. As we passed, I reached out to touch his arm—a gesture of congratulation.

"Was the tape I made okay?" he asked.

# 15

*"Besides, Glen is my best friend"*

Carol MacDonald answered the phone in the still unfinished kitchen of the house she and B.J. were renovating in Edmonton's west end.

"MacDonald's Trading Post," she said.

"Has B.J. gone already?" I asked.

"He left about three o'clock."

Carol MacDonald has a seductive upper-class drawl that makes her, as Curt Brackenbury says, "sound half-ripped all the time." Almost everyone—including B.J.—calls her Squawk. It is sometimes difficult to tell what mood she is in. On the phone, she sounded either angry or happy.

"The Canucks are playing in Calgary tonight," she said, "and Blair went down to join them. He'll be home tonight. Or maybe if he goes out with the boys he'll stay there. I guess it depends on how they do."

"That didn't give him much time," I said.

"No. He found out just after noon. Twelve was the deadline. Sather called at ten after. We'd been expecting it, and when Blair answered I could hear him say, 'So you got it in just under the deadline.'"

This was the evening of March 10, the last day for making deals in the NHL. Sather had been busy. For days he had been closeted in his office, constantly on the phone, trying one combination here, another there. Even at home he had made a steady stream of long-distance calls.

On the evening before the deadline he had not left the phone between five o'clock and midnight. With both Buffalo and Toronto he had been on the verge of closing, but both deals had fallen through at the last moment. Scotty Bowman had called from Buffalo one morning at four o'clock Edmonton time, but that deal hadn't worked out either. Bowman, like everyone else, still wanted the kids, and Sather wasn't going to give any away.

Now, he was pleased with the complex package he had worked out. Each part had depended on another part. B.J. had gone to Vancouver, which needed some scoring punch, but the man the Canucks had given in return, a defenceman named Garry Lariviere, had never played for Vancouver; for four years he'd been a Quebec Nordique. Vancouver had picked him up just before the deadline for one of their own defencemen, Mario Marois. A few minutes after Lariviere had been told by Quebec that he was going to Vancouver, he was told no, he wasn't, he was going to Edmonton. The deal had suited all three teams. For Quebec's purposes, Marois, as well as being a solid hockey player, was also legitimately a French Canadian, born in Ancienne Lorette and having played his junior with Kevin Lowe's old Remparts. Lariviere, in spite of his name, was ersatz, having been born in St. Catharines, Ontario.

Throughout the negotiations among the three teams, everyone had been wary of everyone else, and among Sather's phone calls were a number that had helped to smooth the deal between the Nordiques and the Canucks. Now, when he talked about the tripartite agreement, Sather seemed almost as happy about one subsidiary clause as he was about the exchange of the regulars. To Vancouver, he had also dealt the rights for a young Swedish amateur, Lars-Eric Peterson, whom the Oilers had drafted a year earlier. In return, he had acquired those of Ken Berry, whom the Canucks had chosen from the Canadian Olympic team but with whom they had been unable to sign a contract. Berry, as Sather knew, was an old friend of the Oilers' own ex-Olympian, Glenn Anderson. Berry and Anderson had played as linemates from their pee-wee days, and had attended the University of Denver together before leaving to play at Lake Placid. While Anderson, in spite of his Morkian ways, was popular with his professional teammates—he had even begun to wear ties on the road—he was still, essentially, a lone ranger. Sather was confident that Berry would want to be his Tonto and would sign a minor-league contract with Edmonton to prove it; by next year he would be an Oiler.

The Vancouver-Quebec deal alone, however, would have left Sather short of an immediately useful forward and with more defencemen than he could comfortably use. To round out his package, he had made a swap with the Pittsburgh Penguins. From Pittsburgh, he acquired Pat Hughes, a right-winger who had grown up in Calgary and attended the University of Michigan. Hughes had originally been drafted by Montreal, but, not having been able to crack the Canadiens' lineup, had been traded to Pittsburgh in 1979; although he was only two years younger than MacDonald, Hughes had the kind of untapped potential that appealed the Sather. He was a scrapper, but he could score goals. Sather still liked early draft choices whom other people had been disappointed in.

To acquire Hughes, Sather gave up Pat Price. Price was still capable of fulfilling his early promise, Sather knew (for all his experience, Price was still two weeks short of his twenty-sixth birthday), but overall, he decided, Price had become a liability to the club. His first period penalties were more than an annoyance; they were stopping the team's early momentum in too many games. And his talk had become more than Sather thought the team could bear. On the ice, Price continually chattered at Coffey. Coffey was still lapsing into periods of tension, and Sather was convinced Price's habit of over-coaching was an important reason, even though both Coffey and Kevin Lowe, last year's rookie, felt they had learned from him. Lariviere had a reputation as a stay-at-home defenceman who would provide a solid anchor for Coffey, and allow the rookie to take off on the offensive forays that had been his hallmark as a junior. Also, Sather had noticed in the Oilers' games against Quebec, Lariviere kept his mouth shut on the ice.

Before the deadline, Sather made one more deal. Late in February, Stan Weir had injured his wrist in a game against Los Angeles and was still absent from the lineup in March. The Oilers missed his poise and defensive skills at centre. To replace them, Sather picked up the veteran

Garry Unger from Los Angeles. The 1980–81 season was Unger's fourteenth in the NHL, and Edmonton's blue and gold would be his fifth
set of team colours, but in fact he was coming home; he had been born
in Edmonton and had married a girl from Calgary. He had broken in
with Toronto in 1967, been quickly traded to Detroit (to the dismay
of Toronto fans, who liked his style) and then on to St. Louis, where
he settled in comfortably for eight seasons. He bought some farmland
near St. Louis and went into the cattle business. A non-smoker and
non-drinker, he had continued to invest his salary in his business, and,
now in his mid-thirties, was a prosperous businessman. As a youngster,
Unger had been one of the first professional hockey players to wear his
hair long, and Detroit had ordered him to go to a barber. Later he wore
one of the NHL's first beards, which, perhaps in deference to the youth
of his new teammates, he shaved off before leaving for Edmonton. Now,
he confined his penchant for attracting attention to his wardrobe, which
included a number of gaudily coloured silk shirts, some feathered cowboy hats, and a poncho. He was a practising Christian.

Partly because of his clean living, no doubt, Unger had run
up the longest uninterrupted string of unmissed games in NHL history—914—before he was finally benched by the team to which St.
Louis traded him, Atlanta. He had actually been dressed for what
would have been his 915th and had sat patiently on the Atlanta bench,
awaiting a summons to the ice from the Flames' coach, Al MacNeil.
It did not come. As the game drew to a close, and with the Flames
comfortably ahead, Unger's teammates, conscious of his record, began
taking themselves off and gesturing to Unger, but MacNeil kept shaking his head. Finally, with Atlanta two men short because of voluntary
withdrawals, Unger had risen to leap over the boards. From behind,
MacNeil grabbed his sweater to restrain him, and the string was
ended. MacNeil's explanation was that Unger had for some time been
more aware of extending his record than of playing hockey, and was
so anxious to avoid an injury that he had been playing tentatively. But
Unger had been hurt by the decision, and was happy to be traded to
Los Angeles. Now, he was even happier to come home to Edmonton,
and to rejoin Sather, who had briefly been a teammate in St. Louis. Los

Angeles, for their part, had wanted to make way for two veterans they had acquired from Buffalo, and were so willing to clear Unger away that they had agreed to continue to pay part of his salary, which was close to $200,000 a year.

Everyone was happy with the results of the wheeling and dealing. For both Pat Price and Pat Hughes it would mean a fresh start after a season that had not been going well. Hughes had felt as underused in Pittsburgh as Price had felt frustrated in Edmonton. When Price heard he had been traded, he cheerfully went downtown and gave the first derelict he encountered his $150 ticket to a celebrity dinner the Oilers were holding that evening. For Garry Lariviere, the move would be to an environment in which he felt more comfortable. Quebec City in 1981 had not been a good place to have a French name and an English background. Among other things, he would now be rejoining his old friend Brackenbury.

For the MacDonald family, the transfer would be a traumatic one. As Carol explained on the phone, Blair had been building up some solid business contacts in Edmonton, where, as captain, he had cut a considerable swath. The Canucks, however, were a good organization, whose average age—twenty-seven years and six months—was much closer to B.J.'s own. He had friends there, including Soupy Campbell, whose dismissal from the Oilers MacDonald had been among the first to protest.

"I wanted him to be traded earlier," Carol now said on the phone. "Vancouver will be a good place to live, even though I'll hate to sell this house. And at least we won't have to put up with the crap about age any more."

The Oilers had not been playing well. Of the ten games that followed Gretzky's triumphant night against St. Louis, they had won only three, including, as was their habit, one upset—a 6–2 victory over Philadelphia—and one loss of a game they ought certainly to have won; Colorado beat them 3–1. Gretzky had continued his brilliance, and by the day of the trades was eighteen points ahead of the scoring pack. By now, in fact, it was entirely possible that he could break Phil Esposito's record for points in a single season, 152, and perhaps even Orr's for assists, 102. He had 131 points, of which 82 were assists, with thirteen games left to play.

All the young players were improving steadily. Coffey was now an important part of the team, a fully qualified NHLer who had lived up to his shave. Anderson was soaring, and seemed ready on any night to burst into a scoring spree. Messier was playing with dedication and energy. And Kurri, his English improving day by day, was fitting in well with Gretzky.

Still, there was something missing. On the day of the trading deadline, the Oilers were tied with Toronto for sixteenth place, by no means assured of a playoff spot. And for the time being, not all the trades looked as good as they ought to have. At his last practice in Pittsburgh, Pat Hughes had sprained his back. If the injury had occurred before the trade had been consummated, he would have been returnable, damaged goods. As it was, the Oilers were now without B.J. and without the man Sather had obviously been counting on to replace him. Playing with their new lineup for the first time, they were shut out by the Rangers, 5–0.

The next day, a story spread across the wire services that ruffled a few feathers around the Oilers. Pocklington, off to Calgary for a speaking engagement on the benefits of positive thinking, had been asked what he thought of Hugh Campbell, the coach of the Edmonton Eskimos, the city's highly successful football team. Pocklington said he was an admirer of Campbell's and, given a chance, would "hire him in a second." What about Sather? he was asked. He replied that while Sather had made progress, "dealing with people [was] not his strong suit." By the time the story spread into the east, it had turned into a job offer. I phoned Sather.

"Oh, for Chrissake," he said. He was laughing as he said it, but there was anger in his voice too. "Damn Terry Jones."

Jones, a columnist with the Edmonton *Journal*, had had a running feud with Sather for some time. A clever writer and a hardworking reporter, he was nevertheless not as close to the Oilers as the two regular beat men, Jim Matheson of his own paper and Dick Chubey of the *Sun*.

Both Matheson and Chubey were knowledgeable hockey men, and not above criticizing either the team's play or the decisions of its management. Chubey, in particular, a heavy-set gruff westerner, was a fan of a rougher hockey than the Oilers sometimes played—he was a close friend and ardent supporter of his fellow westerner Pat Price—and would sometimes let his dissatisfaction with the way things were going show in his copy, although Matheson, the son of the venerable Jack Matheson, matched him phrase for phrase in integrity. Matheson and Chubey, however, lived their daily lives on the periphery of the team and were partisan to the men they had breakfast with every day. From his columnist's perch, Jones was more likely to launch thunderbolts, especially at Sather.

This network of relationships is a common situation in professional sport. Sports writers almost always know more about their subjects than, say, most drama critics know about drama, but, unlike their colleagues on the theatre page, they watch the subjects of their work read their notices. Some reporters are bothered by this closeness, and few hockey men realize how lucky they are with its results. Hockey executives would prefer (as who would not?) to have each day's reports filed by their own publicity departments. Once, when a television crew, anxious to show some of the Oilers' off-ice lives, talked Hicks and Lumley into being interviewed in a bar, Sather simply told their producer that if he ran that part of his film, he would be in danger of losing his right to broadcast the Oilers' games; the film was not aired.

Sather disliked Jones intensely. Although he allowed him into the dressing room—by the protocol of the NHL he would have had a hard time doing anything else—he frequently ignored him. The story about Hugh Campbell, which had gained its widest circulation in a Jones column in the *Journal*, drove a nail into his attitude.

"I've already talked to Peter," Sather said on the phone. "And everything's cleared up. He's apologized to me and he's apologized to Annie. He's told us both there was nothing to it, but I think Annie's still mad. Peter's really upset. Give him a call," he said. "You might cheer him up."

I dialled Patrician Investments. As usual, Pocklington took his own call.

"What are you trying to do, get into the football business?" I said. There were rumours that Skalbania was buying into the Alouettes.

"The CFL," he said, "has a future about as long as my you-know-what."

"Well, what's this Campbell stuff?"

"Oh, for Chrissake," he said. "I've been getting calls from all over North America. Of course I'd hire Hugh Campbell if I could. Wouldn't you? He's won four Grey Cups in a row. But that remark was taken all out of context. How could I offer Campbell a job? He's not a hockey man. Besides, Glen is my best friend. You know that. Anyway, we're really going to start to win now. These new guys are just what we needed."

Two nights later, the Oilers tied Calgary, 3–3, and the night after that, they did start to win, beating Pat Price and his new teammates from Pittsburgh 7–6 and following it up with a 5–3 victory over Minnesota. Against Minnesota, Gretzky collected four assists, tying him with Bobby Clarke for the greatest number ever achieved by a centre, and bringing him within even closer range of Esposito and Orr.

But in the Oilers' minds, Gretzky's accomplishment was far overshadowed by an event that, taken in the context of what had gone before, was the most devastating of the season. Eddie Mio broke his hand. During the warm-up before the Minnesota game, Peter Driscoll fired a shot that appeared to be heading for Mio's shoulder. Mio raised his stick hand. Unexpectedly, the puck dipped. With unhappy accuracy, it flew under the rigid padding, cracking into the second finger and breaking it just below the knuckle. Mio would be out for the season. Since Low's departure in December, Mio had become the Oilers' undisputed number-one goaltender. He had held his goals-against average to a big-league 3.87. He had been in goal for sixteen wins and nine ties. Even in the games the Oilers had lost, he had kept them close. Now, the recycled Gary Edwards would move up to number one. As a backup, Sather turned once again to the unproven Andy Moog.

BOSTON GARDEN, BOSTON, MASSACHUSETTS, MONDAY, MARCH 23: Everything is old here. From the rafters of this rickety arena, with an ice surface so small the burly Bruins have been able to confine the opposition to head-knocking range for more than fifty years, hang the banners honouring their retired sweater-numbers: Eddie Shore's 2, Orr's 4, Dit Clapper's 5, Johnny Bucyk's 9, Milt Schmidt's 15, and Lionel Hitchman's 3. Lionel Hitchman? Even Billy Harris doesn't know who he was, although he guesses, correctly, a defenceman of the early Shore era. This year's edition of the team has the highest average age in the NHL: nearly twenty-eight. Their wives have just brought out a cookbook, called *What's Bruin*, and tonight they hover at tables around the Garden, selling copies. Compared to the Oilers' young women, they look like suburban matrons—although, being hockey wives, they are exceptionally attractive ones. At least one of them could be Vickie Moss's mother.

The new Oiler players still seem vaguely out of place in the dressing room. Garry Unger says he's having trouble keeping the Finns apart and "there seem to be a lot of guys named Dave." There are, too—Hunter, Lumley, and Semenko, although to us oldtimers they are Hunts, Lummer, and Sammy, or Semenk. Unger should talk; besides him, the Oilers now have Gary Edwards and Garry Lariviere, whom Unger today called Lavallee. Most out of place still is Andy Moog. Although he turned twenty-one last month, Moog looks younger than any of the kids. With his shirt off he is the least athletic-looking athlete I have ever seen, resembling not so much a Grecian statue as the Pillsbury Doughboy. He is chubby and, I'm afraid, kind of cute. But, with his calm, intelligent manner he will no doubt make a place for himself when he gets more playing time.

He is getting some tonight. In the first period, he looks solid, stopping all fourteen of the Bruins' shots. But the Bruins are all over the Oilers, holding them to six shots on Rogie Vachon. The period ends scoreless, but in the second Boston makes it 3–0 before Edmonton even gets a good chance. None of the goals is Moog's fault. Although the Oilers struggle back to make it 3–2, there does not seem to be much hope. Gretzky assists on both Edmonton goals, one by Anderson, one by Kurri. He had 145 points coming into tonight's game, including 93 assists. Tonight makes him 147 and 95. Both Esposito's and Orr's records are in striking range, and he has moved himself into that position in the arena in which Esposito and Orr played so many of their games. Everyone is watching him closing in on history, and counting him down. The pressbox is full. Tomorrow morning he is due on the *Today* show, and ABC is following him with a camera crew. No one anywhere is watching him more closely than Steve Kasper, a rookie the Bruins have designated as his shadow. Kasper is almost inside the Kid's suspenders—we may see him on the *Today* show too—but he is playing cleanly. At 18:37, Boston scores again, and in the third period, they rap in three more to win 7–2. The Oilers now have six games left and are tied with Toronto for the last playoff spot, with Washington only a point behind. They'll *have* to start winning now—preferably Wednesday night in Hartford.

Before they leave for Connecticut, Gerry Cheevers, one of the all-time great goaltenders, who now coaches Boston, makes a rare gesture of sportsmanship. He visits the Oilers' dressing room to compliment Moog. He also tells Sather that Moog's stick looks too short, and offers one of his own models for Moog to try.

**16**

*"He never did get used to the world outside hockey"*

Hartford, where the Oilers would now continue their perilous progress toward a playoff berth, had a special meaning for Wayne Gretzky in the spring of 1981. There, he would continue his quest for an important place in the record books in front of the man who still dominated those books, and who had meant so much to Gretzky all his hockey life: Gordie Howe.

Hartford was now Howe's home. He had been lured out of retirement in 1973 by the Houston Aeros of the WHA, who had had the ingenious idea of offering a contract not only to him, but to his two sons, Mark and Marty, and to his wife, Colleen, as well (Colleen agreed to act as an officer of the club). After four years in Houston, the Howes had seen that franchise collapse, and had moved, still as a unit, to Connecticut. For two years, Gordie had helped to keep the New England Whalers alive in the WHA. During those years he had become known as an athletic phenomenon that transcended hockey. No matter how much younger the average age of the game's younger players, he had managed to hold his own grey head up among them, becoming only toward the end what he himself called "poetry in slow motion," and continuing to score goals and rack up assists, not at his old rate, but at one that would have done many other players proud.

When New England became the Hartford Whalers of the NHL, the league re-acquired its own most enduring legend, and Howe, in the year that he turned fifty-two, still found enough energy in his remarkable body to score fifteen goals and twenty-six assists. When he finally retired in the spring of 1980, his records loomed like wonders of the world: 1,767 games played in the NHL over twenty-six years (with an eight-year gap between the twenty-fifth and twenty-sixth); 419 in the WHA; 2,358 scoring points in both leagues, with more in the playoffs—more of everything than anyone had ever dreamed of. But Howe, an intense family man, had always seemed at least as proud of playing with his sons as he was of his longevity and the accompanying numbers. When the Whalers sent his younger son, Marty, down to their minor-league affiliate in Springfield, Massachusetts, Howe was even more bitter than he had been over the shabby treatment he had received from his old NHL team in Detroit, who had given him an office job, but who, he once said, had treated him like a mushroom—"every once in a while they open the door of my office and throw in some crap." Speaking at a dinner the citizens of Hartford put on just before the Oilers arrived, he had been warm and funny, but when it came time for him to say he wished "the other fellow"—Marty—could have been there, he wept.

Gordie Howe was not the only retired superstar of hockey to be unhappy with his fate in the season of 1980–81, which was a notable one for underlining what has happened to some of the men who once dominated the game. The most public troubles were those of Bobby Hull, whose disastrous divorce proceedings with his wife Joanne were the subject of gossip and comment throughout the league. The hearings were held in Winnipeg, where the press treated them with the gleeful attention it had usually reserved for Bobby's escapades on ice. One irate Sunday school teacher wrote to Murray Burt, the editor of the Winnipeg *Free Press*, about the inordinate display of the Hulls' dirty laundry: "I'm not even a Bobby Hull fan, so I can imagine how incensed are those of your readers who are." Burt replied, in part: "Fans were happy and interested to see Hull pictured at Portage and Main when he arrived in Winnipeg and signed a $1 million contract. They may not be as happy, but they are certainly interested, to see their hero must face the anguish and tribulation that many mere mortals undergo."

Burt was right, but the Hulls' anguish and tribulations seemed more severe than most mortals suffered outside soap operas. As the hearings dragged on, with each charging the other with adultery, with each claiming the other was in contempt of court, with Bobby firing his lawyer in the courtroom and trying to conduct his own case, with their squabbles about money spattered across the front pages, the Hulls became, for a while at least, the most talked about Canadian couple since Pierre and Margaret Trudeau.

Some of the exchanges in court made telling points about the way Hull had been regarded, and what was happening to him now. On one occasion he questioned Michael Gobuty, his friend and business partner in both the Winnipeg Jets, part of whose shares Hull had acquired, and in Victorian Leather, some of whose coats Hull used to model.

HULL: Is it not true to assume that you made a statement that I am invaluable to your business because you and I are such good friends?

GOBUTY: I think I said you were valuable because of what you are. I think you were invaluable to the hockey club and the city of Winnipeg because of what you are.

HULL: If I was so valuable then why have you lost the Sears account?

GOBUTY: Well, to be truthful, 'cause you stopped playing hockey and your name was tarnished with some of the things that are transpiring today.

On another occasion, Hull was crossexamining Joanne with such zeal that Joanne's lawyer, a bearded Winnipegger named Arthur Rich, objected.

"He doesn't know any tactics other than those in the corners of the hockey rink," Rich said.

"And he's good at those tactics," interjected Mr. Justice Louis Deniset.

In October, Deniset ruled that Hull would have to pay Joanne sums that totalled close to $600,000. Hull said he didn't have anything like that amount of money, and prepared to launch an appeal.

Not long after the judgement was announced, I called Hull in Picton, Ontario, where he was living not far from the village where he had spent his boyhood. On the phone, he was dispirited and sour, although there was enough magnetism still in his voice to be compelling. He sounded as down as he had once been up. He was bitter about Joanne, and called her a vile name—"although I was worse," he said. The real villains were the courts. "I don't know how anyone could hand someone $600,000 of someone else's money," he said.

All of his luck had seemed to turn bad at the same time. The woman with whom he had been living since he and Joanne had separated had been in a terrible car accident in the United States—"all because of the goddamn law that allows goddamn Mexicans to drive seventy-five miles an hour," he said. According to stories I had heard around the league, he had been looking after her with loving care; in the days of her worst debilitation he had carried her to the bathroom and had brushed her teeth for her. Since this went against his image as a swashbuckling and self-centred man, I asked him about it. "Anyone who is surprised by the way I'm treating her just doesn't know me," he said. I asked if I could come to Picton to visit. He said he'd prefer that I didn't.

Shortly after, I went to see Joanne in Vancouver, where she had taken up residence. She had chosen Vancouver, she said, because their daughter ("who has Bobby's legs") was a promising figure skater, and the best instruction was on the west coast. To make financial ends meet, Joanne was trying —with little success when I visited her—to sell insurance. She is an attractive, poised woman with frosted hair and a fashionable look. She had been a figure skater herself, a professional, when she met Bobby. She was more comfortable discussing her marriage than I had expected. There was a tough streak in her. She was bitter about the financial affairs. "I still haven't had any money from him," she said. But she seemed to have an understanding of what had happened to her former husband and almost a sympathy for him, although there had been, she said, physical violence between them.

"He never did get used to the world outside hockey," she said. "He just didn't know how to handle himself and sometimes he took it out on me. He resented people with a better education than he had. That's why he hates lawyers. He dropped out of school at grade ten, you know. He wasn't even as well educated as some of the athletes he'd meet from other sports. I remember once when he took me to Hawaii where they were shooting those bathing suit commercials. The baseball and football and basketball players who were there had all been to college, or so it seemed, and Bobby got so uptight that he and I had a fight that went right out into the hall. Later, it got worse. In Winnipeg, where he was one of the biggest men in town, we'd get invited to all the best homes. But not twice. When the conversation got over Bobby's head he'd just turn it filthy. He'd try to outgross everyone at the table, with his Nose Cohen jokes and his dingle-dangle dirty stories. And it would turn people off."

We have not been as kind to our hockey heroes as we think we have been. When they were young, we singled them out for special attention. We asked them to gamble the possibility of an education against a chance of glory. In Bobby Hull's day, which is just barely over, only 17 percent of NHL players finished high school. When they won their gamble (or lost it, as some may feel) we gave them more than they could have asked for in the way of money, fame, women, adulation. Although they are skilled only at our boyhood game, we paid them to be our guides at everything from the charities we supported to the tonics we put on our hair. We made gods of them. Hull, wrote a society columnist named Tish Baldridge in the Chicago *Daily News*, was a man who "inspires sighs in every maiden, and envy in the blood of every man." And then, when they were thirty-five or forty, as Hull had turned just before he left the game, we took it all away from them at once. Jean Béliveau, the former altar boy, is a well-paid and distinguished vice-president of the Canadiens with an ambassadorial air ("It's been some time since I visited your fair city," he said to me in Montreal). Bobby Orr is reported to wish he had more to do, and, after an unsatisfactory attempt at being a league executive, has taken to representing young players in their business dealings. But he is, at least, comfortably wealthy. Morenz died.

These were the superstars. For the men who had been in the ranks behind them, it was sometimes worse. When the cheering stopped, so did everything else—including the money.

"Excuse me, aren't you …?" quickly turned to "Didn't you used to be …?" and then to "Oh, really, and who did you play for?" Suddenly, the people who used to say, "The bus leaves at 8:30, wear a tie," were no longer there, and men who had never really made any decisions now had to make them all. A few, like Billy Heindl, collapsed. Others turned to booze or lethargy, living out of scrapbooks. And even the greatest, sometimes, had trouble coming to grips with what they had lost.

In Toronto, just before I left for the Oilers' trip to New England, I had seen Maurice Richard. The National Film Board had made a wonderful film of Roch Carrier's short story "The Hockey Sweater." In it, Carrier's mother had sent away to "Mr. Eaton" to replace his hockey sweater, the beloved number 9 that he and all his friends wore on the rink at Ste. Justine. Mr. Eaton, unfortunately, had sent back a replacement in the colours of the Toronto Maple Leafs. The NFB thought it would be appropriate to hold a reception for the film "The Sweater" at Maple Leaf Gardens, and to bring Richard down from Montreal to attend it. I had seen Richard only a couple of years previously, when he had been a guest on the television show on which I then worked. On that show, during which we had shown him for the first time an excerpt from Rick Salutin's *Les Canadiens*, he had received the largest, loudest standing ovation any of our Canadian guests had received in a studio. The reception from the audience—many of them too young to have seen the Rocket play—moved him. He accepted it graciously, in spite of the reputation he had had during his playing days as being curt and uncomfortable with the public. After the show, I had asked if I could look him up some time, and he had given me his calling card. The card was an advertisement for Grecian Formula, the hair dye he was promoting in television commercials.

At the Maple Leaf Gardens reception, he looked overweight and out of shape, but healthy. Not long before, he had been appointed a "special ambassador" by the Canadiens, and his finances were obviously now in hand, although it had not always been so; in his prime, the Rocket had been paid less for playing hockey than some of his successors had got for one television endorsement. Stan Obodiac, the Gardens' public relations director, introduced him to the crowd who had assembled to see the film. When the Rocket stepped forward, Obodiac asked him to try on a Maple Leaf sweater—"just for a few pictures." For a moment, I thought Richard was going to kill Obodiac. He was fat and his hair was artificially coloured, but he was still the Rocket, and for a brief instant the old fire blazed forth from his eyes.

Now, in Hartford, I arranged to meet with Gordie Howe. On schedule, he appeared in the lobby of my hotel, and invited me to ride with him to his new restaurant, Gordie's Place, featuring the Elbow Room. On the way, we would pick up Gus Badali, who was following the Oilers to see Gretzky break the records, and whose friendship with the Howes dated back to the days when their son had boarded at Badali's house in Toronto.

Howe looked middle-aged. His greying hair was thin. He had gained three pounds since he'd stopped playing, he said; he was up to 211. For a while, when he had stopped playing, he had run to keep in shape, but found it wasn't worth it. He said he'd look better now if he pulled his stomach in to where his chest used to be. He is a marvellous anecdotalist, telling stories—sometimes, as we drove, with cues from Badali—the way the Canadian author W.O. Mitchell does, as if they are folktales to be relished anew each time they are retold. Mitchell calls it "replaying old tapes."

Gordie's Place, bright and cheerful, turned out to be one of the most impressive hockey museums imaginable, with all the memorabilia dedicated to Gordie and his sons. Each wall of the several dining and drinking areas was covered with photographs, plaques, telegrams, letters of appointment to august bodies, certificates of honorary citizenship of half the world. One wall in the main dining-room was festooned with sweaters: an old, dirty, white Red Wing sweater with the neck trimmed in red; an NHL all-star sweater; a Houston Aero sweater; a WHA all-star sweater; a New England Whaler sweater; a Team Canada '74 sweater. All of them bore the number 9. As we passed this display—he had insisted on giving Badali and me a guided tour—he mentioned that he wore 9 because it was the lowest number available when he joined the

Red Wings; single-digit numbers got lower berths. He had worn 17 in Omaha, where he had played when he was Gretzky's current age. There was a photograph of him in Galt, in the days when he had to wear a headband to hold back his hair. Now, he said, he had only three ambitions: to have dandruff, to get a zit, and to go offside.

"Offside?" I asked.

"I'd just like to be fast enough," he replied. "I can still handle drop passes, you know. It's just that I used to give them, and now I receive them."

Colleen joined us for lunch, and in her presence, Gordie edited the naughty words out of his anecdotes. She is a handsome, confident woman who bears her middle years well. Gordie calls her Mother Howe. It was evident that she runs the business of Howe Enterprises. She reminded Gordie of some appointments he had that afternoon and of some errands he had promised to run. Interrupting his string of stories, he nodded agreement.

Howe Enterprises holds contracts for various personal services with the Colonial Bank, Chrysler, and Anheuser-Busch, but its heart is with Amway, which sells health care, cosmetics, jewellery, and gardening materials directly to the consumer. When the Howes talked about Amway, they sounded the way recent converts to Moral Re-Armament sound about their religion. Several rooms in their spacious home in a Hartford suburb had been converted to office space, which was, Colleen pointed out, tax deductible, as were portions of their gas and telephone bills.

Gordie still did some work with the Whalers, and the talk turned to hockey. Howe seemed reluctant to be nostalgic; he would deflect questions about the old days as easily as he had once deflected passes toward the goal, and he would respond with a comment about the current season. He was still bitter about Marty's fate, and it was evident that there were hard feelings between the Whalers and the Howes over the demotion. But he spoke glowingly of the other young players. "For the first time," he said, "I think they're having fun, and hockey has to be fun. People used to ask me how I could get up for a game after so many years and I'd tell them I didn't get up, I just played it, and enjoyed it as much as I could."

Colleen joined in the hockey talk, too, and was less reluctant to chat about times past. For a while, the talk ranged over their days in Detroit, the bad feeling they had had when they left the town that Gordie had once seemed to own. Gus should tell Wayne some of these things, Gordie said, and for a moment his brow furrowed.

"Do you know how long they'll remember you if you don't fight?" said Colleen, with a burst of energy.

She dipped her finger into her water glass. Then she pulled it out.

"As long as it takes that hole to fill up," she said. She turned to look directly at Badali. "Tell Wayne to enjoy himself now," she said. "These are the good years."

"I hope he's having fun," said Gordie Howe.

**17**

*"He'll do it," says Walter Gretzky in the stands*

Preparing to play the Whalers in Hartford, the Oilers had six games left in their schedule and every chance of finishing ignominiously out of the playoffs. Although they were tied with Toronto for the last playoff spot, Washington was breathing down their necks, and even Hartford was not out of the race. Any one of these teams could start to win and push the Oilers out. Their only sure route was to start winning themselves, and that route did not look easy. Four of their last six games would be on the road. They had not been playing well; in March they had won only three of eleven games. The stage was set for Sather, and many of the players were sure he would mount it with Knute Rockne-like fervour and try to fill them with his own competitive fire.

Instead, he took them to dinner.

On the evening before their game with the Whalers, they assembled, at Sather's direction, in a Hartford seafood restaurant where pictures of sailing ships hung on the wall and fishnets stretched from the low, dark ceiling. Many of them walked to the restaurant through the spring rain and some had left their jackets and ties at the hotel. They sat at long wooden tables laden with plates of fresh bread and sweating pitchers of draft beer, and when the waitresses were slow with their orders, some of them began wadding missiles out of the bread and threatening to start dough wars. Sather told them to order whatever they wanted, and most asked for lobster dishes or heaping bowls of steamed clams, or both, and plates of French-fried potatoes. Matti Hagman, no fan of shellfish, had trout stuffed with shrimp, and several of the players sitting near him nibbled at it and pronounced it better than their lobsters. For once, the three Finns spread themselves out among the rest of the team.

No one talked hockey, the conversation ranging instead over plans for the summer, the purgative effects of seafood, and—as always—women. There were no speeches of any kind, and after coffee and cheesecake or hot apple pie and ice cream, they pushed themselves back from their tables and returned to the hotel or, in a few cases, out into the Hartford night. Gary Edwards, now the senior goaltender, left first and alone; the others filed out in twos and threes. On their way out the door, each stopped by Sather's chair to thank him formally for his hospitality. Only Garry Unger remained after dinner, sitting with Sather and Billy Harris, a grownup friend of the family.

"There's nothing I can do now," Sather said as he waved for another round of coffee and lit a cigar. "It's all up to them."

The next evening, at the Hartford Coliseum, the Oilers began the string of games that was to carry them so far in the playoffs and into the hearts of so many fans. From that night, March 25, until their season at last came to its dramatic finish a month later, the Oilers played like a different team from the one that had been so fitful and unpredictable all season long.

The drive began on an odd note. The Oilers jumped off to a 3–0 lead over Hartford on goals by Kurri, Anderson, and Callighen. When Hartford made it 3–1, Anderson quickly replied, with Gretzky picking up his first assist of the evening. In the third period, however, Hartford counted its second goal and the score remained 4–2 until the last minute of the game, when the Whalers' coach, Larry Pleau, decided to pull his goaltender and go all-out for a tie. As so often happens, the Oilers scored instead, with Mark Messier intercepting a pass and feeding it to Gretzky, who scored his fifty-third goal of the year into the empty net. That seemed to be that, and the fans who had not already left began to stream out of the Coliseum.

Pleau then did a curious thing: with the game patently out of reach, he left his net empty. Gretzky's goal had come at 19:04. Fourteen seconds later, Coffey harpooned a Whaler pass, fed Gretzky, who in turn fed Messier for the open shot. 6–2. Still Pleau left his net open. Later, on television, he explained that he had not given up hope that the extra attacker would help his team to a tie, and the loss in fact did eliminate Hartford from the playoffs. But the move still seemed spiteful.

For Gretzky now, every point, and especially every assist, was an historic one; he was within easy reach of Esposito's points total and within sight of Orr's record for assists, and, as he said later, he would take points any way he could get them. With eleven seconds left in the game, he collected another one, this time taking Messier's pass and, rejecting an opportunity to score himself, giving the puck to Anderson for the free goal. The play was reminiscent of the game more than five months ago when he had given Semenko his hat-trick goal against the Rangers, but it also gave the Kid his ninety-eighth assist of the season. With five games left to play, he was four assists behind Orr and, with his four points against Hartford, just one behind Esposito.

The media now turned their full attention to him. In Canada and the hockey cities of the United States, sportswriters carried long dissertations on what now appeared to be his certain accomplishment. Did the fact that he played on a team that was much weaker than the one on which both Esposito and Orr had played, and therefore was given more ice time, mean his record would be tainted? Or did that actually make it a greater achievement, since Esposito and Orr at least had each other to set up? Of all the commentators, the most insouciant was Esposito. From New York, where he had retired to a life of broadcasting and the promotion of Sassoon sportswear, Esposito reminded reporters that he had known about Gretzky since the Kid was fourteen, and said he wished Gretzky luck. "You can't stop progress," he said.

Beyond the sports pages, Gretzky's march toward the records was attracting attention too. He had not been good on the *Today* show. A polite story producer, not much older than Wayne himself, had picked him up at dawn at his hotel in Boston and chauffeured him to a small satellite NBC studio. There, he had been planted among some mordant greenery and told to speak to the camera when Tom Brokaw, from New York, asked a question in his earphone. Brokaw called him Mr. Gretzky;

Wayne was self-conscious. Asked about his salary, he said, "We look after Mr. Pocklington on the ice and he looks after us off it." He sounded embarrassed. Other occasions, however, he carried off with his usual aplomb. Later in the day of his NBC appearance, Dick Schaap showed up to film an interview for ABC. Schaap and his film crew took Gretzky across the road from the NBC building and stood him on the sunny banks of the Charles River. Crews from Boston universities rowed their way across the background, and police helicopters buzzed overhead. Gretzky stood by for the interruptions, kibitzing with the crew, and picked up the thread of each question when the interview resumed. He was still more relaxed with people from the world of sports, as Schaap was, than he was with interviewers of a more general background, as Brokaw had been. When the filming was at last over, Schaap, who had once shared the hosting duties on a television talk show with Joe Namath, declared Gretzky among the easiest subjects he had ever had to interview, and said he was sure the piece would delight everyone who saw it.

Well out of sight of the press and television on the night after their victory over the Whalers, Gretzky and several of the other younger Oilers celebrated by attending a Hartford discotheque, where two things happened to surprise them. The first was that the band stopped playing for a moment so that Gretzky could be introduced from the stage. The second was that they found themselves in the unexpected company of Peter Pocklington and a group of his business associates, who had flown in on Pocklington's Lear jet to catch the game before a meeting they had in Montreal the next day.

"What the hell," said Pocklington, and bought his young minions a beer.

Back at the hotel, though, events were taking place that, at least in Glen Sather's opinion (loath as he was to admit it at the time), marked the true coming-together of the team. The sparkplugs were two members of the Swat team, Brackenbury and Semenko. The Swats had returned to their own room directly from the Coliseum. Then, working quickly and stealthily, they invaded all the other rooms on the floor, moving suitcases, bedding, toilet articles, and whatever furniture was not fastened down into the halls and onto adjoining fire escapes. When their teammates returned to this chaos, they retaliated by sticking the nozzle of a fire-hose under the Swats' door and turning the water on with enough force to remove half the stippling from the walls and ceiling.

The next morning, Sather, who had heard laughter in the halls when he returned to his own room, was apprised by the hotel management that the cost of the damage was a cool $1,800. Sather instantly and sternly fined Brackenbury and Semenko $900 each. But, as he said much later when he chuckled over the night's events, "I'm pretty sure everyone chipped in. It was just like the old days, when you really had a sense of a team."

JOE LOUIS SPORTS ARENA, DETROIT, SATURDAY, MARCH 28: On his first shift of the game, Gretzky breaks in alone on Larry Lozinski, the Red Wings' goalie. In the stands, Walter Gretzky silently hopes that Wayne will fake first and then shoot. But Billy Harris has told Wayne that Lozinski stays back in the net on breakaways and his best chance is to shoot quickly. He aims for the low corner and releases. Lozinski jabs out with his skate. The puck nicks his blade and bounces off the goalpost and out. Esposito's record will have to wait.

At 8:37, Dale McCourt puts Detroit ahead. Almost immediately afterwards, Gretzky steals the puck from Detroit's Brent Peterson and fires it to Dave Hunter in front of the net. Hunter, as if taken by surprise, bobbles the pass. The crowd groans. With the Red Wings well out of playoff contention, they are here to see the scoring record.

At 14:33, Doug Hicks ties the game. Although Gretzky is on the ice, the assists go to Callighen and Kurri. Before the period ends, Gretzky sends Kurri in alone, but Kurri, holding the puck an instant too long, misses the corner of the net, and the period ends 1–1, with Esposito's record still intact.

"He'll do it," says Walter Gretzky in the stands.

If he doesn't, it won't be for lack of ice time. Sather sends him out to start the second period, leaves him out for a second shift, takes him off briefly, and then sends him back out. In all, he plays five of the first six minutes.

"Go, Gretzky, go," chants the crowd.

At 9:55, Kurri scores to complete a clever passing play, and the announcer gives assists to Callighen and Gretzky. The crowd roars its approval and begins to rise in tribute. But Gretzky has been on the bench during the play, and now he starts to laugh. He leans over to Kevin Lowe. "I think he said it out of habit," he says.

The crowd boos.

At 12:24, with everyone's attention focused on the bench, Anderson makes it 3–1, and the Oilers' playoff hopes take an upward turn.

Early in the third period, Gretzky sets up Callighen, but Callighen, as Hunter and Kurri have before him, misses his chance, and again the crowd ooohs in disapproval. Detroit scores to make it 3–2.

Just past the halfway point of the period, a fight leaves both teams short two men, and Gretzky goes out to play on the uncrowded ice. With the penalties still in force, he carries the puck deep into the Detroit end, swoops across the front of the net, sees Siltanen come skittering in from the point, and whips the puck across to him. Risto scores, and Gretzky now shares Esposito's record.

CIVIC ARENA, PITTSBURGH, PENNSYLVANIA, SUNDAY, MARCH 29: After a scoreless first period, Gretzky sets up Anderson, and Esposito's record is broken. As the game winds down, he sets up Callighen and then Kurri, as the Oilers win 5–2, and Bobby Orr's record is tied. In seventy-seven games, Gretzky has 155 points, fifty-three goals, and 102 assists, more than any other player has ever scored in the same number of games. Afterwards, the newspapermen crowd around him to record his unassuming comments.

Almost unnoticed, two other significant events have occurred in the evening's game. One is that the Oilers, in defeating the Penguins, have moved a full game ahead of Toronto, and within a point of Pittsburgh; they are in fifteenth place, as high as they have been all season, and climbing. The other is that Andy Moog, who has played goal, has been outstanding. In stopping thirty-two of thirty-four shots— nearly twice as many as the Oilers have fired at Greg Millen in the Pittsburgh nets—he has looked cool and confident. Although Sather has said nothing to the press, it has occurred to him that he may now have the backup goalie he will need for the playoffs, and with him, the possibilities of a dramatic move. But it is still too early to think ahead.

NORTHLANDS COLISEUM, EDMONTON, WEDNESDAY, APRIL 1: At 1:33 of the first period, Gretzky reaches out to nudge the puck with his extended stick just before Kurri swipes it past the veteran Glenn Resch in the Colorado goal. Kurri digs the puck out for him and Gretzky skates with it to the Edmonton bench, where he tosses it over to be kept as a souvenir. The Edmonton crowd gives him a standing ovation. In the second period he sets up Kurri again, every point now a record. But the Rockies, who are doomed to finish ahead of only Detroit and Winnipeg but whom the Oilers have not been able to beat all year, play with the easy nonchalance of players bound for their summer holidays, and hold Edmonton to a 4–4 tie. In goal, Gary Edwards looks adequate, although the four goals that get by him are scored on fewer shots than the Oilers get on Resch. Sather wonders if adequacy will be enough in the playoffs.

PACIFIC COLISEUM, VANCOUVER, FRIDAY, APRIL 3: They are in! The Oilers roll easily over the Canucks, piling up four goals before Vancouver replies, and coast to a 7–2 win. The two points push them ahead of Pittsburgh and out of reach of Toronto and Washington. Gretzky picks up a goal and an assist, and once again the hometown fans rise to salute him, but, once again, there are other developments that Sather finds more significant: Moog has played with cool steadiness in the nets and Glenn Anderson has scored his thirtieth goal, his ninth in seven games. At long last, Anderson seems to have forgotten the Olympics.

When the game is over, B.J. MacDonald, who has been shut out by Moog, skates over to congratulate his former centre, Gretzky, and to wish playoff luck to the team of which less than a month ago he was captain.

NORTHLANDS, SATURDAY, APRIL 4: In the last game of their long schedule, it is the Oilers' turn to be nonchalant. They are playing Winnipeg. With a place in the playoffs assured—although they will not know who they face in the first round until everyone else finishes tomorrow night—they are as loose as they looked at training camp, and Gretzky is having a field day. In the first period, he sets up his roommate, Kevin Lowe, then his linemate Callighen; in the second, he feeds Kurri, who passes to Siltanen, who scores; in the third, he scores himself—his fifty-fifth goal of the year—and sets up Siltanen again, for his 109th assist. The crowd is merry, exulting over their favourite's banquet of points, and the game rolls toward its finish at 7–2.

In the last minute, though, there is an incident that will leave a bitter taste in the Oilers' champagne. Over the season, and almost unnoticed amid Gretzky's accomplishments, their stalwart defenceman (and now captain) Lee Fogolin has scored four short-handed goals, which tied *him* for a record held by Bobby Orr. With the final game of the year cinched, the Oilers decide to set Fogolin up for a record-breaker. First, of course, they have to be short-handed, and with less than three minutes left to play, Dave Semenko takes a penalty. Asked about it later, Semenko will say the penalty was accidental, but when he does so the other players smile ruefully.

Now, jubilantly, Fogolin accepts a pass and skates for the net. He is going too fast. Half checked, he hurtles into the boards and crumples in pain. Peter Millar leaps over the bench, and the crowd falls silent as Fogie is helped off.

In the dressing room, the news looks bad. Fogolin's thigh is swollen and throbbing with pain. Without x-rays, no one can be sure, and Peter Millar tells Sather not to worry, but to Billy Hams, who has seen a thousand injuries over his career, the leg looks broken. In two years, Fogolin has never missed a game. His solid play on the blueline and his captaincy both on and off the ice, have been fundamental to the Oilers' powerful finish. Now, with a playoff series imminent, he may be out for the year.

Sather joins the dressing-room celebration, and smiles his confident smile, but he is already thinking he will have to bring Charlie Huddy up again from Wichita, and the playoffs will be no place for a minor-leaguer.

After the 1980–81 season, the NHL will be broken into divisions whose internal results will determine combinations for the playoffs. But in

1980–81, the pairings were still determined by overall finish, with the top sixteen teams qualifying. In each round, the highest finisher played against the lowest, second-highest against second-lowest, and so on. For the Oilers, who through the luck of scheduling completed their season ahead of almost everyone else, this scheme meant that there was a mind-boggling number of possibilities as they waited for the results on the final night of regular-season play, Sunday, April 5. Their win over Winnipeg had lifted them higher in the standings than they had been all year, to thirteenth place, but a win by the New York Rangers could push them back to fourteenth. At the top of the league, the standings were almost as crowded, so that various combinations of wins and losses could have them play any of Los Angeles, Buffalo, or Montreal.

As he contemplated these permutations, Sather played the traditional role of pretending not to care whom he played. In private, he was as clear about his preferences as any of his most partisan fans. Los Angeles, obviously, was his first choice, for the Kings, after an impressive start, had faded badly and would go into the playoffs without their premier winger, Charlie Simmer, who had been injured. He was confident his young Oilers would threaten and perhaps even beat Buffalo; the Sabres still had a habit of folding in the playoffs. Montreal, he preferred not to think about at all. He was aware of the Canadiens' awesome record in the playoffs and of the pride they would bring against whatever opponent they faced.

In the meantime, there were the past few weeks to relish. Since the dinner in Hartford, the Oilers had gone six games without a defeat. During this stretch—their longest and most satisfying of the year—they had played the way Sather had hoped they would play all year, and for a time at least, much of the pain he had suffered, from his confrontation with Bryan Watson to the unpleasant incident arising out of Pocklington's remarks about Hugh Campbell, was outweighed by the satisfaction he felt now. The decisions he had made through the year—sending Murdoch down, getting rid of Price and MacDonald, and, perhaps most of all, sticking with his kids through their own worst moments and the heaviest pressure to trade them—now looked to be the right ones.

Most of all, there was Gretzky. Sather was lucky to have the Kid in his lineup, and he knew there wasn't a coach in the league who didn't envy him that luck. But, he wondered now, could any coach have given Gretzky a better year? Could anyone imagine Gretzky, anywhere, playing with *anybody*, having had a better season than he had just completed? The hockey world was agog over the figures. His total of points, 164, was a record, of course, and so was his total of assists, 109. The distance between his winning scoring total and that of a runner-up, 29 points, was also a record, and so was the average number of points he had accumulated in each game. In the wartime league of 1943–44, Bill Cowley of Boston had scored seventy-one points in thirty-six games, for an average of 1.97, slightly better than Esposito's 1.95 over the seventy-six games of his record-setting year. Wayne had averaged 2.05, and excepting such prehistoric figures as Joe Malone (Malone had scored 2.20 goals per *game*), he was the only player ever to break the two-point barrier. In two years, he had gathered 301 points; only one other player, Mike Bossy, had ever achieved even *two* hundred. All in all, Sather thought, a year to be proud of—especially in comparison to how everything had looked in the fall.

He called John Blackwell, a former trainer who was now running the team's computer program and looking after the team's playoff arrangements.

"Book us in everywhere," he said. "L.A., Buffalo, Montreal. Might as well book us back, too. We'll be away for two games for sure and we know when we'll be coming back." The first playoff round would be three games out of five; thus, even though the Oilers, finishing lower than whatever team they would face, would play the first two games away, they would be assured of at least one game at Northlands.

Then Sather had an idea. "No one else knows where they'll finish either," he said to Blackwell. "They won't have made any travel arrangements to come here. You might as well book us onto every flight back to Edmonton from all those places too."

"Every flight?" said Blackwell. "How can the other guys make reservations?"

"They can't," said Sather, as his cheeks began to flush.

## 18

*The team's reaction to its triumph was almost as surprising as the victory itself*

On the final night of the regular season, while the Oilers watched on television (or in some cases, since they could do nothing about the results anyway, took advantage of a rare Sunday night off to enjoy the social pleasures of Edmonton), the New York Rangers and Montreal both won their games, Los Angeles tied, and Buffalo lost. When the league had finished its tally, and settled even positions by granting the higher position to the team with the greater number of wins, the complete standings for the 1980–81 season were entered into NHL history:

|  |  | WINS | LOSSES | TIES | POINTS |
|---|---|---|---|---|---|
| 1. | NY Islanders | 48 | 18 | 14 | 110 |
| 2. | St. Louis | 45 | 18 | 17 | 107 |
| 3. | Montreal | 45 | 22 | 13 | 103 |
| 4. | Los Angeles | 43 | 24 | 13 | 99 |
| 5. | Buffalo | 39 | 20 | 21 | 99 |
| 6. | Philadelphia | 41 | 24 | 15 | 97 |
| 7. | Calgary | 39 | 27 | 14 | 92 |
| 8. | Boston | 37 | 30 | 13 | 87 |
| 9. | Minnesota | 35 | 28 | 17 | 87 |

|  |  | WINS | LOSSES | TIES | POINTS |
|---|---|---|---|---|---|
| 10. | Chicago | 31 | 33 | 16 | 78 |
| 11. | Quebec | 30 | 32 | 18 | 78 |
| 12. | Vancouver | 28 | 32 | 20 | 76 |
| 13. | NY Rangers | 30 | 32 | 14 | 74 |
| 14. | Edmonton | 29 | 36 | 16 | 74 |
| 15. | Pittsburgh | 30 | 35 | 13 | 73 |
| 16. | Toronto | 28 | 37 | 15 | 71 |
| 17. | Washington | 26 | 36 | 18 | 70 |
| 18. | Hartford | 21 | 41 | 18 | 69 |
| 19. | Colorado | 22 | 45 | 13 | 57 |
| 20. | Detroit | 19 | 43 | 18 | 56 |
| 21. | Winnipeg | 9 | 57 | 14 | 32 |

Sather's worst fears had become real. The Oilers would meet Montreal. On Monday morning, he cancelled his reservations for Los Angeles and Buffalo and gathered his team together to leave for eastern Canada; although they would not play until Wednesday night, he wanted them to spend as much time as possible acclimatizing themselves, to get their bodies accustomed to the eastern time zone and their minds, in practice at least, accustomed to skating under those twenty-two looming Stanley Cup banners.

The Oilers had lost every game they had played in Montreal, beginning with their first timorous visit in January of their first year in the NHL. In spite of the astonishing upset in their last meeting of 1980–81 (the 9–1 victory at home in January), they could not dismiss from their minds the ease with which the Canadiens had skated past them in their two encounters in the Forum. Neither could the public handicappers. On every broadcast outlet that offered predictions for the Stanley Cup, and in almost every newspaper, the Oilers were solid underdogs. In Toronto, the Globe and Mail, summing up experts' opinions from coast to coast, set the odds against the Oilers winning the Cup at 100 to 1 and those against Montreal at 3 to 1, second only to the Islanders' 5 to 2. The best chance any non-Edmonton columnist gave the Oilers was of perhaps winning one game in the series when they returned home. The only exception to this national pattern was Paul Rimstead, who published his column in various Suns, and who cheerfully predicted the Oilers would win in three straight games; the consensus among even the Oilers' most rabid supporters was that Rimstead, when he had been shaved by the Oilers the previous year, had also had part of his brains cut out.

Sather, however, was determined that his team would go into the series with as much fire as he could engender, and at the Edmonton airport he made one last decision that reflected his own chippy mood. In all their previous visits to Montreal, the Oilers had stayed at a small residential hotel near the Forum called the Manoir LeMoyne, and Blackwell had made reservations there again for the Stanley Cup. At the airport, Sather learned from the team's regular battalion of media men that his enemy Terry Jones of the *Journal* would be following the team to Montreal and that, although he would come on a later flight, he had also made a reservation at the LeMoyne.

"Then we're not staying there," he said.

"Are you serious?" said Blackwell.

"Yeah. Absolutely," Sather said. "Get us in somewhere else. Get the same number of rooms downtown, at the Chateau Champlain. We'll let Jones interview himself."

THE FORUM, MONTREAL, WEDNESDAY, APRIL 8: The statistics handed out in the pressbox underline the differences in what nearly all the reporters here are convinced is a mismatch. The players dressed in the *bleu, blanc, et rouge* of the Canadiens tonight have played, among them, 1,111 playoff games; the Oilers, in their visiting blue, gold, and white, have played 160, and that includes Gary Unger's thirty-nine. Four of the Canadiens in the lineup—Larry Robinson, Serge Savard, Bob Gainey, and Guy Lafleur—have won Conn Smythe trophies as the most valuable players in the Stanley Cup. Lafleur alone had led the league in scoring three times, has been on six first all-star teams, and has twice been selected the league's most valuable player.

Lafleur is wonderful to watch, the last superstar we'll see without a helmet; his long hair billows in the jet-stream as he whizzes around in his patented upright style. Here, in his own province, he wears the mantle of Richard and Béliveau, but he has trimmed it to fit himself. He has a recording out that is a strange, Québécois combination of disco and hockey instruction; while he reads tips, a chorus of girls throbs in the background: *"ou, ou, con-tin-ue,"* and *"oui, comme ça."* Rod Langway, his teammate, says he doesn't sweat.

This has been a terrible season for him. He has been injured. He has been held to twenty-seven goals, the first time in seven years he hasn't scored fifty. Worst of all, his personal life has gone to smithereens. His marriage, to a former stewardess whom he told to lose fifty pounds before the wedding (she lost thirty), is reportedly in trouble. He owes the income tax department $150,000. And, just three weeks ago, on his way home from Crescent Street, he ploughed his $28,000 Cadillac Seville into a sign post at two o'clock in the morning. A picture in the Gazette the next day showed the wreck of his car, with the sign post driven through the window and through the inner arc of the steering wheel; Lafleur suffered the loss of part of his ear and much of his proud image. Robert Picard, a teammate who had been drinking with him, said he'd tried to take Lafleur's keys away before he left Crescent Street. The police, however, did not give Lafleur a breath test.

Since his return to the lineup, however, he has reportedly looked like the Lafleur everyone respects; he has scored five goals and collected six assists in the Canadiens' last six games.

Of the nineteen Oilers who dressed in Buffalo six months ago, only thirteen are in uniform tonight to face Lafleur and his teammates, but even with the newcomers among them, they are more of a unit, more cohesive than they have ever been before.

Number 2 is still Fogolin, his sweater now emblazoned with the captain's c. The break everyone feared has turned out to be a charley horse, but it was as bad a case as the trainers have ever seen. Right up to the pre-game skate there were doubts that he could play. He came to Montreal on crutches and has not been able to practise. Tonight, Peter Millar wrapped Fogolin's thigh in tight adhesive, then laid an ice-bag against the tape and wrapped the leg again with elastic bandage. As he skates now, Sather keeps a wary eye on him, but from the fierce look on Fogolin's face it's hard to tell if he is in pain. He is the bedrock of the defensive corps, and the captaincy has deepened his intensity.

Number 4: Kevin Lowe. Through the year, Kevin has stood in the penumbra of his roommate's limelight, helping to open the mail, sharing in the bonanza of gifts and offerings and perks, answering the phone—and living with the nuisance of having to change even an unlisted phone number. The experience has helped to mature him, and to conquer his own gentlemanly reticence. Next year, Gretzky plans to buy a condominium in Edmonton, and Kevin will share it. Right now, Montreal suits him. The press here has made much of the fact that he is a Quebecker, and he has been giving interviews in his fluent French. "For some reason," he said this morning, "I seem more at ease in French than I do in English." Because of his quiet poise, it is sometimes difficult to remember how young he is, and that on most other teams he would be the baby. Next week is his twenty-second birthday, but there are five Oilers dressed tonight who are younger. From time to time, though, Kevin sends out reminders of his youth; today he arrived at the Forum to begin the pre-game ritual that made such an impression in Toronto. He put on Hicks's sweater and climbed to the highest seats, where he sat for a while in silent contemplation. Then he returned to the dressing-room area, and began the formalized game of road hockey.

Number 5, Doug Hicks, was also a part of that game, as he is a part of so much of the Oilers' off-ice life. Seldom mentioned in postgame dispatches, Hicks is nevertheless an important cog in the Oilers' machine. During the times he has been injured (he has sat out twenty-one games), he has been missed. Sather is counting on him tonight more than even Hicks may know, for Hicks has been in Stanley Cup action before, playing with Minnesota and Chicago. He has another kind of experience that may help; with the neat beard he has worn all year he may be able to give advice on grooming to some of the younger players who have decided not to shave until their undefeated streak comes to an end.

Number 6, Garry Lariviere, is, so far, the most valuable of the newcomers. A rugged six-footer with thinning hair and gaps in his teeth, he has filled two roles left vacant by the departure of Ron Low: as the team's heaviest smoker of cigarettes—only Semenko among the others even touches them—and as its leading user of profanity. There are, of course, other claimants to the latter crown—the otherwise pious Fogolin, for one. But Lariviere is world class: he uses the game's most common swearword, or its gerund, between the words of his sentences the way a good bricklayer uses mortar. He is happy to be with the Oilers, and the Oilers are glad to have him. They have quickly picked up his inexplicable nickname, Bimbo, which Brackenbury remembers from their days together in Quebec. He is providing exactly the kind of balance Coffey needs.

Number 7, Paul Coffey, is, along with Mark Messier, the most obviously changed of the Oilers. He has finally confessed that at the beginning of the year, when he was playing ineffectually and sitting out as many games as he was in, he was in constant terror of being sent back to Kitchener to play Junior A; because of his youth, he could have been. "And if I'd gone down there I don't know if I'd ever have made it back up," he said. The confession would have been beyond him six months ago, when he would never have presumed to talk about himself—or, for that matter, to speak so long a sentence without pausing. Now he is out of his shell, an accepted member of the team, a player in airplane card games, a participant in the banter of practice, at which he often arrives with his hair in unkempt splendour, as if a high wind had blown through the apartment he shares with Jari Kurri. Now, black stubble ages his swarthy chin, and the Oilers hope that he will look old enough to avoid some of the marginal penalties they feel referees sometimes call on the players they instantly spot as rookies. Anchored by Lariviere, Coffey has become a vital part of the Oiler attack, and the smoothness of his skating pleases the eyes of the fans.

Number 8: Risto Siltanen. The long season has taken its toll on Risto's short, stocky body, but he still dances up the ice in his short, choppy strides often enough to be a potent offensive threat—he is by far the highest scorer among the defencemen and is well ahead of many of the forwards—and his pixie smile still lights up his private conversations.

Number 9, Glenn Anderson, is Andy now and not Mork, and he is close to fulfilling the potential the scouts saw when they signed him. As he went on his late-season scoring spree, he was named the *Hockey News* player of the week, an honour that among the Oilers had theretofore been reserved for Gretzky, who was so named an unprecedented four times. One of the newspapermen here, Tim Burke of the *Gazette*, is convinced Anderson is cut from the mould of Maurice Richard—like Richard, he shoots left-handed and plays right wing—and Sather is concerned with that comparison as he was in the fall with the comparison between Anderson's skating abilities and those of Lafleur.

Number 10 is Matti Hagman, who, with the exception of the players who have disappeared to the minors or to other teams, has been the season's biggest disappointment. Alone among his countrymen, he seems reluctant to go into the corners, and his three-second buzzer is still in operation: he gets rid of the puck as quickly as he can. On the line of which he is now the centre this doesn't matter as much as it might in other combinations, for the wingers he gets rid of it to are Anderson and Messier, both of whom are playing the best hockey of their lives. In the last twenty-five games of the season, the two of them collected sixty-nine points, so Hagman must be doing something right. Over the year, he has stayed within the reformed guidelines he set for his social life when he went back to Finland, but he has not made many close friends among the non-Finnish Oilers.

Number 11 is Mark Messier. Of all the factors that have turned the Oilers around in the last few weeks, from the trades to the midnight raids in Hartford, none has been more important than Mark's decision to apply himself. The reckless abandon of the early months had now turned into a controlled fury on the ice, and in many games he has been the Oilers' most exciting player. He kills penalties and adds zest to the power play. Although he has been converted from a centre to the left wing on Matti's line, Sather still sends him out for crucial face-offs, and it is a favourite ploy to send him out with, for example, Stan Weir, then have Stan deliberately mix it up with the opposing centre, get waved off by the referee and hand over the face-off duties to Messier to take against another winger. No one knows for sure what has turned

Messier around, although it appears more than coincidence that he began his new dedicated approach at about the same time his cousin Don
Murdoch was banished to the minors. So many of the other youngsters
take their moods from him that there are those who believe he will one
day be the captain of the Oilers.

Number 12: Dave Hunter. Although Hunter has been among
the least noticed of the Oilers all year, he will be a focus of attention
tonight, for Sather has assigned him the job of checking Lafleur. With
his curious, elbows-in skating posture, he will never be able to stay even
with Lafleur on the open ice, and he will have to spend the evening
trying to keep things closed down, hitting and grinding. On the team,
there is no one who is physically better suited to the job, but there is
also no one who would appear less suited for the villainous aspects of
the role; Hunter is the most unassuming of the experienced Oilers, and
even on the night in Boston last month when Sather sat him out, his
only comments in the pressbox were on what a great player Gretzky is
and how pleased he was to be a member of the same team.

Number 17: Jari Kurri. The youngest Finn has had a spectacular
season. On the ice, he has clearly staked out for himself the coveted
place on Gretzky's right wing—and he had done so even before B.J.
MacDonald's departure. He has accumulated seventy-five scoring
points, which, while still eighty-nine short of Gretzky's incredible total,
ranks him second on the team. He is so much at home in NHL play
that in Hartford, when he scored his twenty-eighth goal of the year, he
actually did a little dance, raising one knee and punching the air with
his fist. Even more amazingly, after that game he gave his first interview
in English. Much of the credit for his newfound extroversion belongs
to his roommate, Paul Coffey, who night after night plays cards with
Jari and painstakingly works on vocabulary drills. The Oilers' publicity
department would have people believe that Kurri has been learning his
English from *Happy Days*, but both he and Coffey prefer game shows.

Number 18, Brett Callighen. With the contact lens he now puts in
his injured eye, Brett has 20/15 vision; he can see as well from twenty
feet as the average person can see from fifteen, and the improvement in
his play reflects the improvement in his sight. Even with the Plexiglas

visor he now wears on his helmet, he was tentative when he first returned to the lineup, but he quickly regained the aggressive style that gained him the spot on Gretzky's left wing in the first place. Playing in only fifty-five games, he finished the season with twenty-five goals and thirty-five assists, behind only Kurri and Messier.

Number 20, Dave Lumley, has not had a good year. On and off the bench all season—and fighting himself in either situation—he has scored only seven goals, less than half the number he got last year as a rookie. Now, when he does play, he is largely confined to a defensive role. If he is sulking, however, he is not showing it. He is a moving spirit of the pre-game road hockey, and he is sprouting a beard for luck. He has worn the same argyle sweater to the arena for every game since Hartford, and as an ex-employee of the Canadiens, he is aching for a chance to get at them.

Number 21, Stan Weir. Weir remains a loner. Unable to win from the Oilers the kind of contract he feels he deserves, he is playing out his option and hoping to be somewhere else next year. For all this, though, he is an important part of the team; the line he centres, with Hunter and Lumley on the wings, has only thirty-nine goals in total—fewer than Kurri alone—but the Oilers rely on their dogged checking to spike their opponents' biggest guns, as tonight they will have to spike Lafleur. While Hunter gets the specific assignment, the experienced Weir will set the tone for this line.

Number 27, Dave Semenko, has been dressed for more games (fifty-eight) than anyone else on the Swat team and, with eleven goals, has done the most scoring, but he had seven of those goals before the end of October. Except for the birth of his second child—which he almost missed because of his temporary demotion to Wichita—1980–81 has not been a good year for Semenko. Curiously, he may be the second most recognizable of the Oilers: his size and his looming ferocity make him a stereotype of the NHL's traditional tough guy, and people notice him. The trouble with that stereotype—from every point of view—is that he hasn't fought very much this year, and he has served only eighty minutes in the penalty box; six other Oilers, led by Curt Brackenbury, have served more. Partly, Semenko's gentlemanly record survives because no one wants to challenge him. But the truth is that he also doesn't want to fight; he'd much prefer to make the kind of plays he spoke of so longingly at training camp. Tonight, his number is circled on the game sheet, which means he will play on the first shift with Gretzky and Kurri, and the only person who can believe that he is being sent out to score a goal is probably Semenko himself.

Number 77, a new number, is Garry Unger. Through most of his long playing career, Unger has worn 7, but with the Oilers he has had to concede proprietorship of that number to his senior in the Edmonton service, Paul Coffey. In uniform, Unger, who is letting his beard grow back in for the playoffs, still looks as youthful as any of his teammates except perhaps the chubby Andy Moog. In Hartford, a television crew followed him for an entire practice thinking he was Gretzky. But away from the ice, as when he sat with Sather and Harris after dinner, the generation gap shows; with his flashy clothes and his demure Christian air, he seems to be from another time and place.

Number 99. More, if anything, than last year, Gretzky is the heart of this team. Of the team's eighty games this year, he failed to score a point in sixteen, and as they did last year, the Oilers lost all the games in which Gretzky was shut out. In Esposito's record year, he was involved in 38 percent of Boston's goals; Wayne this season was involved in exactly half of Edmonton's, another record. He had twenty-six more scoring points than the two next highest Oilers, Kurri and Messier, combined.

Despite his brilliant season, however, Gretzky still has something to prove here at the Forum, where memories of Morenz and Richard and Béliveau do not fade easily, and where Lafleur still reigns. This year, Gretzky has assisted on the only goal the Oilers have scored in their two visits here, and except on television, that's all the sophisticated Montreal hockey fans have seen from him. Even in the pressbox, with statistics spread out before every chair, there is a feeling of "show us."

The Montreal press and fans are not alone in their misgivings about Gretzky's place on the scale of greatness. The NHL has assembled a team to play in the world championships in Sweden over the next couple of weeks, taking players from the five eliminated teams. Before the Oilers assured themselves of a spot in the playoffs, Gretzky was asked if he'd go to Sweden if he were eligible. When he expressed some reservations, Trent Frayne, one of Canada's most experienced and eloquent sportswriters, blistered him in the Toronto *Sun*. The night before the playoffs opened, Dick Beddoes, another veteran, said on television in Hamilton, Ontario, that Gretzky "might just have made third-string centre on one of the good Leaf teams of the past."

That broadcast upset Walter Gretzky, who watched it in Brantford, and is here tonight. Tomorrow, Walter and Phyllis will drive to Cornwall, Ontario, to watch their second son, Keith, play in a bantam tournament. Partly because of the 7-UP commercial in which he co-stars with Wayne and partly because of the name he wears on his back (as well as because, at fourteen, he is an excellent young hockey player himself), Keith has become a celebrity this year, and Badali is now receiving invitations for him to attend banquets. But Walter continues to be largely unrecognized. This morning, Forum security men barred him from the Oilers' practice. The slight, coupled with Beddoes' remarks, has Walter in an uncharacteristically belligerent mood tonight.

The Kid himself is up. This afternoon at the Chateau Champlain, he bought coffee for some visiting friends and seemed as relaxed as if he were on his way to watch Keith's bantam game. "If Montreal loses," he said as he bit into a sugarcoated doughnut, "do you think they'll ask Lafleur to play for the team that's going to Sweden?" Now, on the ice, taking one last sweat-breaking sprint in his chicken-hawk skating style, he looks intent and determined.

Gary Edwards, clad in his goaltender's armour, wears sweater number 33, since no one wants to usurp Ron Low's 30 or Eddie Mio's 31. His family is settled in Edmonton now, and he has made himself a part of the team, as much as practitioners of his solitary trade ever do. Since he has become the team's starting goalie, in fact, he has recorded a lower goals-against average than either Low or Mio, and the team has become convinced that it can win in front of him. But the real news tonight is that he will not be starting. Sather has decided to go with Andy Moog.

"Sather must be thinking of Dryden," says someone in the pressbox when this startling news makes the rounds. Ken Dryden stepped into the Canadiens' net late in the season of 1970–71, an unheralded rookie out of Cornell University, and went on to win the Conn Smythe trophy in the playoffs.

"That's a lot of thinking," says someone else. "Dryden had the Montreal Canadiens in front of him."

"So has Moog," says the man from the *Journal de Montreal*, pronouncing it, correctly, to rhyme with rogue. "It's just that they're coming the other way."

Moog began to suspect at practice this morning that he might start, even though Sather often left his decision until the last possible moment. Then, after the team meeting at the hotel, Sather called him aside and asked him if he could handle it.

"No problem," Moog said, in his unemotional way.

Now, as the Oilers fire their last warm-up shots, he looks incongruously small. As he juggles a shot from Stan Weir, it is necessary to remind oneself that he does not play as well in practice as he does in games.

In the pressbox, Peter Driscoll tries nervously to light an unaccustomed cigar. Along with his fellow Swat Brackenbury, Driscoll has been sitting out through much of the Oilers' stretch drive, and he is aching to be back.

"You must almost want them to lose," says the man next to him.

"Hell, no," says Driscoll. "I get my share of the money anyway."

He leans over the pressbox ledge to try to catch Semenko's eye.

"They're really going to be hitting tonight," he says. "That's the kind of hockey I like. Never mind the money."

Down the pressbox, Brackenbury stands beside Billy Harris. He has his coat off already, and is jumping up and down in excitement. He has playoff stubble. In all his years as a professional, Brack has never been in a Stanley Cup playoff game, and tonight Sather let him dress with his teammates for their first skate, while the crowd was still filing in, before telling him what Brack already knew, that he wouldn't dress for the game.

Charlie Huddy came close, too. Called from Wichita, he was to step in if Fogolin's leg collapsed. Now he sits calmly beside Driscoll, wondering if he will go back to the minors yet again.

Pat Hughes, who has not yet found a place to fit in with his new team, is somewhere in the crowd, sitting with friends from Montreal.

Just after eight o'clock Montreal time, which is just after six in Edmonton, referee Bruce Hood, into whose dressing room Sather has diplomatically smuggled an autographed Wayne Gretzky Titan stick, drops the puck and the Stanley Cup playoffs of 1981, eighty-nine years since the first series was played in this historic city, are underway.

On his first shift, Lee Fogolin, as if to test his injured leg, tries to muscle the titanic Larry Robinson off the puck, and to the amazement of everyone who knows how badly he is hurting, succeeds. Right away, Fogolin's determination inspires his teammates, and they pour in on Montreal, playing with poise, beating the mighty Canadiens to the puck, ignoring the twenty-two banners over their heads. After Fogolin's encounter with Robinson, Dave Hunter bumps Lafleur. When Brian Engblom, one of the Canadiens' strong young defencemen, tries to retaliate, Hunter stands up to him. They both go off. Like Fogolin, Hunter has proved his point: the Oilers will not be intimidated.

At 6:41, Gretzky sends the high-flying Anderson in for the series' first score and, astoundingly, the Oilers are ahead. Five minutes later, Steve Shutt ties it up, but the Oilers won't quit. Gretzky sends Kurri in alone, and Kurri chooses to hold the puck, feint, feint again, then drill it high over the shoulder of Richard Sevigny in the Montreal goal. He turns to punch the air.

"I'm not sure he knows enough to be nervous about this game," says Billy Harris.

At 17:36, it's Kurri again, again assisted by Gretzky, and the period ends 3–1. Gretzky's three assists in one period have equalled a record that dates back to 1941. As the crowd mills about during the intermission, there are murmurs of appreciation.

"But he still hasn't had a shot on goal," a Montreal newspaperman points out at the pressroom bar.

"Maybe he doesn't have to," says an Edmonton supporter.

The second period is scoreless, hard fought and chippy. Two incidents illustrate the frustration of the Canadiens and the glowing confidence of the Oilers. Dave Hunter gets into a fight—more of a pushing match, really—with Guy Lapointe, a one-time all-star defence-man who has lost the support of the fans through a mediocre season. When Hunter has him clearly beaten, he tears off Hunter's helmet and begins pummelling him over the head with it. Hunter gets a major penalty; Lapointe gets a minor, a major, and a game misconduct. The crowd boos, more displeased with Lapointe's display than with the referee's call. In the other incident, Mark Messier stands eyeball to chin with Larry Robinson, who—even when Messier stretches to his full six foot one—looms over him. Both get minor penalties. In the intermission, Billy Harris tells Messier in the dressing room that he thought he was going to fight Robinson. "Not out in the open," says Messier of one of the game's all-time great—and tough—defensive stars. "I'm going to wait till I get him against the boards and then I'll beat the crap out of him."

Throughout the first two periods, with his team outshot 19–18, Moog has been as cool and dependable as Georges Vezina, the Chicoutimi Cucumber who once guarded the nets for Montreal, and Sather has looked like a genius.

Early in the third period, Gretzky sets up Callighen to make it 4–1. With the announcement of his fourth assist, the crowd gives a lukewarm round of applause, reluctantly coming around to believe in the new superstar. By now, the Edmonton lead has lost its fluky overtones. Even the most partisan Montreal fans are aware their team may be facing a stunning upset. The wheelhorse of the team that is beating their favourites is the Kid. He is at the top of his form. Even when he is not directly involved in the play, he is a factor, for the Canadiens must always be wary of him. On one rush, he puts on a brilliant flash of stick-handling that ties up two defenders and the crowd applauds again, this time even more warmly. Then he takes the puck from Larry Robinson as cleanly as a pickpocket on the Main. He is winning even the cynics of the pressbox over to his side.

Almost as important as Gretzky's heroics is the play of the line of Weir, Hunter, and Lumley. Shift for shift, they have been matched against Lafleur's line, and they are winning. Weir fights for every inch. Lumley is digging as energetically as if he had just finished the greatest year of his life. And Hunter has not let Lafleur get a step ahead of him.

Seven minutes into the third period, Sather makes his first coaching mistake. He sends out Unger to take only his second shift of the game. Unger flings himself into the play with the energy of a rookie but he does not seem up to the pace of the game; he is a beat behind the play of his young teammates. Doug Risebrough takes the puck from him and scores. 4–2.

Moments later, Coffey restores Edmonton's three-goal lead. At first, Gretzky is given an assist, and the announcer says, in both languages, that this ties a record, too: only five men have ever had five assists in one playoff game; one of them is Maurice Richard. The crowd applauds vigorously. They have given the game up as lost, and they acknowledge the mastery of the Kid. When the announcer says the record-tying point has been taken away from Gretzky—the decision is correct—they boo. At 16:55, with Unger on the ice again, Réjean Houle makes it 5–3. But at 19:21, with Sevigny out for an extra futile attacker, Callighen scores into the empty net. This time, Gretzky has clearly earned the assist, and the crowd rises in noisy appreciation. He has converted the unbelievers, and without a shot on goal, he has led his team to one of the most remarkable opening-game upsets in the history of the Stanley Cup.

The team's reaction to its triumph was almost as surprising as the victory itself. In the dressing room, they were happy and light-headed but remarkably subdued. Gretzky sat for nearly half an hour undraped on a bench, answering the same questions—"how does it feel to …?"—over and over again. Like everyone else, he was more intent on the task of the next night, when they would face the Canadiens again. Reserved, the players dressed and left for the hotel, many of them on foot. Only Andy Moog was in no hurry to leave. Longer even than Gretzky, Moog sat in a corner, still in his heavy pads, sipping a soft drink. For most of the time he, too, was answering questions from the press, and, in doing so, showing the same poise he had displayed in the nets. He had faced thirty-one shots to Sevigny's twenty-nine and now he was able to recall all of them and to give the reporters an articulate, Drydenesque explanation of what he had done. As he finally began to strip off his sweat-drenched uniform, a friendly reporter commiserated with him on having been left off the game's three-star selection.

"Oh, that's all right," he said. "I'll get a star tomorrow night."

Outside the dressing room, the scene was less phlegmatic. Walter Gretzky spotted a visiting writer and asked him immediately if he knew Dick Beddoes.

"Sure," said the writer.

"Then I'll see if I can get you five pucks," Walter replied, "and you can take them to him and stuff them one by one down his throat."

Tim Burke, the *Gazette* columnist who had been so impressed by Anderson, saw the game in more historic terms.

"Do you know what this could mean?" he said. "I won't say Montreal's not going to beat them. I can't believe that. But if they do … well, we've got an election here on Monday, and if the Canadiens lose this series, the Péquistes will win it for sure."

Only Pocklington, holding court in a special VIP room down the hall from the dressing room, seemed unmoved by the evening's drama.

"I never doubted it," he said. "Never doubted it at all. We should have started Moog a lot earlier in the season."

THE FORUM, THURSDAY, APRIL 9: Today, the ritual of the corridors was carried out with the formality of the Mass. First, Kevin Lowe came to the dressing room just after four o'clock, while Peter Millar was beginning to tape Fogolin's leg. (Garry Lariviere has joined the early-arrival club, too, and was working on his stick when Lowe arrived.) Lowe hung up his tweed jacket and went directly to Hicks's locker, pulled Hicks's uniform sweater over his dress shirt and, without saying a word, climbed into the stands. Then Lumley arrived, his argyle sweater now a familiar sight, to don the goalie's catcher and blocker and make the puck out of adhesive tape and the stuffing of a shin pad. And finally Hicks came in, to complete the lineup for the road-hockey game in the long hall that leads from the dressing room to the historic ice. For nearly half an hour, their game raged on, while a photographer from the *Journal de Montreal*, which today reflected all the local press by its headline about *Gretzky le maître*, clicked away to record the ceremony.

The game, however, belongs to Andy Moog. Early in the first period, he puts his stamp on the play when he blocks a shot from Rod Langway at the point and the rebound goes right onto the stick of the Canadiens' Doug Jarvis. Jarvis snaps it instantly toward the open side of the net, but Moog's glove hand reaches out with the quickness of a rattlesnake to pick the puck out of the air.

The rebound to Jarvis was in itself a rare error, for the mark of Moog's confidence is that he is not only stopping Montreal's first shots but is almost always managing to steer the puck harmlessly into the corner or toward one of his own players.

At 5:24, Coffey, unassisted, puts the Oilers ahead, and as Moog continues his wizardry—the Oilers are outshot once again—the period ends 1–0.

Early in the second period, Gaston Gingras, who has been dressed in place of the disgraced Guy Lapointe, shoots from the blueline, and the puck takes a lucky bounce off Stan Weir's stick and goes in behind Moog. Rising to his feet after the goal, and sweeping his crease with his stick, Moog looks unfazed. Less than three minutes later, Siltanen, accepting a pass from Gretzky, scores from the point and puts the Oilers back in the lead. Shots after two periods of play: Montreal 30, Edmonton 22.

In the third, Moog remains unflappable. "Tonight," says Jim Matheson of the Edmonton *Journal*, "he could stop rice." One after another he beats Langway, Shutt—on a supernatural, fallaway glove save, and Pierre Larouche. Finally, at 14:21, Kurri gets his third goal of the series, on Gretzky's seventh assist, and the game is effectively out of reach. Incredibly, the Oilers have done it again, and as the siren sounds for what may well be the last time of the 1980–81 season in Montreal, they rush to embrace their pudgy hero Moog.

In the dressing room, Moog is as unperturbed as ever. "I felt before the game that I had to make one or two big saves early so the crowd would shut up," he explains patiently. "And that's what happened."

His save on Jarvis?

"Well, I had no time to think, so I just reacted."

But how could he play so confidently in a Stanley Cup when only a few weeks before he had been in Wichita?

"Wherever you play," he says, "you have to stop the puck."

When at last his press conference draws to an end, he spots the writer who had sympathized with him the previous night on his failure to be named a star—an oversight the selectors have rectified tonight by putting him first.

"I knew I'd get one sooner or later," he says. He takes another sip of his soft drink and, half an hour after the game has ended, begins to strip off his soggy uniform.

Edmonton International Airport is nearly an hour's drive from the centre of the city—when it was built in pre-boom times, someone thought it would also serve Calgary, 250 miles to the south—but when the Oilers arrived there on Friday afternoon a crowd of close to a thousand was on hand to greet them, along with a thumping rock band and platoon of police.

The flight back had been a long one (although not as long as the one the Canadiens, who found all the most convenient flights booked, would later take): the Oilers changed planes in Toronto and most of the players who lived in the east and whose families had been unable to get to Montreal called home from the airport. Those who did were amazed at the excitement they had caused, as if only now, as they heard their relatives or friends crowing with delight, did they become aware of what they had done. From Toronto, several newspapermen dashed out to the airport for quick interviews with Gretzky and Moog, and from other parts of eastern Canada, journalists who had spent the season with other teams—principally the Maple Leafs—joined the western cavalcade.

The Oilers were becoming a national phenomenon, as more and more fans sensed their impending victory. The Leafs, having staggered into the playoffs, were being swept away by the Islanders, and even in Toronto television fans were pleading with the CBC to concentrate on the Edmonton-Montreal series. In the west, the Oilers were heroes, and when a stewardess on their flight to Edmonton welcomed them aboard over the PA system, waves of applause swept through the plane.

Perhaps the least excited people involved in their march to fame were the Oilers themselves, as if they alone realized the difficulty of the task that still faced them. Sather had prepared them painstakingly for the Canadiens, sitting them down with videotapes of the Canadiens' games and sending them home from each practice with sheets of their statistics. Homeward bound, as the Oilers sat soberly playing cards or trying to listen to their headsets, he wondered if he had gone too far, if, on the verge of victory, they would be seized by the magnitude of the moment.

The well-meaning crowd at the airport seemed to make things worse. As the Oilers filed through their supporters, escorted by the smiling police, some of them looked tense and embarrassed.

At home that evening, Sather watched a sportscast on ITV, the network that carried Oiler games through the year. Billy Harris had gone directly from the airport to the television studio and, as Sather sipped a rum and Coke at his west-end house, nodding approval, Billy on television was going through replays of all nine Oiler goals in Montreal, pointing out the highlights of each play.

NORTHLANDS COLISEUM, SATURDAY, APRIL 11: Ron Low is in the crowded pressbox. He drove from Manitoba overnight to watch this final game. Along with Eddie Mio, who had stayed on in Edmonton after his injury, he has been with his teammates all day. Low and Mio are an odd couple; Low is now clean shaven for the summer, and Mio, unable to wield a razor with his injured hand, has grown a beard.

"That crazy bugger's really got them going," Low says. "Sather. He's really got into them now."

"You should see what's happening," says Mio.

"He's got a tape," Low continues. "He's got every one of their goals against Montreal on tape, and he's put them all together into one long show. In the background he's put on that song, you know, 'The Impossible Dream,' and while it plays they can see themselves scoring.

One ... two ... three ... just pouring them in. It's the goddamnedest thing you ever saw. But is it ever working!"

"Those guys are so high you wouldn't believe it," says Mio.

"They're going to win this sonofabitch," says Low.

In the stands, the crowd behaves like 17,499 Krazy Georges. The Oilers are greeted with a standing ovation, and the noise, pumped up by the sound of the organ, continues as the play begins. Just six minutes into the first period, Matti Hagman picks up a rebound from a shot by Anderson and, without waiting for his buzzer, drills it past Sevigny. The crowd raises the volume of its roar.

Then, less than a minute later, there is a sickening interruption. Dave Lumley, caught in a clean check, somersaults in the air, hitting the ice with the back of his head. He lies still too long. Dr. Gordon Cameron, the team's physician, is summoned from the stands. When Lumley finally and shakily does get up, there is blood on the ice. Garry Unger takes his place on Stan Weir's line.

At 15:34, Gretzky, heavily checked, pushes a one-handed pass out to Coffey, who zooms in on the right wing and scores. 2–0. Just before the period ends, a new war-cry is born. Moog makes a brilliant save and, swooping the puck up with his glove, brings the play to a halt.

"An-dee. An-dee," chants the crowd. "An-dee. An-dee."

During the intermission, Dave Lumley sits up in the Oiler dressing room. "All I could think," says Lumley, "is that I was going to spend the summer in a body cast. Now, I'd like to get back out there." Dr. Cameron has put eleven stitches into his skull.

At 8:15 of the second period, Gretzky scores from Coffey and Callighen. Even though the Canadiens make it 3–1 less than a minute later, there is, at last, a sense that victory is possible. For two and a half games, the Oilers have been outplaying the Canadiens; in their rare lapses, Moog has answered every challenge. But until now, no one has really believed they could win the series. In Montreal, the feeling, however they disguised it, was first, "wow, we've won a game," and then, "we've actually beaten the Canadiens twice on their own ice." But the idea that the Edmonton Oilers, two years into their NHL history, could *eliminate* one of hockey's mightiest teams has been so far beyond everyone's imagination that only now, as this home game heads for its denouement, does the crowd really believe what it is witnessing. John Hunter, the Coliseum organist, breaks into Bob Dylan's "'The Times They Are A-Changin'."

At 15:33 Shutt makes it 3–2, but there is no stopping the Oilers now. Just before the period ends, Gretzky intercepts a pass and goes in alone on Sevigny. As calmly as if he were on the driveway in Brantford, he comes in from his own left side, fakes to the near corner and drifts a lazy shot that catches the inside of the goalpost, much as he had done in his *mano-a-mano* victory over Liut. 4–2.

By the middle of the third period, Montreal is hurling itself into every rush, desperately trying to avoid humiliation. The Oilers' defence is content to break up the play however it can and lob the puck to safety.

"Go, Oilers. Go."

The players stand at the bench, raising their fists in exultation.

"An-dee. An-dee."

Sather's face is as red as a Montreal sweater, but his expression remains solemn.

With just 1:14 left on the clock, Montreal pulls Sevigny and sends out a lineup that resembles an all-star team: Napier, Shutt, Robinson, Savard, Gainey, Lafleur.

Sather responds with the forward line that has meant so much in the whole series: Weir, Hunter, and, his head now bandaged, Dave Lumley.

With just thirty-seven seconds left Lumley scores into the empty net, his aching head now forgotten.

And with Sevigny still out, Gretzky, for once finding no one else to give a hat trick to, completes his own. The game ends 6–2; the series 3–0, the first time Montreal has been eliminated without a victory since 1952. It is the most incredible playoff upset anyone can remember.

**19**

*... one more ripple in the onrushing wave of the future*

"Way to go, Peter Puck."

If no one else had been certain of the Oilers' ability to beat Montreal on Saturday night, Peter Pocklington was. After the game, as Pocklington strode through the restaurant where he had reserved a room to celebrate, many of the diners rose to salute him and applaud.

"Let's fire up some champagne," he said as he entered his private room, with Eva on his arm. His guests, who included friends and acquaintances from other parts of his life as well as Glen and Ann Sather and Dr. Gordon and Gwen Cameron, proposed a toast to him. He accepted it proudly, although without making a speech. "How about that Moog?" he said instead. "I told you we should have used him earlier."

At the one end of the table, Sather smiled quietly. Unwilling to jinx the team by ordering champagne for the dressing room—"We'll save that for the Stanley Cup," he had said—or to allow the television people to set up lights and cameras inside his inner sanctum before the game, Sather had shared a beer with his players after their victory, speaking quietly and individually to as many of them as he could. He had scrawled a note on the blackboard about an optional practice and a team meeting the next day.

"Do you know what I said to Moog?" Pocklington was saying from his seat at the table's centre. "I told him if they won tonight I'd fly his parents in from b.c. I will, too, wherever we play. His father's a bus driver, you know."

"A goaltender, too," someone said.

"Really?" said Pocklington.

"Sure. Played with Penticton the year they won their world championship in the fifties."

"I heard something about that," Pocklington said. Pleased as he was with the victory, which would mean at least two more home games, with their quarter-million-dollar gate receipts, for the Oilers, Pocklington seemed unaware of the historic overtones of what his young mercenaries had accomplished.

Sather, on the other hand, had been touched not only by the resonance of the occasion, but, more personally, by the grace of some of the Montreal veterans who had come into the dressing room to congratulate the Oilers and wish them luck in their next series.

"They're a class organization," he said of Montreal now.

"Well, they're a beaten one," said Pocklington, raising his glass of champagne. "And it's on to whoever we play next."

When the dust settled from the scores around the NHL that night, it was clear how much the balance of power in the league had moved from the older teams to the new: four of the five old-guard teams who had made the playoffs—Detroit having fallen in the regular season—were eliminated in consecutive games: the Canadiens by Edmonton, Boston by Minnesota, Chicago by Calgary, and Toronto by the Islanders in a series that was as humiliating as the Edmonton-Montreal result had been surprising, the Leafs having given up twenty goals while scoring four. Only the New York Rangers remained, locked in a struggle with the Los Angeles Kings.

Once more, the Oilers had to wait until the results of all the other series were in before they would know whom they faced next. The Islanders lay in wait for the lowest ranked team to survive the first round. So far, Edmonton had that dubious honour, but if Pittsburgh, which was giving second-ranked St. Louis a surprising battle, emerged victorious, the Penguins go to Long Island, and Edmonton would face the winner of …

Only Billy Harris seemed to understand it, and Harris, as usual, was taking everything philosophically.

"As long as we don't have to play Colorado," he said. "They gave us as much trouble as anybody. It's a good thing they didn't make the playoffs."

On Sunday, nearly everyone showed up at the Coliseum for the practice Sather had called optional, although not all of them wanted to skate. Dave Lumley stayed at home nursing his head wound, and some of the others came in just to shower and, if they were not growing playoff whiskers, shave, and to lounge around the dressing room, watching a tape of the previous night's game. Only the Swat team put on full uniforms to skate. The others wore sweatsuits. There were some unexpected skaters too: Eddie Mio in his reinforced goalie's skates and, at one end of the ice, Sather's sons Shanon and Justin. Gradually, some of the Oilers began playing with the two youngsters in a game that covered half the ice, and when someone threw out a tennis ball to replace the puck, an informal game of shinny was formed, with one net moved up to centre ice to cut the rink in half.

In the seven months since I had skated out so stiffly among them to pose for Joe Black's bubble-gum photo, the Oilers had appointed me to a kind of honorary position. I was their writer. When they would see me pop up on television promoting a book or appearing as a panellist on *Front Page Challenge*, they would give me avuncular reviews—"Is that the only suit you've got?" They made a point of introducing me around the league. "He's writing a book about us," they would say smugly and possessively. I, in turn, had become their total and perfervid fan. I liked them and I cared about their fortunes; through the Montreal series I had joined with those who were not shaving, and I pledged, with Coffey and Lumley and Lowe and Unger and the others, not to shave until they lost a series or won the Stanley Cup. Until now, my experience with teams, as player or coach, had been with amateurs, and I had wanted the part that hockey played in their—or our—lives to work out well. With the Oilers, the game, and their success at it, *was* life, and I found my concern about them deepening proportionally. As the year wore on, my own moods began to vary almost as much as theirs, depending on the hockey scores.

Still, it was the game itself that had brought me to the Oilers: the game of Dickson Park and the Richibucto River, of Sprague Cleghorn and Joe Malone, of Syl Apps and Howie Morenz, of Gordie Howe and Billy Heindl and Curt Brackenbury and Wayne Gretzky and Peter Pocklington and Glen Sather and—now, as I looked at the makeup of the pickup session—of Shanon and Justin Sather, too.

"Jeez, I'd like to be out there," I said to Sather.

"Go ahead and join them," Sather said. "I told them it wasn't a serious practice."

Peter Millar dug me out some clean underwear and a jockstrap. I found a sweatsuit that had belonged to Don Murdoch—"Any dope in the pockets?" Doug Hicks asked—and a stick of Lumley's. Hicks lent me a pair of gloves and Garry Unger found a pair of Tacks in his bag that were big enough to fit me. As soon as I clumped out to the ice, I realized that Unger's skates were, as Vic Hadfield's had been in September, sharper than any I had worn as a boy, and as I wheeled into my first turn, I had to thrash Lumley's stick onto the ice to keep my balance.

I was told to join the team composed of Glenn Anderson, Hicks, Shanon Sather, and, as a very roving centre, Wayne Gretzky. In opposition were Peter Driscoll, Pat Hughes, Dave Semenko, Unger, and Justin Sather, with Eddie Mio in goal.

The action swirled back and forth, as I skated in wide arcs around its periphery. Because of the unpredictability of the tennis ball, passes launched with perfect accuracy arrived like bounding jackrabbits. The various speeds of the players made organized rushes difficult. And there were games within the game: Peter Driscoll, rushing to clutch Hicks in an illegal but friendly embrace, would suddenly have to swerve to avoid a tottering child or a stationary middle-aged man; Anderson and Gretzky would get carried away on a passing play and head together for the open end of the ice. But gradually patterns emerged, and the game established its own internal rhythm of swoop and turn, sprint and glide. Old rules came back. Anderson threw his stick along the ice at a breaking-away Semenko—how graceful he looked from this perspective!—and Semenko was awarded an automatic goal. Driscoll was called for goal-sucking.

Once, I almost scored. Gretzky parked himself behind our opposition's net. Anderson bounced him the tennis ball. The Kid faked once and flicked a pass to where I stood in front of the goal. Unable to cup the ball, I swiped at it, and watched it zip wildly past the corner I thought Mio would have left open.

It didn't matter. With the greatest player of his time on one side of me and a nine-year-old boy on the other, I was transported to my own boyhood. However awkwardly, I was playing exactly the same game I had first played nearly forty years before.

Personnel changed as we played. The Sather kids retired, and Brackenbury, weary of his own serious drills on the open ice, joined us. Brett Callighen came to play on Gretzky's wing, then switched places with Driscoll. Mio changed ends. Finally, out from the dressing room skated, with surprising grace, Peter Pocklington, his beard jutting into the wind. The players greeted him with whoops of joy, and instantly started taking fake runs at him.

The game waged on. "Next goal wins," someone would say, and then score it, and someone else would decide it was two out of three, or three out of five. Sooner than I would have wished, a lifetime of cigarettes caught up to me, and I panted to the bench. Sather came down to open the door to the Oilers' bench.

"Thanks," I puffed.

"Yeah," he said. "You looked like you were have a pretty good time out there."

"I was," I said. "I was."

NASSAU VETERANS MEMORIAL COLISEUM, UNIONDALE, NEW YORK, THURSDAY, APRIL 16: On the first trip the Oilers made to this big, noisy, dirty arena this season, there was a ceremony to honour the Islanders' Stanley Cup victory of the previous spring. The ceremony would commemorate, said an announcer who strutted out onto the ice, "the noight Lo-wid Staaanley came to Long Gyland." Lord Stanley didn't. The Right Honourable Sir Frederick Arthur Stanley, Baron Preston, Knight Grand Cross of the Most Honourable Order of the Bath, came to *Canada* in 1888, the Dominion's sixth Governor General. Already a devoted follower of horse-racing, cricket, and soccer, he fell in love with hockey, and sponsored a team playing out of Government House, the Rideau Rebels, which featured, among other players, his sons, the Honourable Algernon and the Honourable Arthur. Lord Stanley went back to England in 1895. He never set foot on Long Island in his life.

Historic sentiment aside, the players who are defending his Cup tonight are worthy heirs. The Islanders came into the NHL in only 1972, and they started out as if they were going to offer to their fans the same appeal as the early New York Mets; they lost even more games in their first year than Winnipeg has lost this year. But, by building carefully on their draft choices, they moved steadily upward. Last year they finished fifth and went on to win the Cup.

This year, they have been spectacular. Mike Bossy, their brilliant right-winger, scored fifty goals in his first fifty games, equalling Maurice Richard's most honoured record, and has finished with sixty-eight. Only the Year of the Kid has kept Bossy from even greater recognition. His centre is Bryan Trottier, with 103 scoring points; Trottier and Bossy make the most effective one-two scoring punch the league has seen since Gordie Howe and Ted Lindsay. Their defence is anchored by Denis Potvin, six times an all-star, and the linch-pin of their awesome power play. What makes them truly awesome, though, is the lineup behind these superstars. With a mixture of experienced veterans like Butch Goring and Clark Gillies and young scorers like John Tonelli, of steady checkers like Bob Nystrom and clever scorers like Anders Kallur, the Islanders simply have no weaknesses. They represent much of what has changed about the NHL, in that they have a leaven of Europeans (Kallur and another Swede, Stefan Persson) and a sprinkling of Americans (Dave Langevin and the former Olympian Ken Morrow). In goal is the competitive Billy Smith. Playing disciplined, patient hockey, they overtook St. Louis to finish in first place and waltzed past Toronto in the playoffs. The Oilers have known since Monday morning they would be facing the Islanders and they are not comfortable with the idea.

Gretzky, moreover, has made an unfortunate remark to the press. In what he intended to he an innocent tribute to Montreal, he has called the Canadiens "the greatest team in hockey," and in New York the papers have played up the remark as an insult to the Islanders, who have some of the clippings on their dressing-room wall.

Now, they are playing as if they will avenge Gretzky's comments and everyone else who has ever doubted them all at once. Nystrom scores; Goring scores; Tonelli scores; a youngster named Hector Marini scores, and Denis Potvin scores on a power play. When Gretzky finally manages to break Smith's shutout, the Islanders start again: Gillies, Gillies again, Potvin again. Even after Matti Hagman beats Smith again, the game ends 8–2, and Lord Stanley's Cup looks, for this playoff round at least, safe in its foreign clime.

While the Oilers had been preparing for the Islanders, the New York Rangers, the only member of the old six-team league still in the play-offs, had squeezed by Los Angeles. With the one-sided nature of the Islanders' first win, many New York writers began looking forward to an early semi-final confrontation between Long Island and Manhattan. They spoke too soon. The Islanders won the second game in Uniondale, but its complexion was much different from the 8–2 humiliation. For two periods, the Oilers played the Islanders evenly, holding the score at 3–3: only a questionable penalty call against Jari Kurri as the first period began led to the final result, 6–3. The Islanders' advantage in the game was their power play, and the key to that advantage was the performance of Denis Potvin, who scored three goals while Edmonton was short-handed, including the decisive one with Kurri off, and assisted on two others, to join, along with Gretzky, the list of players who had accumulated five points in a single game. Gretzky was held to one assist.

It was now evident how the Islanders planned to stop the Kid. "We're using a kind of zone," Potvin explained. "We know if we give him enough time and enough targets, he'll blow our doors off. So we're concentrating on covering his wingers, and getting to him quickly to get him off the puck." In reply, Sather continued to use Gretzky in various line combinations—he played twenty-eight minutes and twenty seconds of the game—but, overall, the most effective line the Oilers iced was that of Hagman, Messier, and Anderson, who scored two of their goals.

On the plane home, the Oilers were businesslike. They had, they felt, deserved a better fate in the second game. Playing to this mood, Sather devoted much of their preparation time to studying films of the Islanders, in particular their devastating power play. On the ice, the Oilers practised killing penalties. If they could key on Potvin as well as the Islanders had keyed on Gretzky, Sather figured, they could get back in the series.

On Easter Sunday night, in front of their own frenzied fans, they more than fulfilled their game plan. With his wings shut down, Gretzky blew the Islanders' doors off by himself, scoring three times, including once on a power play. His teammates shut Potvin down. Moog played steadily and with poise, and the Oilers won 5–2, to bring themselves within one victory of tying the series.

The hockey public, meantime, had taken the team into its heart. The clamour to watch them that had begun during the Montreal series now reached a crescendo. For one thing, the eight cities still represented in the playoffs now included only one other in Canada, Calgary, and to many fans the Calgary Flames were still identified with their Atlanta background. For another, there was the Oilers' flair for the dramatic; even when the CBC decided to follow the series Calgary was waging with Philadelphia, the Oilers had a way of stealing their thunder. Early in the telecast of the Calgary-Philadelphia game on Easter Sunday, an announcer dolefully told his audience that Gretzky, who was now leading all playoff scorers, had left the game with an ankle injury—"and all of hockey wishes him a speedy recovery." Gretzky had, in fact, been slapped across the ankle by Billy Smith during a goal-mouth melee, but by the time the television broadcast was able to announce his return to the play it also had to show him breaking in on Smith alone and notching his first goal of the night. From that moment, it was difficult for the CBC to pay any attention to Calgary at all. The Oilers seemed to have appeared by magic to enlighten an otherwise dull round of playoffs for Canadian fans, with a lot of players no one had heard of before but who were suddenly in the thick of a spirited fight with the mighty Islanders. As the time approached for the fourth game, which could very well tie the series, *Hockey Night in Canada* once again had the most anticipated program in the country.

NORTHLANDS COLISEUM, EDMONTON, MONDAY, APRIL 20: Not content with the standing ovation with which they welcome their own heroes to the ice, the Edmonton fans boo the Islanders.

Al Arbour, the Islanders' coach who has helped to build their disciplined system, has chosen to rest the belligerent Billy Smith tonight and, perhaps hoping to catch some of Andy Moog's magic, has chosen to start his own rookie, Roland Melanson. Sather is sticking with Moog, whose entry onto the ice, followed only by a sprinting Gretzky, has raised the crowd's welcome to spine-tingling proportions. Moog's Pillsbury body is splattered with bruises now, but if he is feeling fatigue from his six consecutive playoff starts, it is not showing in his face. If anything, he looks younger than when he started. The newspapermen who have flocked to this series vie with each other for new ways to describe his apple cheeks and baby-fat body, but after each game he holds court for them with presidential aplomb. He does not yet seem to realize that this is the Stanley Cup he is starring in, and, with his equally dispassionate father, who has taken a few days off from his bus-driving job to fly east at Pocklington's expense, he seems to take his stellar position as his due. Those who expected him to collapse under the pressures of the Cup underestimated the technical soundness of his game. Although he has the reflexes of a mongoose, his style is neither spectacular nor acrobatic, and sometimes he can make the most difficult saves look routine. He is, of course, a mainstay of the team now, but his phlegmatic manner keeps him apart from many of their high jinks—or maybe they are just in awe of him, and don't wish to break his spell.

This time, it is the Oilers' power play that jumps on the first opportunity, and Paul Coffey puts them ahead with a clever solo effort. In New York, Coffey talked about what a thrill it has been for him even to play on the same ice as Denis Potvin, but as the series wears on, Coffey is becoming almost as important to the Oilers' progress as Potvin is to the Islanders'.

Moments later, Gretzky accepts a pass from Lariviere and sets up Kurri. 2–0. But when first Anderson and then Coffey draw penalties, leaving the Oilers two men short, Potvin scores with frightening ease, and before the period ends Bob Nystrom makes it 2–2.

Early in the third period, a combination of two youthful errors

sends the Islanders in front. Glenn Anderson trips Butch Goring need-
lessly at centre ice. Then, killing the penalty, Messier unforgiveably tries
to stick-handle when he is the last man back, and Bossy filches the puck
from him to go in and score. Within two minutes, Messier makes up for
his mistake: he takes a pass from Hicks, who has broken up an Islander
rush, and, from an obtuse angle, fires it behind Melanson, and they are
tied again.

Now two other kids make blunders. First, Moog, mistaking a
delayed offside signal for an impending penalty, begins to leave the ice
for an extra attacker with the play still underway, and has to scramble
back when he discovers what he has done. Then Gretzky leaves the ice
for a line change with the play in the Oilers' end and John Tonelli takes
advantage of the lapse to score. 4–3, with only a period left.

Six minutes into the third period, though, Sather expresses his
confidence in the Oilers' youth. When Gord Lane is called for tripping,
he sends out a power-play combination no one has seen before: Gretzky
at centre, with Callighen on one wing and Anderson on the other; on
defence are Paul Coffey and Jari Kurri. When Coffey gets control of
the puck in his own end, he seems to forget that he is missing his usual
anchor Lariviere and takes off up the ice, carrying deep into the Islander
zone. Gretzky trails the play and then, seeing the defensive gap Coffey
has left, slips back to the point himself. Coffey spots him and sends him
the puck. Gretzky to Anderson. Anderson out in front to Callighen.
Callighen scores, to tie the game again. He is the only Oiler on the ice
who is over twenty-one.

For the rest of regulation play, every Edmonton fan's heart is in his
mouth. Hunter takes a penalty. Messier, killing the penalty again, loses
his stick, and the deadly Islander power play buzzes around the net. But
Moog coolly snatches the puck out of the air and gives Messier a chance
to re-equip himself; they survive. Coffey loses the puck in front of his
own goal, but Lariviere covers up for him with a sliding block. Finally,
the buzzer sounds the knell of regulation play, and the teams retire to
prepare for overtime.

In the seven years they have made the playoffs, the Islanders have
been involved in eighteen overtime games. They have won fourteen of

them. The Oilers last year took Philadelphia to overtime twice, and lost. As the teams return, even the staunchest Edmonton supporters have a sense of doom.

Early in the play, though, the Oilers lift their spirits and their cheers. Matti Hagman carries the puck across the Islanders' blueline, is heavily checked, and watches the puck skitter free. Suddenly, Glenn Anderson spurts out of nowhere, flying across the line and headed unimpeded for the goal. He scoops up the puck and ...

The linesman whistles it dead, ruling that the puck has come outside the line and, with Hagman still sprawled in the offensive zone, Anderson is offside. Later, a television replay, which the Oilers watch bitterly in their dressing room, shows the puck has never left the Islanders' end. But the whistle seems to have taken the heart out of the Oilers and the game marches to its inevitable conclusion: with less than six minutes elapsed, Bossy shoots, Moog saves, Trottier shoots, Moog goes down on his back, the puck squidges out behind him, Fogolin tries to clear it, Unger swipes at it, it bounces back to Ken Morrow at the point and Morrow misfires a shot that bounces between the legs of a kneeling Fogolin and into the net.

In the dressing room, Moog, as unperturbed as he has been even in his most triumphant moments, says: "Our guys had it in front and I figured they'd get it out of our zone so I relaxed. But it landed on Morrow's stick and he shot it back. I didn't see what happened until they started dancing, and I didn't like that."

So close to tying the series, the Oilers are now two games behind, with the next, and possibly final, game scheduled for Long Island.

Late in the evening of their heartbreaking defeat, Risto Siltanen called Winnipeg to speak to his agent, Don Baizley. Risto wanted to settle some income-tax matters before the team left for Long Island. To the surprise of Baizley, who had watched the game on television, his Finnish client didn't sound at all dejected.

"Maybe the opposite," said Risto in his careful English.

"But you must be disappointed to have been so close," said Baizley.

"Oh, sure," Risto replied. "But we've learned something, too. We can play these guys at their own game. They're a great hockey team. But we didn't give anything away to them. We're not out of it yet. And even if we lose, we've done something good."

"I'm glad to hear you say that," Baizley said. "It sounds as if you're personally very up."

"Well, it takes a long time, you know," Risto went on. "To come here from Europe is very frightening. It doesn't matter how good you have done at home, when you come here you're aware that this is the National Hockey League, and you know all their names, while they have never heard of you. It can take a long time just to realize that you play the same game. Look at how far Jari has come. When he was first with us in the fall, he wasn't sure he could even play here. But now he is playing like he always played, and doing fine."

"I guess you're all doing fine," Baizley said.

"All of us young guys are," Risto said. "Sure. Now we know we are good, we will just play like we have always played, and we will do fine."

That mood was evident among all the Oilers as they flew back to Long Island. No longer did they have anything to prove. As Sather put it to anyone who asked: "With a couple of breaks in the refereeing, we'd be *ahead* 3–1. If Kurri hadn't got that bad call when we were tied in the second game, I think we could have won it; we were sure playing as well as they were. And that offside against Anderson, well, look at the tapes."

More than at any time since their remarkable turnaround had begun in Hartford nearly a month ago, they were able to enjoy the results of what they had already done—anything else would be icing on the cake. Since Hartford, they had lost only to the Islanders, winning eight of their other nine games along the way and tying their nemesis, Colorado. The attention they were getting pleased them. "Canadians are caught up in national pride," Al Strachan had written of them in the *Globe and Mail*, and in Edmonton, a city that was growing blasé about its perennially successful football team, they had become daily front-page news.

"It's like a dream come true," Paul Coffey told his parents, and Brett Callighen said: "I don't know what it's like to win the Stanley Cup, but it can't be much more fun than we're already having."

Incredibly, the fun continued on the ice, and at the Nassau Coliseum, the Oilers beat the Islanders to carry the series on yet one more game; and bring another quarter of a million dollars into Pocklington's box office. The game was a brilliant one, marked by furious rushes and miraculous goaltending by both Moog and Billy Smith, who returned to the Islanders' goal in spite of Melanson's overtime win. Doug Hicks opened the scoring on a pass from Gretzky. Seven minutes later, Trottier tied it. Then Bossy, scoring his seventh goal of the playoffs, put the Islanders ahead. But before the first period ended, Callighen passed to Gretzky behind the goal. As Gretzky began his bobbing and weaving, Bob Lorimer, an Islander defenceman, extended his stick along the ice as a roadblock. Gretzky simply flipped the puck over it and onto the stick of Glenn Anderson, exactly as they had practised so many times at training camp, and Anderson poked it home to tie the score.

Sather had made some lineup changes for this game. Stan Weir was out, partly because of a case of the flu that had struck him in Edmonton, but also because, since Montreal, Sather had been disappointed in his play. Lumley was rested, too, and to replace his usual checking line of Weir, Lumley, and Hunter, Sather put together Semenko, Garry Unger, and, in a rare start, Pat Hughes. Keeping his other lines intact, this left him with two estimable Swats for reserve duty: Dave Hunter and Curt Brackenbury, who had scarcely been dressed at all since the good times started. Early in the game, Pat Hughes signalled his eagerness to become part of the team by getting into, and winning, a slugging match with the Islanders' tough young forward Duane Sutter.

Just before the second period, Callighen put the Oilers ahead, and the team went to the dressing room as euphoric and confident as it had been all season.

Then, in the third period, a stirring thing happened: the Oilers began to sing. Mark Messier started it. Sitting on the bench, his stick clutched like a spear in his gloved hand, he began to chant, "Here we go, Oilers, here we go." Down the line, Kevin Lowe picked it up. Then Brackenbury. Then everyone else, and all through the arena, amid the din of the suburban Long Island crowd, you could hear them singing.

"Here we go, Oilers, here we go."

With twelve minutes left, Sather sent out Gretzky with two fresh wingers, Hunter and Brackenbury. Gretzky won the face-off and passed to Brackenbury. Brackenbury, his energy pent up from nearly a month on the bench, started to flail his way toward the Islanders' goal but, seeing Hunter open, passed instead. The players on the bench leaped to their feet, their chant turning to screams of encouragement as a scoring chance appeared for two of their least heralded teammates. Hunter missed, but the fervour on the bench continued.

"Here we go, Oilers, here we go."

At 15:19, combining with Messier and Anderson, Matti Hagman made it 4–2. A valiant last-minute goal by Bossy was too late, and once again the series was extended.

On Friday, April 24, with the organ crashing and the cheers of their fans echoing in their ears, the impossible dream ended for the Oilers. The Islanders, older, more experienced—and now with their lips clenched in determination not to let their embarrassment go another game—were simply too much for them. The Oilers played valiantly, and once pulled from behind to tie the score, but they could never get ahead, and the game ended 5–2. As they lined up for the often perfunctory handshake that concluded the series, the Islanders were full of praise for the young Oilers, and their compliments continued in the dressing room afterward. "They're a splendid young team," Al Arbour said.

In their own room, the Oilers felt a mixture of frustration and pride. Sather, Harris, Pocklington, and a number of less formally connected well-wishers moved among them, shaking their hands, ruffling their hair, patting their shoulders, and repeating that they had nothing to be ashamed of. They hadn't. But they had been tantalizingly close to victory, and the dream had affected them all.

In the days that followed the end of their dream, nearly all the Oilers made a run for the exits of Edmonton, seeking an early start on their holidays, which would last until training camp began in the fall. The Finns went to Finland (although the increasingly cosmopolitan Jari Kurri told his roommate Paul Coffey to expect a postcard from Spain during the summer), and the Canadians spread throughout North America: Doug Hicks to Phoenix, Dave Lumley to Cape Cod, Brett Callighen to his cottage in Ontario, Kevin Lowe to his mother's home in Quebec. Among the exceptions to this exodus were Mark Messier, who planned to spend much of the summer re-exploring his home turf, and the married men who had bought houses in town. Even among that group, however, there were those who needed to roam. Driving the unexpected alliance of Glenn Anderson and Curt Brackenbury to the airport, from where they would depart for Hawaii, Dave Semenko suddenly found himself in heed of a Hawaiian vacation, and went with them. On the trip, none of them wore ties.

For Andy Moog, who still appeared unmoved by the emotional ups and downs of the Islanders series, there was still more hockey to play. As his parents returned to British Columbia, where he would join them later, Moog left for Wichita, where he was still eligible to tend goal in the playoffs. The Wichita team was doing splendidly in its own post-season play. But for the Oilers, this news was overshadowed by the performance of one player; Don Murdoch, who had seemingly put his life together, was playing with an excitement that reminded some people of his rookie days in New York, and in the playoffs was leading all minor-league scorers.

Eddie Mio, Ron Lowe, and Gary Edwards watched Moog's departure with mixed feelings. On the one hand, all of them liked Moog, and admired the way he had risen to stardom in the last few weeks. On the other, they realized that only two names from the list on which Moog had now so firmly implanted his own would be on the Oilers' roster when the next season began. To add to their tension over the summer, word was that Barry Fraser's scouting system was even higher on a new prospect than it had been on Moog. The prospect was Grant Fuhr, a young black who had grown up in Edmonton, and who, at nineteen, seemed yet one more ripple in the onrushing wave of the future.

For Wayne Gretzky, at the crest of that wave, prospects for the summer were dizzying. In July, he would move into a new two-storey condominium in a fashionable part of Edmonton's west end. He and Vickie were already drawing up a guest list for a black-tie party to mark his homewarming. In August, Wayne would report to training camp for Team Canada, a collection of the NHL's best players (to which, because of his playoff performance, Paul Coffey would also be named) for an international tournament, but before that he would scarcely have a moment to call his own. In the meantime, Gus Badali had planned an almost unbearably busy schedule of public appearances for him. Badali was also talking about asking Peter Pocklington to raise Wayne's salary for the next season to $800,000, which would make him the highest paid player in the history of the game. Wayne was thinking about having his blond hair permed; as word of this possibility spread, Glen Sather for the first time expressed concern about the Kid "going downtown." "I suppose it's inevitable," Sather said, "but I still hope it doesn't happen."

There was business to be done before anyone left town. On the morning after the last game, Sather, who planned to take Ann to Nairobi to photograph some wildlife and get, for a time at least, as far away from his telephone as possible, called Callighen, as players' representative, and Lee Fogolin, as captain, to his home for one last and congenial meeting. There, the three discussed how to split the $105,000 the team had won as its share of the playoff spoils. They quickly decided to give a full portion to each man who had taken part in the final drive. Before the meeting began, Fogolin proudly announced that his wife, Carol, was now pregnant. Callighen, deciding it was an inopportune moment, did not announce that he had heard of another pregnancy as well: Carol MacDonald, wife of the long-departed B.J., was expecting a baby almost exactly nine months after Blair's trade had been announced.

That afternoon, the Oilers gathered for a last team picture at the Coliseum, some of them still sleepy from their celebrations of the night before. Paul Coffey, to no one's surprise, still sported the dark whiskers he had worn for the playoff drive; Doug Hicks, to almost everyone's, had in a moment of elation shaved off his distinguished beard. Their mood during the picture-taking was not a solemn one—Dave Semenko, muttering mock imprecations in his bass voice, kept turning his back before the film could be exposed—but there were overtones of gravity too. During the summer, everyone knew, Sather would wheel and deal; some players, notably Stan Weir, faced the end of their contracts, and others, including all the members of the Swat team, faced challenges for their jobs. In the months ahead, many of them would run into each other at baseball games and golf tournaments, and even at some formal occasions—Pat Price's wedding, or, as they would soon sorrowfully learn, the funeral of Don Ashby, who was to be killed in an automobile accident on his way home from Wichita. But for the team as an entity, so dramatically changed from the one that had assembled for Joe Black's camera in the fall, the spring afternoon in the Coliseum was a last moment together. The team in the photograph would never exist in precisely that way again. For the men looking into the lens, the occasion marked the end of a time in their lives. And that time, with all its frustrations, disappointments, and adventures, and—gilded by the unforgettable achievements of the still-innocent young superstar who had played among them—with its ultimate happy end, was now a part of the history of their game. In the years to come they would relive many of its moments, and there would be other moments and other seasons to supplant it. But it was a time that would not recur.

## 20

*" … in whatever decade he played, he would have been the scoring champion."*

The Oilers' 1981–82 season, which had such a dramatically different ending from the year in which I had first followed them, was nevertheless an extraordinary one for the team, most notably for Wayne Gretzky. Gretzky set records for both goals and assists and, of course, a record for their total. This combination had a special glimmer in the light of hockey history; virtually every player before him who had led in one or another of these statistics had done so with the help of at least one teammate. In 1970–71, when Phil Esposito set his points record with seventy-six goals and seventy-six assists, Bobby Orr collected 102 assists, also a record, and many of them on goals by Esposito, as well as scoring thirty-seven goals himself, many of them set up by Esposito. In 1944–45, when Maurice Richard scored his fifty goals in fifty games, the league was led in total points not by Richard but by his linemate Elmer Lach. Mike Bossy had Bryan Trottier; Gordie Howe had Ted Lindsay; Bobby Hull had Stan Mikita. Even Marcel Dionne shared the best of his scoring seasons with his linemates Dave Taylor and Charlie Simmer. In recent years, only Guy Lafleur managed to lead the league in scoring without having one of his linemates or a frequent playing partner join him in the top ten—and even Lafleur had done so only once in the three years he won the scoring championship.

In 1981–82, many of the Oilers achieved impressive statistics. Mark Messier scored fifty goals. Glenn Anderson had 105 points. With twenty-nine goals and sixty assists, Paul Coffey emerged as one of the league's most prolific defencemen. But none of the three played regularly on Gretzky's shifts. In all, the Oilers scored 417 goals in the Year of the Kid—in itself a record—and once again Gretzky was involved in half of them (this time raising that league record to 50.84 per cent). But he distributed his largesse, playing sometimes with such defensive specialists as Dave Hunter or his protector, Dave Semenko, and sometimes with players whose styles matched his own, Jari Kurri or his old partner Brett Callighan. Inevitably, he sweetened their statistics. When Dave Lumley joined him at right wing for one extended period in the fall, Lumley went on a scoring rampage and came within a whisker of tying Charlie Simmer's record for scoring in consecutive games. But when the season's totals were totted up, no two Oilers combined approached Gretzky's figures, and no single teammate who had played regularly with him even approached the league's top ten. Gretzky was on a plateau by himself. He scored ninety-two goals. He set a record for three-goal games—ten of them, including three four-goalers and one five. He led the league in game-winning goals and shared the lead (with Michel Goulet of Quebec) on those scored while his team was short-handed. On top of all that, he collected 112 assists, playing his own Orr, as it were, to his own Esposito. It was as if a football player had led his league in throwing touchdown passes and in catching them. No one had ever seen anything like it before.

For a while, some of the men who had cavilled at Gretzky's quick rise to fame continued to disparage his exploits. Stan Fischler, in the *Hockey News*, wrote several columns early in the season hinting that the rest of the league was going easy on the man Fischler dubbed Mr. Waynederful. Fischler also suggested that the combined offensive and defensive skills of at least one other player, Bryan Trottier, made him more valuable than Gretzky. And Dick Beddoes, undaunted by the reaction to his Gretzky-baiting of the previous year, kept jibing at Gretzky on Hamilton television, claiming that what Gretzky was accomplishing could not have been accomplished in the old, six-team league. Undoubtedly, this was true. Even those of us who had celebrated Gretzky from the beginning would not have argued that he could have run up such unbelievable statistics before expansion watered down the opposition. What we did argue, though, was that he would have been a special player at any point in the game's history, and that whether or not he was the most remarkable of all the players in our pantheon of heroes, he had certainly established his place among them.

Well before the season ended, the most convincing statement on either side of this argument came from an unexpected, if unimpeachable, source: Maurice Richard. The year before, when Mike Bossy had been closing in on Richard's record of fifty in fifty, the NHL had tried to trot the Rocket out of retirement in Montreal to witness the occasion; but even in the formal acknowledgement Richard had given the press when Bossy eventually tied him, he had sounded somewhat grudging. Now, as it became evident that Gretzky, too, would have a chance to tie or break this most hallowed of records (he scored thirty-one times in the Oilers' first twenty-six games), many of us were speculating on how Richard would react.

Gretzky gave him little chance to prepare. In the first four games of December, he was shut out, then four times in a row he scored one goal each, bringing him to thirty-five in thirty-four and, for a while, cooling the media fever. For many of us, the hope was that if he were to achieve the record it would be in game number forty-seven, which was to take place in Toronto, in January, not only on national television but also in front of his parents and his family. Gretzky himself had set his sights on this game before the season began, saying in a private moment that he would like to break the record there. Through the Christmas season, however, he went on a spree that caught all of us—including, he later admitted, himself—by surprise: three against Minnesota in game thirty-five; two against Calgary in thirty-six; one against Vancouver (a late and apparently meaningless goal in a 6–1 romp); four (including two short-handed) against Los Angeles in game thirty-eight. Still, the next game was against Philadelphia at home on December 30, and most of us were convinced we would wait until the new year to see him break the Rocket's record.

At 7:47 of the first period, a rebound of Paul Coffey's shot jumped off the backboards onto Gretzky's stick. Forty-six. Less than three minutes later, leading an Oiler break, he blasted a slapshot past Pete Peeters. Forty-seven.

Halfway through the second period, he scored on a breakaway. Forty-eight.

"Gretz-kee, Gretz-kee," chanted the fans, reminding onlookers of the way they had hailed Andy Moog in the playoffs the year before.

Five minutes into the third period, he scored again. Forty-nine.

Halfway through the period, he missed one chance when Coffey sent him in alone.

"Gretz-kee. Gretz-kee."

With a minute to play, the Flyers, trailing 6–5 and less interested in stopping the record than in tying the game, pulled Peeters. Glenn Anderson scooped up a Philadelphia rebound and headed for centre ice. Gretzky broke toward the open area. Only Bill Barber stood between the two young Oilers and the open net. Anderson to Gretzky. From the blueline he drifted a shot. His fiftieth goal—in thirty-nine games.

From Montreal, Richard, whose thirty-seven-year-old record was now shattered, sounded almost effusive. "I have now seen Gretzky enough," he said, "to say that in whatever decade he played he would have been the scoring champion."

Although the Oilers went into a mild slump after the exultation of Gretzky's scoring explosion, losing to Vancouver the next night, they turned into the new year far ahead of the pace even their most ardent supporters had dared hope they would set. Of their first forty games—half the season's total—they had won twenty-five, lost nine, and tied six. At the same point last year, they had won only nine. They were so far ahead of their own division of the newly reorganized league that first place was virtually assured. Even more astonishingly, they were ahead of the entire league. Buffalo, Boston, Montreal, and, of course, the Islanders were all playing as well as anyone had expected, but they were in a race for second place. The rest of the league was strung out behind, with Colorado, Washington, Detroit, and Hartford in much the same positions they had finished the previous spring, and Toronto, even more inept than in 1980–81, and Los Angeles, having apparently fallen on disaster, threatening to join them. Winnipeg, now coached by Tom Watt, the former university coach whose teachings had inspired so much of the return of pretty hockey to the NHL, had risen to the middle of the pack. But the season's most exciting story was the Oilers. By mid-season, at least one knowledgeable commentator, Dave Hodge of *Hockey Night in Canada*, was suggesting that Glen Sather would be the coach of the year, Gretzky the most valuable player, Coffey the outstanding defenceman, and that the rookie of the year and the leading candidate for the all-star position was Grant Fuhr.

Fuhr had been surprising the experts well before the season began. By tradition, and never more so than in the offensive-minded 1970s, general managers had used their first draft choices to bolster their scoring power, or at least to acquire, as the Oilers had acquired Kevin Lowe, good, solid two-way players. Only one goaltender—John Davidson, chosen by St. Louis—had gone in the first round, while such now established stars as Mike Liut and Billy Smith had been taken fifty-sixth and fifty-ninth among their year's crop, and had been allowed to mature in backup roles. Sather, in spite of the Oilers' apparent depth in goal, took Fuhr at his first opportunity, seventh in the league. Behind his reasoning was not only Fuhr's Edmonton boyhood—he had played on the team coached by Mark Messier's father before leaving for Junior A in Victoria—but his exceptional ratings on Barry Fraser's charts. On the ice, Fuhr displayed marvellous technical skills. Even the untrained eye could perceive that his style was more one of control than of desperate reflex, that after nearly all his saves the puck went into a neutral corner or toward one of his own teammates. But away from the ice he had another quality that even Fraser's charts found difficult to measure. In manner and in conversation and in spite of his tender years he was as cool as ice and as imperturbable as a prairie slough.

The NHL never had a legal barrier like the one that kept blacks out of baseball until the 1940s. It didn't need it. As long as professional hockey remained a Canadian monopoly, it remained white. A few blacks—Hibby Galloway, the Carnegie brothers of Toronto, a whole team that barnstormed out of St. Catharines, Ontario—appear in the annals of the early minor leagues, but there is no suggestion of the equivalent of Josh Gibson or Satchel Paige blooming unseen in the winter air. Nor was Willie O'Ree, who finally broke whatever restrictions the league had in 1957, a Jackie Robinson; O'Ree played in forty-three games over seven seasons with the Boston Bruins, departing with four goals and ten assists. But even in the early 1980s, Fuhr's race set him apart. Until his arrival with the Oilers, Tony McKegney of Buffalo had been the only black in the NHL.

In July 1981, the Oilers gathered for a softball tournament in Niagara Falls, Ontario, one of the few times they saw each other over the summer. Despite his recent arrival, Fuhr's position as the team's number-one draft choice entitled him to be taken along. On the evening before the tournament began, some of the older players celebrated their reunion with typical off-season enthusiasm, and the next morning a few of them needed surcease from the bright Niagara sunshine. Brackenbury and Semenko, among others, showed up for their first game with black boot-polish smeared under their eyes. Billy Harris asked to take a picture; and Brackenbury went to drag the teenaged Fuhr from his bed. When he appeared, his dark cheekbones were covered with white polish, and in the photo, he appears as a negative image of his new teammates, but already a member of their exclusive fraternity.

With broadcasters and the press, Fuhr showed a still more remarkable facet of his personality. He would answer questions as if he had never learned the language of "the interview"—the ritual by which hockey players would phrase wordy and predictable answers to wordy and predictable questions. Fuhr answered what was asked of him, no less but certainly no more. Asked if he found NHL play much tougher than Junior A, he would not say, as the ceremony demanded, "Well, they're faster here and they shoot harder and I'm playing against guys I used to read about and dreamed of playing against, but I just try to do my job one game at a time; and if I hang in there I think ..." Instead, he answered, "No." Had it surprised him when Sather had shown so much faith in him? "No, not really." Well, did he like playing on the same team as Gretzky and the other young stars? "Sure," he would say, and look quizzically at his interrogator, as if the question had not been serious.

There was no arrogance in these exchanges; Fuhr simply talked the way he played goal—coolly and giving up no easy rebounds.

By the end of training camp, he had established himself as Edmonton's leading goalie, allowing just five goals in 140 minutes of play. Andy Moog, the hero of last year's playoffs, was unable to recapture the brilliance he had displayed in the spring, and to Sather's eye at least, he appeared to loaf in practice. Sather sent him, still just twenty-one, to Wichita. Gary Edwards, his role as emergency replacement now redundant, was left unprotected when the team listed its playing roster, and he was snapped up by St. Louis, where he would fill the same role he had played in Edmonton. After much deliberation between Ron Low and Eddie Mio, and after weighing the relative cost of their contracts (Low had a "one-way" clause that would have made sending him to the minors much more expensive), Sather traded Mio to the New York Rangers for a minor leaguer, and the team opened the season with its youngest and oldest goalies, Fuhr and Low.

Otherwise, the lineup that opened the 1981–82 season was essentially the same as the team that had come together so dramatically in Hartford in March: on defence, Fogolin (the captain's c now a permanent fixture on his sweater), Lowe, Lariviere, Coffey, Siltanen, Hicks, and Huddy; at forward, Anderson, Hagman, Messier, Hunter, Brackenbury, Pat Hughes (his health restored), Kurri, Callighen, Lumley, Weir, Semenko, Unger, and Gretzky. From the previous year's Wichita team, Tom Roulston now seemed to have found a regular berth, and Mike Forbes, a handsome, blond twenty-four-year-old journeyman from Brampton, Ontario, was kept up to fill in on defence.

After a brief stumble at the starting gate—Fuhr lost the first game he played—the Oilers picked up the momentum they had shown in their gallant displays against Montreal and the Islanders. While the older teams rolled slowly into shape, the Oilers soared, playing with the new confidence their triumphs of the spring had instilled. If they were indeed the team of the NHL's future, the future seemed to have arrived ahead of schedule, and brought with it an era that was dominated by their free-wheeling, nonchalant play. Gretzky was on top of the league in scoring before the end of the first week. Anderson, Hagman, and

Messier played brilliantly. Pat Hughes added fresh aggressiveness. Gary Unger, in spite of two sudden and severe injuries to his cheek (he reluctantly donned a helmet after the first one, but ripped it off at the first opportunity to fight), seemed to have found his own fountain of youth in Edmonton. Brackenbury chirped encouragement. Semenko loomed. Coffey carried the puck as if his initials were carved on its surface and, with twenty goals before Christmas, found himself among the league's top ten scorers. No one, it appeared, could do anything wrong. Only an injury to Hughes kept Lumley, who had sat out thirteen straight games, from being sent to Wichita, but when he did crack the lineup, he scored fourteen goals in the next twelve, foregoing an opportunity to maintain his streak by passing to Lowe for the winner against Calgary and then, two nights later, scoring his first NHL hat trick. In goal, Fuhr was uncanny. Many close games the Oilers might have lost the previous year were turned around by his cool domination. The rebounds kept going to his teammates. His interviews remained short. After his opening defeat, he went twenty-two games without a loss, closing in on yet another NHL record.

Sather installed a ping-pong table in the dressing room, and, as the team rolled east for its first long road trip of the year, the world seemed coloured in white and blue and glowing Oiler orange.

Shortly after one o'clock on the afternoon of January 15, 1982, Gretzky strode through the swinging glass doors of the Westin Hotel in Toronto, carrying his suitcase, In spite of the punishing cold that had dogged the Oilers through the first days of their eastern trip, he wore only a trench coat over his beige suit, white shirt, and striped tie. His hands were bare. Just before leaving Edmonton, he had had his hair trimmed, and the summer perm was now scarcely evident; an unruly forelock fell across his eyes, and the neat shag folded back over his temples to reveal a generous portion of his ears.

Gretzky had continued to score goals and accumulate assists after breaking the Rocket's record, and now, with 123 points in forty-six games, he was so far ahead of the rest of the league (his nearest rival had seventy-four) that the remainder of the season would be only a matter of seeing how many more records he would set. Away from the arena, he had moved as far ahead of his hockey colleagues in celebrity. He was lionized beyond any of the heroes who had preceded him. His popularity now transcended that of hockey itself. Part of this, of course, could be attributed to the era in which he played, with its commercial endorsements and public appearances. By the middle of the 1981–82 season, no Canadian who read newspapers or magazines could be unaware of who Wayne was or what he looked like. His image adorned billboards and posters everywhere. (On their way in from the airport the Oilers had passed a sign endorsing the hotel they were travelling to that declared only STAY AT WAYNE GRETZKY'S PLACE in large black letters.) But part of it, too, had to do with the becoming way in which Gretzky was handling his status. He was now, if not comfortable with being the constant centre of attention, at least not made uncomfortable by it. The only exceptions to this rule would occur when, in public or in private, the conversation would stray from his own universe to politics or other worldly affairs. Then Gretzky, who did not read widely, would stumble and blush. But on his own turf —the ice—he was secure. With reporters and fans, he unfailingly showed the patience and good humour that had been his hallmark since Walter had lectured him in Kingston more than a decade earlier. Nearly all the people who wrote about him—Stan Fischler and Dick Beddoes notwithstanding—came to cherish him, his modesty, and his lack of pretension. At a time when so many heroes of more serious pursuits were failing, Gretzky remained unblemished, and in the winter of his twenty-first birthday—eleven days off when he arrived in Toronto—he was the most celebrated Canadian of his time.

The team's arrival in Toronto, the media capital of the country, marked the peak of this phenomenon, and now, as Gretzky walked across the lobby, he was being followed by a retinue of reporters and photographers that rivalled the trappings of a royal tour—or, more accurately, those of a touring rock group. Cameras whirred and clicked in his path. Earlier in the week, because of an unmanageable number of requests for private interviews, the Oilers had set up a formal press conference for him, and when the requests continued to pour in—the 132nd was filed the night before his arrival—they moved it to the Governor General's suite on the Westin's mezzanine. Since eleven o'clock, reporters and photographers had been milling around the suite, drinking coffee and asking questions of Peter Pocklington, who had flown in from Edmonton to witness the occasion and to complete negotiations on a new contract for Gretzky, and Gus Badali, who had driven down from suburban Don Mills for the same purposes. At the front of the room, nineteen microphones had been strapped to a podium to receive Gretzky's words, and a semicircle of camera tripods, lights at the ready, awaited his entrance.

Gretzky looked tired and preoccupied when he came into the suite, but as he moved toward the podium, the cameras still whining and clicking in accompaniment, he smiled in salute to the press. Several times, he spotted special friends, men who had written about him before his fame had grown, and with one or two of them he exchanged private glances, rolling his eyes upward as if to say, "Isn't this incredible?"

When he reached the podium, however, the press was flummoxed. For all their preparation, there was now little left to ask Gretzky that he hadn't answered before. Jim Hunt, a veteran of the media wars who now handles sports for radio station CKEY in Toronto, sought a way out of this dilemma by saying, early in the ceremonies: "Wayne, is there anything you haven't been asked about?" And Gretzky, after joining in the common laughter, said, "Well, when I was in Washington yesterday, a woman asked me something I hadn't been asked before. She wanted to know who of all the people around me I would miss the most and I said that would be my father." He looked up, seeking new questions. But Hunt, sensing a dialogue, went one step further. "After all," he said, "we can't ask you about beating your wife, since you're not married. I mean, if you were Bobby Hull ..."

Hunt's colleagues in the press made sounds of embarrassment, and Gretzky, blushing, did not laugh.

When the press conference ended, Pocklington and Badali retired together to the offices of Rose, Persiko, Arnold, and Glieberman on the nineteenth floor of the Toronto-Dominion Centre. Rose et al. were

Gretzky's lawyers, and one of the partners also served on the board of Pocklington's Fidelity Trust. The office provided a convenient meeting ground to resume the contractual discussions that, over the course of the season, had grown thornier than either side would have wished. Curiously, much of the difficulty arose from Pocklington's generosity toward his young superstar. While the contract that Wayne had signed so ceremoniously at centre ice in Edmonton on his eighteenth birthday was still legally in force, Pocklington was among the first to agree that its terms—which gave Gretzky roughly $180,000 in 1981–82—were unworthy of his accomplishments. And especially after it was announced over the summer that Marcel Dionne had just signed for $600,000 a year, Pocklington would willingly have torn up the twenty-one-year contract and offered a more munificent replacement. Before he could do that, however, Gretzky let it be known through Badali that he would like one million dollars a year. Pocklington felt pressured; it would have suited his regal style to grant the extra money, but it did not suit it to be *asked*. For a time over the summer, feelings had grown so intense that Gretzky declined to show up for a fishing trip Pocklington had planned for the Arctic, and Sather, who negotiated with other players or their agents, washed his hands of dealings with Badali, saying that he could not act as Wayne's coach if he was caught in a squabble over money.

While Badali and Pocklington talked in Toronto, Wayne slipped away for a few rare hours in Brantford with his family and some childhood friends. The media were not told where he had gone. That evening, the group at the Gretzky home watched a videotape Walter had prepared of some of Wayne's goals and of a debate on the CBC's *Journal* in which Wayne's merits were disputed by Dick Beddoes. Beddoes, in Wayne's opinion, had looked foolish, and still laughing at the energy of the debate, Wayne retired, full of pizza, to the bed he had slept in for the first fourteen years of his life.

Badali and Pocklington ultimately resolved their differences. Pocklington convinced himself that he had won by keeping the annual salary figure below one million dollars—at least until the Oilers could raise their ticket prices and enjoy some revenue from television. But lest the settlement appear stingy, Pocklington threw the title to a shopping centre into the deal, and the agent and the owner shook hands.

MAPLE LEAF GARDENS, SATURDAY, JANUARY 16, 1982: Gretzky made it to practice today, but in keeping with the tenor of his weekend, he had to leave early. With his hair still wet from the shower and still followed by the cameras, he made his way from the dressing room to the Hot Stove Lounge, where Daoust skates, which he endorses, wished to make a presentation. Before the ceremony, King Clancy, seventy-eight years old and one of the great figures in NHL history, asked the Kid for an autograph. "For my grandchildren," he said. Then a man from Daoust presented Wayne with a bronze replica of Wayne's feet. Wayne said he didn't much like the look of them and handed them to his father. Walter Gretzky handed them to Lefty Reid, the curator of the Hockey Hall of Fame. They will, presumably, remain there, part of the growing collection of artifacts and mementoes that one day may require a wing of their own.

Just after the ceremony, Bobby Hull, in town for *Hockey Night in Canada*, also asked Wayne for an autograph. Now, in the pressbox, Milt Dunnell, the sagacious columnist of the Toronto *Star*, remarks: "If that kid can play a hockey game tonight, it will be a miracle." But earlier, Dunnell, who has covered hockey since Howie Morenz played for Stratford, asked for an autograph too.

There is an unusual crowd here tonight, much younger than the Gardens regulars, many of whose boxes are paid for by corporations. Tonight is for the real fans. Scalpers have been selling gold tickets for $300 a pair, and there have been classified ads in the *Star* all week offering to buy or trade for "a pair of Gretzkys." Oiler sweaters are in evidence everywhere, nearly all with 99 on the back. The Oilers' 99 now outsells the Leafs' 27—Darryl Sittler's number—in Toronto.

Constrained by television, the game does not start until seven minutes after eight. Very early in the first period it does not look good for the Oilers. Before thirty seconds have gone by, Fuhr gives up a disastrously generous rebound. Wilf Paiment gobbles it up for Toronto and passes to Normand Aubin. Moments later, Michel Larocque makes the first of a series of brilliant saves in the Leaf goal. His teammates keep firing at the now obviously shaky Fuhr, and halfway through the first period it is 3–0 Toronto.

Then, with ten seconds left before the intermission, Mark Messier sets up Gretzky on Larocque's doorstep. It is reminiscent of the Oilers' last game here, when, at a similar time and with a similar score, Gretzky launched an Edmonton comeback. He whirls, fakes Larocque—and shoots wide of the open net. It is hard not to think of the hectic weekend he has put in. As the game goes on, Gretzky's frustration mounts. At 10:33 of the second period, Toronto's Bob Manno grabs a puck in his own goal crease. Penalty shot. Sather assigns it to Gretzky. The crowd tingles; this is what they have come to see. Skating in slowly, Gretzky fakes once, twice, and flips the puck between Larocque's knees. But in the last fraction of a second, it catches the inside of a pad and drops harmlessly onto the goal-line. The crowd rises in ovation—for Larocque.

Two minutes later, Gretzky does score, on a clever backhand. But it is already evident that the team's—and his—spirits have been broken, and although nearly all the 16,390 people who have paid to watch the Oilers stay until the end, the Leafs win easily, 7–1.

Occurring, as it did, before the lens of national television and under the pressure of Gretzky's media parade, the loss to Toronto was the low point of the year to date for the Oilers. Viewed from the perspective of what happened later, it may indeed have been a more frightening portent than it was taken to be at the time. But it didn't faze them for long. Home from their eastern trip, during which they set several attendance records, they resumed their winning ways. Although the older teams—in particular the Islanders—played more seriously in the season's latter half, the Oilers managed to stay in front until very near the end.

In Toronto, Sather had resolved to put a barricade between Gretzky and his pursuers. But with Wayne's disarming inability to say no (except to *Playboy* and to a religious magazine that wanted him to attribute his puck sense to the Almighty), such dictums were easier said than enforced. As the Kid closed in on Esposito's record of seventy-six goals in a season, *Maclean's*, which had ignored him only two seasons earlier, ran a cover story on "The Glory of Gretzky." The *Sporting News*, hitherto more interested in baseball or National League football, named him its athlete of the year. At the all-star dinner in Washington, President Reagan made jokes about him ("We'd trade two draft choices and the state of Texas for him"); the 7-UP commercial he had made with Keith became the first in which a hockey player sold goods in the United States, and only a snowstorm kept him from the ultimate accolade of American celebrity, an appearance on the *Tonight Show*. As Morenz had fifty years earlier, he was raising hockey's appeal in the rich markets of the U.S.A.

Gretzky's rush past Esposito's record was not as spectacular as his shattering of Richard's, but he added a fillip to set it in the minds of all who saw it. On February 19, he scored a hat trick against Hartford—his eighth of the season—to bring himself within one. Number seventy-six came in Detroit, after he had run up four assists. Esposito, following along to watch his disappearance from that page of the record books, joined the caravan to Buffalo. Late in the third period, with the score tied 3–3, it appeared that everyone would have to carry on to the next game in Pittsburgh, until suddenly Gretzky stole the puck from Buffalo's Steve Patrick and raced in to flip the puck between Don Edwards's legs. Then he scored again at 18:14. And then, putting his stamp on the evening, once more at 19:43.

In March, with a break in the schedule allowing the team to steal away for a brief respite at a California resort, Sather, as he had the previous season, completed a number of intricate deals to finetune his team for the playoffs. On the day before the trading deadline, he sent two minor leaguers to Toronto in exchange for Laurie Boschman, a twenty-one-year-old who had been the Leafs' first draft choice in 1979. Boschman's was an interesting case. After a bright beginning in the NHL, he had run into frustrating times, most recently when Harold Ballard, the Leafs' owner, had blamed his complacent play on his conversion to

Christianity. Sather cackled gleefully over his acquisition, which, while hardly fitting his pattern of reclamation, would give him one more chance to watch a player live up to his early promise.

More sadly, Sather dealt away two of the veterans who had been with him through all his campaigns as a coach, Doug Hicks and Stan Weir, Hicks to Washington for a rookie left-winger named Todd Bidner, for whom Sather expressed high hopes, and Weir to Colorado for a minor-leaguer. Neither had been playing regularly in 1982, and Weir in particular, who had gone thirty-one games without a goal, was obviously written out of the future in Edmonton. For both, it would mean not only the end of the friendships they had made in Edmonton but the loss of playoff bonuses. "At least I'll get to play now," said Weir as he left for his fourth NHL city.

Even more sadly, for those of us who had come to look on him as a vital part of the team's spirit, Curt Brackenbury was sent down to Wichita. The faster and more sophisticated the play in the NHL became, and the more the Oilers became a serious contender rather than a team playing on youth and reckless abandon alone, the less Brack had belonged. The game, as Sather said, had passed him by. In the fourteen games he dressed for in 1981–82, he had scored no goals, earned two assists, and drawn twelve minutes in penalties. He had just turned thirty when he went down, and even among those who were fondest of him there was little hope he would be back.

In the final weeks of the season, the Oilers played adequately at best, and the Islanders, looking ever more likely to win their third consecutive Stanley Cup, moved inexorably past them in the overall standings. Gretzky fell off the pace that had threatened to propel him past the unheard-of total of 100 goals. One reason for their slowdown was simply exhaustion. Blood tests showed that four of them—Kevin Lowe, Semenko, Messier, and Gretzky himself—were dangerously close to anemia; the long season, with its fierce pressures (and, to be sure, their own sometimes carefree approach to diet and rest), had worn them down. Sather instituted strict new rules about vitamins and sleep, and their iron levels rose. The laboratory results, however, could not entirely explain their erratic play. Coffey, as healthy as he had ever been, began making some of the same mistakes he had made at the beginning of his rookie year, and dropped down the scoring list. Coffey's decline was sudden and bewildering. For most of the season, he had played brilliantly, like a character in a Saturday morning cartoon running through the air. Now, as the season and its publicity caught up with him, it was as if he had suddenly realized where he was. He plummeted to earth. His play grew so tense that Sather wondered whether he should dress him for the playoffs at all. Just in case, Sather arranged to bring up Randy Gregg, a massive medical student who had played on the Canadian Olympic team, and in Japan, and who had finally signed a professional contract with the Oilers; Gregg, too, was an Edmonton native.

Other parts of the newly tinkered-with lineup had difficulty meshing. Boschman, struggling with a back injury he had suffered in Toronto, was slow to come around. Many of the others seemed flat and uninspired. Fuhr continued his steady play in goal, supplemented by the old pro Ron Low, but staunch goalkeeping was not the Oilers' style. Only Messier, hurtling toward his first fifty-goal season in spite of his health, and Anderson, skating with all his irrepressible exuberance, were playing as they had in the opening burst of the season.

Still, with their playoff position long since assured, and virtually every record within their reach now grasped—and, most of all, with the memory of their dramatics of the previous spring still fresh in everyone's memory—the Oilers appeared ready to make, at the very least, a strong challenge for the Cup. Certainly in their first round, against Los Angeles, who had limped to a seventeenth-place finish, there would be no problem. No problem at all.

What happened? Through the summer of 1982, Glen Sather, travelling across the continent and twice back and forth to Europe, would face the same dreary, depressing question. Peter Pocklington, his own spring terrifyingly upset by a kidnapping incident in his home (Pocklington was rescued but wounded by a police bullet), would search for answers. The players, scattered once again to their holiday retreats, would grin sheepishly or snap surly replies. The Edmonton press, turning as nasty as it had been gloating a year before ("weak-kneed wimps," Terry Jones called them in one particularly vicious column in the *Journal*), would ponder endlessly, and talk of needed changes they had not perceived before.

The defeat was as stunning as the triumph had been. The roof fell in, the penny dropped, the balloon burst, and the world was shocked.

Nine minutes into the first game with Los Angeles, everything seemed to be going as planned. Led by two goals from Risto Siltanen, the Oilers had a 4–1 lead. Fuhr looked steady. True, Los Angeles was bumping and shoving, but it appeared that the sign Sather had posted in the dressing room listing the number of games the Oilers would have to win to take the Cup—fifteen—would drop a figure that night. Then Semenko sent out an errant pass, Gretzky took a silly penalty, and before the period ended it was 4–4.

After two periods, Los Angeles had an 8–6 lead.

In the third, Edmonton pecked back. 8–8. It was not a playoff score. (No two teams had ever scored sixteen goals in one playoff game before.) It got worse. With five minutes left, Charlie Simmer scored, and the Kings went on to win 10–8. The Oilers were humiliated.

The second game, finally won 3–2 on an overtime goal by Gretzky, did little to restore their confidence.

And in game three, in Los Angeles, the Oilers suffered the most embarrassing defeat anyone could remember in a Stanley Cup game. Leading 5–0 after two periods—with two of their goals having been scored short-handed—and so apparently in control of the game that the Kings' owner, Jerry Buss, packed up his pretty date and went home, the Oilers fell apart. Jay Wells scored. Doug Smith scored on a power play. Simmer jammed home a rebound. Then, with five minutes left, Gary Unger took a major penalty for high-sticking, and the Kings' Dave Lewis drew a minor. The Kings would play short-handed for two minutes (unless the Oilers scored); the Oilers, for the rest of the game. With five men aside, Mark Hardy scored for the Kings. The Coliseum was bedlam. In the last minute, Los Angeles pulled their goalie, and now with six skaters to the Oilers' four they swarmed around the net. With five seconds showing on the clock, Steve Bozek scored a goal he would never forget, sending the game into overtime.

The overtime took two minutes and twenty-three seconds, ending 6–5 Los Angeles in the most astounding comeback in NHL playoff history.

After the game, Sather exploded. As the jubilant Kings poured into their dressing room and began to pound on the wall that separated them from the Oilers, a Los Angeles public relations man came past to taunt him, and Sather tried to hit him. Only the pushing of the crowd kept the incident from becoming much uglier. As Sather closed the Oilers' room, the shouts of victory from next door continued. The players sat in white-faced shock, their elbows on their knees, their hands dangling in despair. Sather realized that, as he never had before, he now had to impose some calm, to take stock, to pull his team—and himself, if he could cool his own anger—together.

It was now evident, he figured, that the Los Angeles strategy involved as much physical contact as they could generate—not so much to intimidate the Oilers, for the Kings were not bullies by nature, but to entice them into playing the same way, to drive them into frenzied retaliation, and to take away from them the prettiness of their game. To get at Gretzky they were employing the same principle; they were not just hacking at him—he had been hacked at before—but bumping him at every opportunity, running into him as he turned from the play, bouncing him when he wheeled near the boards. Little of this was illegal, but it was keeping Wayne a second or two behind his usual pace. And, most seriously of all, it was driving him to a frustrated response. Gretzky, who had taken only twenty-six minutes in penalties through the regular season's eighty games, had eight in the playoffs' first three. "Stupid hockey," the Kid had called the Oilers' play in one of his innumerable media interviews about the earlier loss. Now, Sather thought, Gretzky might be talking about himself. As angry as Sather was, he could not help replaying in his mind the moment that had given Los Angeles a chance to score its final goal. With the Kings' net empty, Gretzky had snared the puck in his own end. Instead of just banging it outside the blue line, he had glanced toward the open goal. In that one fraction of a second, Marcel Dionne had stolen it from him and sent it to Steve Bozek for the tying score.

Well, it was too late to recall that moment now, Sather thought.

"Let's get out of here," he said, and called a team meeting for the next morning.

As in Hartford when they had faced a crisis the year before, in the Los Angeles dressing room, the Oilers heard no fiery speeches, no pep talks, no exhortations. For more than an hour, they just talked quietly about what they had been through together and how much the next hurdles meant to them. That evening, Sather, his cheeks red but his voice low, said he felt more confident of victory than he ever had before. And when game-time rolled around, the Oilers fulfilled his confidence. Even when Dionne sent the Kings into an early lead and the fans into frenzy that approached that of the spectacular comeback, the Oilers remained in control. After a breakaway goal by Kurri, Anderson scored and then Pat Hughes. Playing disciplined hockey, and quietly and de-terminedly in control of themselves, the Oilers held on to win 3–2.

Because of the unexpected length of the series—nearly everyone had predicted Edmonton would win three straight—the Oilers had made no airline reservations for their return to Edmonton, and with the final game scheduled for the next night, April 13, at home, Sather had no choice but to share a charter flight with the Kings. In retrospect, this omission seemed almost as serious an error as his booking all the available flights from Montreal had been a clever tactic. Arriving at Edmonton airport at 5:30 in the morning, the Oilers were exhausted. So, of course, were the Kings, but for the Oilers the necessity of sitting on the same airplane as their nemesis for the long flight had a debili-tating effect. Once so highly favoured, they felt tense and worried; the Kings, with nothing to lose, were loose and relaxed. For perhaps the first time in their lives, the Oilers faced the possibility that they could lose, shamefully, before their own fans.

Sather had one dramatic ploy available to him. After sticking with Fuhr through the first four games, he could switch to the veteran Low—or, even more theatrically, he could recall Moog from Wichita and stage a reprise of last year's plot. He considered each move briefly, and then rejected both. Fuhr, extraordinarily in the light of the football-like scores of two of the games, was playing steadily. None of the goals that had pushed the Oilers so close to the abyss could be blamed on him. As one change, Sather would restore Paul Coffey to the lineup. But in the end, he decided to go with essentially the combinations that had brought the team this far.

The players were flat. Flat and tense. The team that had so long flown on the wings of its own cockiness was afraid to lose, and now, inevitably, they were losing. 1–0. 2–0. Gretzky, even in defeat high among the league's playoff scorers, made it 2–1, but less than ten minutes later Los Angeles scored again. Before the first period ended, Coffey brought the Oilers back to within one, but the second period was all Los Angeles. 6–2.

At 14:24 of the last period, Dave Lumley scored the Oilers' last goal of the year. Too little, too late. The game, and the season, ended 7–4.

As the Montreal players he admired had done last year, Sather went to the winners' dressing room to congratulate them and wish them luck. All over the league, favourites were falling. Quebec had beaten Montreal. Vancouver put out Calgary. The Rangers eliminated Philadelphia. And even the mighty Islanders came within a heartbeat of elimination at the hands of Pittsburgh. But, as they had been all year, the Oilers were the story on everyone's lips. From the bottom of the league to victory over Montreal, to a spectacular season of success and now …

In the end, the Oilers were beaten not so much by Los Angeles (whom Vancouver put out handily in the next round) as by themselves, and the characteristic that led to their downfall was exactly the one that had had so much to do with their success: their youth. Youth had always defined their blithe and freewheeling style of play. With defeat holding no disgrace, they had sung on the bench and laughed on the ice, as so many of us had laughed on the rinks of our boyhood. Their dream had come close to reality precisely because it was impossible. But when it had become possible, and when, concomitantly, loss did mean shame, it had proved too much for them. The moment seized them, and their style lost the joy that had brought them so far. When they had to, they could not summon up the very elements that had made them what they were. And that, too, was a function of their youth. They were still unexcelled at playing the game of their lives. But they were not yet ready for the grim business of winning at it.

The ability to win at games involves much more than superior gifts and skills. And of all the qualities that set champion athletes apart it is the hardest to measure or understand. It is what makes John McEnroe dig in for the tie-breaker in Wimbledon's ultimate set, or Tom Watson sink a chip-shot to win the u.s. Open. In hockey, it sent Bobby Orr flying across the goalmouth in Stanley Cup overtime and gave Maurice Richard the strength to carry an opponent on his shoulders as he roared across the blueline. In the most romantic terms, it is Hemingway's grace under pressure, and away from the playing fields or arenas it is what makes a businessman concentrate all his faculties on the instant of closing an intricate deal or allows an actor to stretch beyond himself. It is seldom inherent, and although there are exceptions—Cassius Clay knocking out the fearsome Liston; Fernando Valenzuela facing the awesome Yankees—it almost always comes, when it comes at all, with age. Chris Evert Lloyd is a greater tennis player than little Chrissie Evert was; Punch Imlach won a Stanley Cup by sending out, for the final shift, a lineup of players over thirty. Even the Islanders, the handiest example of all to the Oilers, lost four times in Stanley Cup semi-finals before emerging as the pre-eminent team of the early 1980s.

The Year of the Kid was a momentous one for the team, as it was for those of us who had watched Wayne Gretzky grow to his now undisputed place in the game's history. Now, that season, too, was over, and the sour taste of frustration was as strong as the glow of achievement had been the year before. In the fall of 1982, the Oilers would begin again, their eyes now focused on redemption. They all knew that eventually—maybe even in the year coming up—they would make it to the top, and that the Stanley Cup would move for awhile to Edmonton. They were a year older now, and much wiser, and it was as if their boyhoods were behind them.